PARTICIPATION AND PREVENTION

*when organizing shift work at company
level in various European countries*

PARTICIPATION AND PREVENTION

*when organizing shift work at company
level in various European countries*

*Hans Jeppe Jeppesen, Magnar Kleiven,
Henrik Bøggild and Colin Gill*

Psychology of power and participation
(The SPARK Research Unit)
Department of Psychology
University of Aarhus, Denmark

AARHUS UNIVERSITY PRESS

Participation and Prevention
Copyright: The Authors and Aarhus University Press, 2006
Printed in Denmark by Narayana Press
Cover design: Jørgen Sparre
Cover illustration:
Unknown Mexican artist

ISBN 87 7934 115 2

AARHUS UNIVERSITY PRESS
Langelandsgade 177
8200 Aarhus N
Denmark
Fax (+45) 8942 5380

White Cross Mills,
Hightown
Lascaster, LA1 4XS
United Kingdom
Fax: 01524 63232

P.O. Box 511
Oakville, CT 06779
USA
Fax: 860-945 9468

www.unipress.dk

FOREWORD

This report deals with the organization of shift work at a local level, the role and importance of the actors involved, the connected organizational processes among the participating companies, the health and safety impacts, and the prevention of shift-work-related problems. The report has been prepared, and the findings are presented, in such a way that the scientific approach and basis are clarified. A further aim is that it can be read by organizational actors and other parties involved in organizing and designing work schedules.

The reader of this report will find that reiterations may occur between the different sections. However, possible inconveniences notwithstanding, the aim here is that the individual sections can be read separately and do not require perusal of previous sections or of the report in full.

Findings from the project have been presented at various international scientific conferences and symposia, including the following: the 15th and 16th International Symposia on Night and Shift Work held in Hayama, Japan 2001 and in Santos, Brazil 2003, the 3rd Annual Conference of the European Academy of Occupational Health Psychology held in Barcelona, Spain 2001, and the 11th European Congress on Work and Organizational Psychology (EAWOP) held in Lisbon, Portugal 2003. Single-company reports have been completed for the companies that participated in the questionnaire phase of the project (see Appendix 10.3), as well as a summary report to Norsk Hydro and the national companies involved.

During the data collection period, EU Council Directive 93/104/EC concerning certain aspects of the organization of working time was valid. This directive has later been replaced by Directive 2003/88/EC of the European Parliament and of the Council, but this has not changed the preconditions of this project, although it did extend the scope of the directive. The findings presented can therefore be assumed to have the same validity and relevance as when the data were collected, and our findings on the themes of employee participation, organizational processes, the dynamics of the involved actors, and health and safety issues continue to be of topical interest.

The local representative participatory bodies were described and analysed according to the information about their conditions, composition, and roles in the participating companies. This information was collected through local fact-finding and project interviews, not deduced from looking at the national regulations. This implies that particular features found to manifest themselves in the description and classification of local conditions may differ from the national regulations or the corresponding regulations at trade level.

We would like to take this opportunity to thank the employees and the management of the participating companies for their contributions, and particular thanks go to the employee and management representatives who supported the activities of the project groups at the individual companies. Special thanks are also due to the involved staff at Norsk Hydro. Without their active contributions, we would not have been able to write this report.

Furthermore we wish to express our gratitude for the financial support granted to the project by Norsk Hydro's Research Foundation and the Work Environment Fund of the Confederation of Norwegian Business and Industry. Also many thanks to the Research Foundation of Aarhus University for their support of the publication of these findings.

We also thank our colleagues, Professor Peter Smith, Central Queensland University's Rockhampton Campus, Australia, and Senior Lecturer Lawrence Smith, Institute of Psychological Sciences, University of Leeds, UK, for their valuable comments on earlier drafts of this report. Similarly, the supporting activities undertaken by librarians Jette Bødker, Rita Jensen, and Betina Sjøstrøm at the University Library, Department of Psychology, University of Aarhus, have been inestimable throughout the process.

It is our hope and our aspiration that through this report we can communicate knowledge that will contribute to improving employee participation, and increasing the attention paid to employee health and safety in the organization of shift work.

Hans Jeppe Jeppesen   *Magnar Kleiven*   *Henrik Bøggild*   *Colin Gill*

October 2006

CONTENTS

1. INTRODUCTION

In recent decades the use of shift work has increased and spread to more and more areas, even while the conditions for organizing shift work have been altered, becoming more complex. In many countries the structure of working time has changed due to reductions in the formal number of weekly working hours and increases in vacation days and periods for special leave. Furthermore, evolving social policies and the dependence of production sectors on well-developed social infrastructures – such as communication systems, transport facilities, child care, and medical services – have increased the level of round-the-clock public service systems, and also extended 24-hour service to new areas. At company level, new kinds of production and work organization have been introduced to accommodate a growing need for frequently re-aligning working hours, jobs, and production – a need that results from the implementation of new technologies and the globalization of the market. On the other side of the equation are the employees, who want their free or "social" time to accommodate changing family structures (two partners working outside the home, altered sharing of house work, and new dynamics in family relations) and changing demands for education.

These common and conflicting desires, needs, and demands to work schedules pose considerable challenges, especially in relation to the adaptability of both employees and organizations. When it comes to shift work, this situation is reflected by an increased complexity in the schedules applied, whereas varying degrees of importance are attributed to the issues mentioned above. In general, two main trends can be identified: increased individualization, and closer links with the organization of work (ILO 1990). A key element in looking at both these developmental trends has been the notion of 'flexibility'. The implications can be traced further in the design of different types of flexible schedules and in various kinds of compressed workweek schedules (Kogi 1995).

Parallel to this development, a greater margin of flexibility has been added to the existing legal framework in many developed countries, and yet another manifestation of flexibility lies in the possibility of deviating from the legal provisions on working time through collective agreements (ILO 1990). Corresponding trends can be seen in the EU directive on working time, whose contents and mode of adoption must be implemented in accordance with national practices, allowing deviation by way of collective agreements (EU Directive 1993). A further incentive to increase flexibility came later, with the European Commission's adoption of a resolution on the 1998 Employment Guidelines. This resolution asked partners to negotiate agreements to introduce flexible and innovative methods of work organization that reconcile company requirements and individual preferences regarding the division of time between work, leisure, and education (European Commission 1998). Regardless of such invitations to negotiate working-time issues, designing work schedules still remains a prerogative of the employer, within the regulatory framework. The design of a shift schedule can thus be seen as indicative of the existing regulations, the degree of compliance exhibited, and the employer's attitude to incorporating employee interests relative to company interests. Another consideration is the potential advantages of flexibility, where questions such as *flexibility for whom*, and *flexibility of which conditions* must also be placed on the agenda if we are to fully understand its dynamics and impact.

However, the design of shift schedules is not just about preferences and managing interests. It is also a matter of considering health and safety. Shift work has adverse effects on sleep, performance, accidents, health, and social life (Waterhouse, Folkard & Minors 1993, Costa 1996, Wedderburn 2000). Night work according to fixed or rotating schedules that include regular night shifts is recognized as an occupational hazard that necessitates the establishment of protective measures (EU Directive 1993).

The overall regulatory development corresponds to the general trends on the labour market, which are moving towards increased local influence. Concurrently, health and safety strategies are changing from detailed technical legislative standards towards framework regulations that emphasize building up systems, programs, and conditions conducive to health and safety, and which stipulate the obligations and rights of the parties involved. Attention is also given to the importance of health and safety interventions at the planning and design stage, and to local activities (Rantanen 1995). Thus, the regulatory framework – national as well as international – not only corresponds to demands from organizations concerning potential adjustments to particular local conditions. It also accommodates the emergence of participatory systems and joint committees aimed to ensure employee rights by influencing company matters, including working-time conditions and health and safety issues (EU Directive 1989).

1.1 RESEARCH OBJECTIVES

The participatory principles and practices set out in the applicable health and safety regulations offer opportunities to tackle shift work issues at different levels, for instance by monitoring strain in the work environment and by observing compliance with prescribed activities. They also suggest possible ways to adjust working conditions and to change how work is organized. In the face of this complexity, with its blend of local, national, and cross-national conditions and prescriptions, and its diverse considerations and interests at local level, we have chosen to focus our research project on the following areas:

- Exploring the influence of participatory practices on designing shift-work arrangements and on health and safety management when shift work is organized at a local level in different European countries.
- Investigating whether different shift-work schedules have different effects on the employees' health, social life and organizational behaviour.
- Identifying potential facilitators and obstacles to ensuring health and safety when organizing shift work in different national companies.

1.2 THE STRUCTURE OF THE REPORT

Here in **Section 1** we have established the context in terms of working-time regulations and research aims. **Section 2** provides the background for the project, discussing shift work as an occupational hazard, and offering a description of shift work as a risk factor through its influence on work functions, social life, and health. We also sum up current knowledge about preventing such adverse effects, and about the significance of participation in doing so – not only in terms of regulations and implementation, but also by redesigning shift schedules at company level.

Section 3 presents information about the development of the project and formulates the problems and research model. This is followed, in

Section 4, by an account of the project's design and organization. Then we go on to describe the nature of the project (a multiple-case study), the participants, and the data sources used. Furthermore, we explain the organization of the project; both the central organization in relation to Norsk Hydro and the individual companies that provided the basis for carrying out the project.

Section 4 then describes the data used for the project, which was mainly obtained in the form of factual information, accident records, interviews, and questionnaires. It also includes a brief account of the data collection process for the different data sources. We also specify when the reporting on the various data analyses was completed, and whether there was in fact an appropriate basis for carrying out particular analyses.

Section 5 contains factual data about the individual participating companies. These data are summarized in three tables that reflect the context in which the results of the interview and questionnaire analyses should be interpreted. The first of these tables outlines the companies' production, workforce, size, and workplace conditions. The second lists the participatory bodies at each company that are relevant to our areas of study. The third table shows some characteristics of the most common shift systems in the participating companies, enabling us to compare the shift systems across the companies.

In **Section 6** we present the findings based on our analyses of the interview data. Most of these analyses focused on the significance of participation and the organizational bodies involved in organizing shift work, on the management of health and safety in shift work, on the process of design, and on the implementation of the applied shift schedules.

The results of our analyses of the questionnaire data are set out in **Section 7**. The findings are divided into frequency or distribution analyses of the participants, depending on the individual variables in the questionnaire. We carried out comparative analyses of shift workers and day workers, and of shift workers in different age groups, and with or without children living at home. Our aim was to determine whether age and parenthood would influence the impact of shift work. Finally, we analysed shift systems consisting of four, five, and six teams, comparing the dependent variables from the questionnaire.

The report concludes with **Section 8**, which summarizes, integrates, and evaluates our findings with a view to drawing conclusions on our study. This leads us to suggest various perspectives for employee participation when organizing shift work and introducing preventive measures. **Section 9** presents references to the scientific literature relevant to the issues this report covers.

Section 10 is an Appendix that supplements the body of the report by presenting the results of the questionnaire analyses from the individual company sites (with each company compared to the other participating companies taken as a group). Here we also more thoroughly describe the methods of analysis, as well as the strengths and options for interpreting the data. The company reports have been organized so that each one can be read individually and distributed at the relevant company. They all end with a list of ergonomic rules for designing shift schedules and a list of process recommendations when working to implement and redesign shift schedules. Both lists are based on empirical research within the relevant area. This approach inevitably means that the report's structure is repetitive, especially in the supplements in the Appendix. Even so, we deem it of the utmost importance that both the supplements and the individual sections can be read independently.

2. SHIFT WORK

The term *working time* denotes the periods of time during which the employee is at work and is at the company's disposal to perform the job he or she is employed to do. An *enterprise's organization of working time* refers to the periods of time around the clock, throughout the weeks, months, and year during which the enterprise's production takes place and the employees perform tasks to achieve production goals. The nature of the company's production and its organization of working time determine which, and how many, groups of employees must work during various time periods. *Shift work* in a company means that one or more employees or groups replace each other after the end of a working period, and that their tasks form part of a continuous process that prolongs the normal working day. A *work schedule*, on the other hand, shows in detail how the employees' working time is organized, placing the working periods to fulfil the given production goals. Derived from this, a *shift schedule* denotes how the working time of the company's employees is organized in order to perform the shift work required.

The essential dimensions of shift schedules, which also demonstrate the concepts used in this report, are as follows:
- Extension of continuity (Is night and weekend work included?)
- Extension of rotation (How many types of shift are used in the rotation, or is work performed in fixed shifts?)
- Speed of rotation (the number of days and nights in a row that people work in the same type of shift)
- Length of rotation cycle (the period worked until people work the same shift again on the same weekday)
- Level of regularity (Is the same pattern repeated in the following rotation cycle, or does the pattern vary?)
- Length of shifts (number of hours in a row in an individual shift)
- Location of the shifts in time (start and end time of the individual shifts)
- Level of flexibility (opportunities for employees to choose, and for the company to vary the design)

- Direction of rotation between the different shifts (In which order do people work different shifts when one shift type ends and another begins – clockwise or counter-clockwise?)

These dimensions can be combined in many different ways when designing shift schedules, and a huge number of different schedules are in use. The systems most common seen combine two-shift schedules, with day and afternoon/evening shifts and weekends off; discontinuous three-shift schedules with day, evening, and night shifts and weekends off; and continuous three-shift schedules with day, evening, night, and weekend work. These basic structures can then be further developed by having a different number of teams succeed each other at different intervals. They can also be composed of different lengths of shifts, with typical work periods (shifts) ranging from 6, or more commonly 8, to 12 hours.

2.1 SHIFT WORK AS AN OCCUPATIONAL HAZARD

The detrimental effects of shift work are linked to the fact that the working periods involved in shift work obstructs the normal biological and social time structures of day-oriented people. The shift worker is therefore forced to try to adapt to time structures other than day work, which are in conflict with this daytime orientation. The demands for adjustment, with continuously varying phase shifts, to different and internally conflicting time frames affect the shift worker's circadian rhythmicity and sleep, most notably during night work. Adjustment demands impose other frameworks for family life, and other opportunities for developing a social life. They also change the conditions and the organizational features of work (Åkerstedt & Knutsson 1994, Costa 1996). These effects apply to all those performing the same shift work.

Whether, and to what extent, such effects adversely impact social life, sleep, health, performance, and safety depends on a number of mediating factors. These factors can be divided into variables related to: (a) individual characteristics such as age, behaviour, and physiological and psychological adaptability to shift work; (b) working conditions such as type of job, tasks, the nature of the work process, and the shift system employed; and (c) social and family-life conditions such as family structure and dynamics, age of children, and leisure activities (Knauth & Rutenfranz 1987, Knutsson & Bøggild 2000).

2.1.1 BIOLOGICAL RHYTHMS AND SLEEP

Most of the biological processes and physiological functions of human beings, such as temperature, blood pressure, respiration, adrenaline, and urine secretion, run in a rhythmical sequence over a 24-hour period, during which levels vary between low and high values in agreement with patterns of activity and rest. The sequences of these circadian rhythms are controlled by endogenous biological clocks, but one characteristic of the rhythms is that they have an interact with, and are susceptible to influence from, external conditions that act as cues or "time indicators". Such cues include the change between light and darkness, social time cues like meal patterns, the time phases of work and rest, and societal activity. Laboratory experiments have demonstrated that without the influence of external time cues the natural period for biological rhythms can be about 25 hours (Folkard 1996). This means that it tends to be easier to postpone a sleep period than it is to begin one prematurely, and easier to adapt to new time zones that lengthen the day rather than shorten it. If the external conditions are consistent, physiological and behavioural rhythms such as sleep maintain an internal synchronicity with one another, and an external synchronicity with environmental conditions such as light and darkness. Therefore under a normal day orientation, the large majority of rhythms peak sometime during the day, whereas sleep, growth hormone, and melatonin, which are connected to sleep, peak at night.

For shift workers, the times for activity and rest are altered, sometimes even inverted, especially by night work. The requirements of the new time phases of rest and activity conflict with the normal day-oriented synchronization. Rhythms try to adjust to the altered functional demands arising from new activity and resting patterns, but simultaneously, and in conflict with these attempts, the dominating external time cues remain unchanged. That is why a complete adjustment of the rhythms to the altered activity–rest patterns does not occur – even in the case of fixed night work. Some argue that such schedules allow for greater adjustment, ignoring the fact that fixed night workers experience regular disruption when phasing their activity–rest periods to readjust to daytime routines on their days off (Åkerstedt 1985). Some experimental studies have changed the external time cues, thereby offering the most favourable conditions for subjects to adapt their biological rhythms. Even so, here too it is evident that even after working a run of 21 nights in a row, complete adjustment of the day-

and-night temperature rhythm does not occur (Knauth & Rutenfranz 1976). After a period of night rhythms, subjects tend to return to normal day orientation relatively quickly, in about 1.5 to 2 days. This is related to the strong influence of the cycle of light and darkness, as well as other social and environmental cues.

The adjustment of rhythms throughout successive night shifts happens gradually, with modest changes taking place during the initial days and nights, when the rhythms largely remain synchronized with day work. Adjustment then increases over subsequent days and nights, but at varying rates for the different physiological functions. Furthermore, rhythms appear to change most during the first week of night work, adapting more slowly during the following weeks when more night shifts occur (Folkard 1996). Research shows that although individuals with longer shift-work experience must continually undergo an adjustment process, they adjust within a shorter time span (Åkerstedt 1985, Knauth & Rutenfranz 1987, Comperatore & Krueger 1990).

The changing activity and rest phases, and the way rhythms attempt to adjust in response, imply that the 'normal' internal synchronization of physiological and behavioural rhythms is obstructed, and that a desynchronization of the functions arises because of variable susceptibility to the altered activity–rest demands, and variable adjustment speeds for the different rhythms. The associated strains are also connected with the fact that the body's physiological functions must continue to operate during the permanent phase shift, and work and sleep functions take place at times that are not in harmony with circadian rhythmicity (cf. Monk & Folkard 1992).

The impact this has on the way shift workers sleep is that the amount of sleep during the day (following a night shift) tends to be reduced by 1 to 4 hours. This time is primarily taken from stage 2 (basic sleep) and REM sleep (dream sleep), whereas stages 3 and 4 are less affected (Åkerstedt 1990). The day sleep of night-shift workers is therefore briefer, and of a poorer quality, than the night sleep of day workers. This also applies to shift workers with fixed night shifts (Alfredsson *et al.* 1991). As a combined consequence of the shortened sleep and the desynchronized circadian rhythmicity, an increased level of fatigue is found in shift workers, which can be further aggravated through the gradual accumulation of a sleep deficit proportionate to the number of successive night shifts worked. The sleep deficit occurring after night shifts tends to increase with age. With fatigue comes an increased risk of briefly dozing off or actually falling asleep on the job, with the safety problems this entails.

Besides its potentially adverse effects on safety, this concoction of desynchronized biological processes, reduced sleep quality, and social disruption impact the health and social functioning of the shift worker. The biological, physiological, and behavioural disharmonies that are established have consequences, both in the short and the long term, for shift workers' emotional condition and reaction patterns, and even for their gastrointestinal and cardiovascular functions. However, the dynamics of the causal relations surrounding the increased risk of illness have still not been fully clarified. Specific personality traits have been investigated to examine whether they might serve to predict problems that might arise, but there is no solid scientific evidence either way. On the other hand, it seems that having the opportunity to choose a given shift system is reflected in shift workers experiencing less strain (Barton 1994). Härmä *et al.* 1994 found that age was significant for adjustment, in that shift workers around 50 years of age were more cap-able of adjusting over the first two night shifts than the control group, which consisted of colleagues in their 20s. However, after three night shifts the older group were more fatigued and had a reduced circadian adjustment ability compared to the younger group, as well as a reduced ability to recuperate after additional night shifts. Furthermore, rhythms in general appear to become more unstable from around the mid-to-late 40s, which may indicate not only that the effectiveness of the adjust-ment process is reduced and that the effects of altered activity and rest phases are amplified, but also that the number of consecutive shifts may constitute part of the problem for older shift workers (Folkard 1996).

Knowledge of the biological processes, circadian rhythmicity, and the interplay of sleep and activity phases has been central to shaping suggestions for prevention through the design of shift systems based on biological and physiological health criteria. This idea has been de-veloped further in a set of proposed ergonomic rules for designing shift schedules. (These rules are presented at the end of the report, and in the supplements for the individual participating companies). Examples of ergonomic rules include minimizing night sequences, with an employee working only 2-4 successive night shifts, and avoiding short intervals of time off between two shifts (no fast double-backs or 'quick returns').

2.1.2 THE RISK OF ACCIDENTS

The correlation between shift work and the risk of accidents is determined by the shift system employed, and also by the nature of the work itself and the conditions under which tasks are performed. Consequently, the risk can vary for different types of tasks, and for the same type of tasks performed in different working conditions. The sleep-deficit duration and the increased fatigue arising in shift work, especially during and immediately after night work, increase the risk of errors and hence the risk of accidents. An increased risk of errors has been found in public work at hospitals (Gold *et al.* 1992) and in industrial enterprises (Smith *et al.* 1994). The size of the risk, however, should always be specifically evaluated at the individual company or organization in relation to the factors mentioned above, i.e. task types, working conditions, and shift system. At the same time we must presume that the risk will vary across the cyclic period in the given shift plan depending, for instance, on the number of nights worked in a row and on the position of rest days in the shift cycle. By way of example, accidents were found to occur more frequently at machine-paced workstations at night than at stations with a human-controlled work pace, and yet accidents occurring in self-paced work tended to be more serious at night (Smith *et al.* 1994).

2.1.3 SOCIAL LIFE

Shift workers have the same amount of social time (time apart from working time) available as day workers. However, because it occurs at different, and varying, times during the day and night and the days of the week, a disharmony arises in relation to societal patterns and the timing of social activities. These societal patterns have been developed in accordance with the prevailing time structures of day work, with social time situated in the evenings and on weekends. Compared to day work, shift work narrows the time frames for engaging in social activities, but at the same time, depending on the design of the individual shift system, it gives one's social life other time frames and time structures. These altered social-life conditions apply to all shift workers. The social consequences for each shift worker depend on the nature of the shift system in use, and on this system's complex interaction with his or her attitudes and interests, age, family situation, and additional social and societal activities. The significance of shift work's influence on social life can be illustrated by various studies, some of which have found that:

- Social problems can be more frequent than sleep problems (Scott & Ladou 1990, Costa 1997).
- Social conditions can indicate the degree to which shift workers will experience satisfaction or dissatisfaction with the working-time system (Escribà-Agüir 1992, Bohle & Tilley 1998).
- Social effects can be the main reason for leaving a shift-work position (Koller, Kundi & Cervinka 1978).
- Social factors are more important than physiological and health issues when choosing a shift system (Orth-Gomér 1983, Kandolin & Huida 1996).
- Conflicts between social time and work time are linked to physical and psychological health symptoms (Büssing 1996, Loudon & Bohle 1998).

Problems can arise from difficulties in making one's family life work satisfactorily, from having less time with one's spouse or one's children after they reach school age, from having fewer opportunities to participate in formalized organizational activities with others, such as parental work at school. This can create potential patterns of conflict, and resulting stress reactions, which may in turn reduce one's health and increase the risk of illness. However, some employees experience shift work as having a positive effect on their social life. Some choose shift work or, for example, a specific shift schedule that gives them more time with their young children. Shift work can also mean better opportunities for cultivating one's personal hobbies, and new possibilities for time off. Finally, shift work tends to provide a higher salary, often for a shorter day's work.

When assessed based on the value of social time over a working week, evening and weekend shifts appear to generate the most significant conflicts with valuable social time. This is why social problems can be more serious on the evening shift (Folkard 1992), and why the experience of disruptions to family life can be more significant in two-shift systems without night shifts than in three-shifts systems (Nilsson 1981). Generally speaking, the time placement of night shifts collides less with the activities of shift-worker families – depending, however, on the start time of shifts. In addition, to properly understand the influence of night work on a shift worker's social life, one must remember that the extent of its impact is related to reduced energy, lack of sleep, and increased fatigue, all of which influence the use of social time (Walker

1985, Bohle & Tilley 1998). In general, assessments of the social effects of shift work are found to correspond to the prevalent time distribution of social activities in European societies, and to a social rhythm that conforms to a time structure defined by day work.

Social effects do not solely reflect individual and family variations, but also the configuration of shift schedules. Shift workers in an irregular system experience the most significant collisions between their schedules and the time patterns of social activity. Like other shift systems, irregular systems break with the social time rhythm of day work, but arguably that is not all they do. They are further characterized by not providing any alternative social-time rhythm, but rather by causing the absence of such a rhythm. This makes it very difficult to plan and handle social activities that involve social interaction and continuity in time. One study conducted among nurses found that social strains increased as a function of the number of irregular shifts besides day work. All of this indicates that besides the irregularity itself, the frequency of the experience also contributes to aggravating the social consequences (Bohle & Tilley 1998).

The consequences of different shift lengths are found to vary. This is probably because the advantages and the strains of 12-hour and 8-hour shifts differ. What is more, as noted earlier, the effects may also be related to both the type of work and the nature of the work environment. A comparison was made in the hospital field between an 8-hour and a 12-hour shift system. The 8-hour system was rated more positively, as employees found that it involved less work strain and less adverse affects on their social life and health (Kundi, Koller & Stefan 1995). Another similar investigation found greater satisfaction with the 12-hour system, even though the employees working 12-hour shifts experienced more fatigue and more adverse health symptoms than those working 8-hour shifts. These studies illustrate the conflict between social considerations and health considerations when discussing 12-hour shifts, and they show how the conflicts relate to the given work and its demands. Compared to 8-hour shifts, 12-hour shifts increase the flexibility of the employee's social-time structure, with more days off and frequent blocks of days off, especially in a fast-rotating system. Such a structure increases the employee's ability to maintain the social-time value of day work, and thereby participate in social activities to a greater extent. The utilization of such time is highly dependent on the time-related flexibility inherent in the family dynamics (Grzech-Sukalo & Nachreiner 1998). At the same time, depending on the work demands, fatigue, sleep disorders, and psychological symptoms can be more serious in those working 12-hour shifts. This, in turn, may mean an increased risk of developing health symptoms over time, and lead to less effective utilization of valued social time.

Regarding the speed of rotation, greater satisfaction has been described with fast-rotating shift systems than with slower, weekly rotating systems (Wedderburn 1993). Another study, carried out 12 months after a workplace changed from a slower to a fast-rotating system, showed that employees experienced more social-time availability and were able to use this time better (Knauth & Schönfelder 1990). Besides interfering less with the harmony of circadian rhythms, a fast-rotating system can yield greater flexibility and let the employee experience more opportunities to engage in social activities. This is achieved with schedules that vary shift types in brief blocks of the same shift, thereby varying the placement of social time within the same week.

Assessments that compare fixed shifts to rotating ones are complex, and difficult to interpret unequivocally, since studies so far indicate that other factors may be significant – as in instances where night work is handled by a specific group that has elected to work nights. Thus, investigations of fixed shifts have typically addressed fixed night work, usually among hospital staff, most of whom also work part time (Jeppesen, Bøggild & Larsen 1997). Furthermore, there can be differences in the length of shifts worked. Research results suggest that, for people with particular personal preferences (Hornberger & Knauth 1993) and particular priorities in terms of the value of available social time (Barton & Folkard 1991), fixed night work is experienced as a more satisfactory working-time system with fewer negative social consequences than rotating shift work (Escribà-Agüir 1992). Another factor assumed to contribute to these findings is that rotating-shift workers maintain a day orientation, which they experience as being constrained, whereas employees who have chosen fixed night work appear more ready to adjust to night orientation. Currently there is no basis for assuming that fixed night work in itself leads to fewer negative social consequences than rotating shifts, although for some employees it might be more socially desirable. Moreover, it should be emphasized that social satisfaction with a shift schedule does not avert the risk of developing the health-related strains that are primarily associated with night work (cf. the following section on health effects).

The influence that personal attitudes and interests, and family structure and dynamics, have on the social effects of shift work shows how an optimal shift system for everyone does not exist (Knauth & Costa 1996). However, certain themes emerge that can be used as social criteria by those shaping shift systems and prevention measures. Optimizing a shift system's social-time availability is largely about attempting to establish the best possible agreement with the valued social time available in normal day work – in short, allowing for weekends off and social time in the evenings.

The predictability of a shift system's social time availability is linked to the shift schedule's regularity and the placement of the shifts, and thereby to the regularity of the employee's social time. This enables shift workers and their families to plan ahead and handle social activities on an ongoing basis.

Flexibility in a shift system implies that the system allows individual shift workers to influence start times, or to choose days off, nights off, and weekends off, as well as allowing individuals to take time off in lieu of unpaid overtime and to exchange shifts. Individual flexibility strengthens the employee's ability to deal with the needs and demands of social life, thereby securing greater participation in social arrangements, better management of domestic and family responsibilities, more effective participation in ongoing activities that occur at certain times every week, and more ready participation in organizational activities.

Autonomy at the individual level in the applied shift schedule design involves offering the individual shift worker a choice among several optional schedules or systems, or offering a choice, within certain frames of reference, between specific system design criteria in order to increase agreement between the person's work and the social needs. However, flexibility controlled by employees can also exist at group level in the form of autonomous shift-work groups (Knauth 1996). The level of freedom for group-designed rotas can vary, and there can also be considerable variation in the features of shift schedules designed with any degree of autonomy. Typically the latitude allowed is also associated with the level of freedom the organization gives in relation to performing work tasks.

It must be pointed out that when a shift system is being shaped, the social themes cannot be considered in isolation as prevention strategies. They should be employed in connection with the biological criteria, and be weighted appropriately (cf. the report supplements on ergonomic rules recommended for designing shift schedules). The aim is to avoid any unintended consequences – say, increased long-term health risks – that priorities in one area might have on another area.

2.1.4 HEALTH EFFECTS

The reasons why shift work can lead to illness are probably linked to biological, psychological, and social factors. Shift work affects circadian biological processes, with an accompanying desynchronization of physiological functions, reducing the quality of sleep and leading to disharmonies in social-time structures (Knutsson & Bøggild 2000). These processes can create imbalances that can initially seem overwhelming to the shift worker. The stress-handling process can begin with attempts to find coping strategies or actions that aim to re-establish balance. The shift worker cannot individually change the shift work causing the imbalance and strain. The possibility of changing shift work schedules implies that the schedules themselves can be a part of the collective and organizational processes aimed at finding prevention strategies (which are further addressed in the following section). Individual shift workers may try to adapt as best they can to the specific life conditions of shift work. How successful they are, and how they adapt, will depend not only on the actions and personal resources of each shift worker, but also on the possible familial and company scenarios in relation to the options offered. So while shift-work imbalances cannot be removed, a certain degree of adjustment and levelling out can be achieved, depending on the situation of the individual. Some choose to leave shift work completely to avoid its negative impacts, depending, of course, on labour-market and socio-economic conditions. Age is also an important factor here, since as one gets older it generally becomes harder to deal with the demands of shift work (Härmä 1996), due to changes in one's resources for handling shift-work imbalances. Different personal situations – and hence different adaptation capabilities – combined with the appropriateness of the action strategies chosen can also help explain why shift work can have different social and health consequences. However, as mentioned above, there is a scarcity of scientific evidence that allows us to differentiate between those who experience health problems and those who do not.

It should also be emphasized that even though shift work represents a time structure for work, it does not, in itself, say anything about the character or nature of the work, or about the conditions in which the work takes place. To reach a deeper understanding of the consequences of shift work, we must therefore also include the nature of the work performed as well as the working conditions. It follows that some situations involve exposure to a combination of strains from shift work and from the rest of the work environment, and in such cases the various influences can enhance each other's effects. Some studies have compared the work environments of day workers and shift workers, finding that there are more strains on shift workers, including higher noise levels and more adverse climatic conditions (Rutenfranz & Knauth 1986). Another investigation (Bøggild *et al.* 2000) also found increased strains on shift workers, with increased noise levels, monotonous repetitive work tasks, and lower decision-making authority.

Psychological health symptoms in the form of irritability, sadness, restlessness, and tension have been found to be present more frequently among shift workers than day workers (Freese & Semmer 1986, Koller, Kundi & Cervinka 1978). Shift workers have also reported more frequent use of tranquillizers in some studies (e.g. Gordon *et al.* 1986).

Shift workers experience gastrointestinal symptoms in the form of nausea, loss of appetite, or constipation more often than day workers (Scott & Ladou 1990, Waterhouse, Folkard & Minors 1993). Several older studies also found that shift work was linked to a higher risk of diseases in the abdomen and intestines, where especially peptic ulcers were found to be more frequent in shift workers (Angersbach *et al.* 1980, Koller 1983, Knauth & Rutenfranz 1987). Hospital admissions because of ulcerative diseases have been reported as more frequent in occupations where work often takes place outside of normal working hours (Tüchsen, Jeppesen & Bach 1994).

New research has underscored the risk of coronary heart diseases (CHD), and two review articles have recently estimated this risk as being increased by approximately 40% (Bøggild & Knutsson 1999, Steenland 2000). One study found a connection between increased participation in shift work and an increased risk of CHD among industrial workers at a sawmill. The risk rose to 2.8 times the baseline in the course of 20 years (Knutsson 1989). Another investigation among nurses found an increased risk of 1.51 for staff with more than 6 years of shift work (Kawachi *et al.* 1995). These studies were adjusted for traditional heart disease risk factors such as smoking and obesity. Other recent studies have found that shift work is also related to a condition labelled "metabolic syndrome", which is associated with abdominal obesity, high triglycerides, high blood pressure, and glucose insensitivity. This condition in itself is linked to a higher risk of heart disease (Karlsson, Knutsson & Lindahl 2001).

In addition, a group of studies has found links between shift/ overtime work and the risk of having premature or small-for-date babies. (Infante-Rivard, David, Gauthier & Rivard 1993, Fortier, Marcoux & Brisson 1995). A further meta-analysis examined the best studies (Mozurkewich, Luke & Wolf 2000). Six studies found the risk of preterm birth to be increased by around 25%. Contrary to earlier studies, for shift-working women no link was found between shift work and premature/small-for-date babies or early miscarriages.

A few recent studies have examined whether shift work is associated with an increased time to pregnancy (the time from a couple plans to conceive and stops using contraceptives until pregnancy). The studies do not show consistent results, and the findings may be attributable to levels of smoking (Bisanti *et al.* 1996, Zhu *et al.* 2003).

Three studies were published in 2001, all of which showed that women on shift work appeared to have a higher risk of breast cancer (Hansen 2001, Davis, Mirich & Stevens 2001, Schernhammer *et al.* 2001). This was in line with an older study (Taylor & Pocock 1972) that found a non-significant risk of death due to cancer in male shift workers. Studies of stewardesses and female telegraphists have previously reported a higher risk of breast cancer in these groups, and animal studies have suggested that the hormone melatonin is protective against breast cancer. The three new studies have methodological weaknesses, in that other factors (such as alcohol consumption) may play a role in the link between night work and breast cancer. This leaves the question of a possible link unsettled, and asserting the existence of a real risk may be premature.

In some studies, the incidence of days lost due to illness is taken to express the strain of a given factor or exposure. A large study encompassing 13,000 sick-leave reports at Norsk Hydro Norway, from the decade 1980-1990, found no increased absence frequency for shift workers with shift-related illnesses (Kleiven, Bøggild & Jeppesen 1998). The study concluded that the number of days lost due to illness could not be seen as an expression of a health risk occurring in conjunction with shift work, but rather that absence due to illness might be related to conditions such as the quality of the work environment and the character of the work culture.

The correlation between specific dimensions in a shift system and health effects has been examined in different studies, often conducted in association with certain changes made in the applied shift schedule. Varying results have been found that indicate the significance of other work conditions and their importance in the strains experienced. In some cases strains have been linked to simultaneous changes made in several rota dimensions (Hornberger & Knauth 1995, Tucker *et al.* 1998, Bøggild & Jeppesen 2001). For two dimensions, namely the speed of rotation and the direction of rotation, improvements tend to follow a reduction in the number of night shifts in a row (Williamson & Sanderson 1986, Hornberger & Knauth 1998), and similar improvements occur after clockwise rotations (Orth-Gomér 1983). Studies that investigated the significance of individual controlled flexibility have reported improved sleep and fewer stress reactions (Kandolin & Huida 1996) and a positive effect on well-being (Barton 1995). A hospital study found that nurses with shift work and a high degree of control were better able to integrate work and social life (Kundi & Wöckinger 2000). One study where a number of changes were introduced simultaneously (including fewer night shifts in a row, an extra day and night off, and only two types of shift) found lower concentrations of risk factors for stress and cardiovascular diseases (Bøggild & Jeppesen 2001). There are no studies that compare the longer-term effects for employees on rotating shifts and those on fixed shifts. The length of individual shifts has been compared (typically 8 versus 12 hours), but improvements found to accompany 12-hour systems, most notably in terms of well-being and satisfaction, are probably based on social factors (Lowden et al. 1998).

2.2 PREVENTION

Activities aimed at reducing the harmful effects of shift work can be applied at different levels and focus on either changing workers' exposure or improving their adaptation to shift work through altered behaviour and coping strategies. In addition, the shift work literature includes recommendations on sleep, nutrition, communication, and social behaviour (Monk 1988) as well as ergonomic rules for designing shift schedules (Knauth 1996). Various studies have also examined the effects of using regulatory measures as prevention strategies, which involves presenting the different characteristics of the regulations, and managing them (Jeppesen, Bøggild & Larsen 1997, Jeppesen & Bøggild 1998). In accordance with the aims of this project, *prevention* is understood as protection against exposure to a hazard. This further implies that prevention is conceived as encompassing the activities aimed at reducing the detrimental effects of shift work by changing the employee's exposure. Such activities can rest on a variety of approaches and strategies, but at the core of changing the exposure to shift work hazards lie three alterable: the conditions for applying shift work, the organization of the shift work, and the design of the shift schedules. Even so, bringing about changes in these areas does not mean that the adverse effects of shift work will disappear. Such changes can more accurately be described as measures aimed at minimizing its adverse impacts.

2.2.1 REGULATIONS

Regulatory measures serve to determine frameworks and conditions concerning when and how working time can be applied. Working-time regulations primarily deal with payment and compensation for those whose working hours lie beyond normal daytime work, and with protecting employees' health and social life. The nature and content of these regulations typically reflect some consideration for production conditions and demands. Some regulations also take employment issues into account. One example is France, where, from January 2000, companies have been offered financial incentives to reduce weekly working hours from 39 to 35 via collective agreements (Jeffreys 2000).

Regulations on working time can be based on different foundations, use different methods, and apply at different levels: 1) at cross-national level via directives/legislation, 2) at national level via legislation, 3) at trade levels via collective agreements, 4) at company level via local agreements, and 5) at a personal level via employment contracts. The EU countries (in this case including Norway, which is participating in the project) typically differ in the degree to which legislation and agreements are emphasized as regulatory foundations, and in the extent to which legislation can be changed through collective agreements.

The terms for applying working time, including shift work, are regulated in the participating countries (EU countries and Norway) through collective agreements, or through a combination of agreements and legislation. Health and safety issues, on the other hand, are primarily a legislative matter. Thus, collective bargaining plays a key role in determining the length of working time in all the countries involved. However, the nature of its role differs widely from one country to the next as far as bargaining level and scope are concerned. By way of example, in the participating countries the collectively agreed normal weekly working hours in the chemical industry – at the time of data collection in 1999 – were:

Sweden	40
Former Eastern Germany	39.2
France	39
The Netherlands	39
Italy	37.8
Norway	37.5
Germany	37.5
Denmark	37

TABLE 1 *Collectively agreed normal weekly working hours in chemicals 1999*
(EIRONline 2000)

Note: In France the statutory 35-hour working week came into force in 2000.

The number of actual weekly working hours may also differ between countries due to variations in shift-work compensation methods, which can involve either financial advantages, reduced weekly working hours, or a combination of the two. Furthermore, in some countries, previous reductions in working time have been introduced through extra days off or cuts in annual hours, leaving the normal working week relatively unchanged. Conversely, the number of holiday weeks and other free periods may vary without significantly influencing the working week. Weekly working hours can also vary considerably around an average during a reference period, which is also reflected in the way conditions for applying shift work vary from country to country.

At the same time, another move towards harmonizing certain aspects of working-time organization are evident in the development of cross-national regulations via the EU Directives on Working Time (EU Directive 1993 and EU Directive 2003). However, there are two prerequisites for understanding the importance of the Directives: First, they are minimum directives, and second, they have played a role in determining and defining variables such as "night work" and "night worker". The Directives still emphasize that implementing standards like daily rests and weekly rest periods, maximum weekly working hours, and length of night work take place according to national traditions and regulations. The Directives also stipulate that "derogations" – deviations from the standards – can be made through collective agreements. In accordance with the development of fewer standard regulations and more 'broad' framework regulations, it might be fair to presume that derogation issues will increasingly be decided by the local actors.

The responsibility of ensuring health and safety at work lies with the employers. Since the 1970s, legislation that emphasizes employee participation in handling health and safety issues in the workplace has been introduced in various ways in the countries involved. At cross-national level this development was reflected in the EU Directive (1989) on introducing measures to encourage improvement in employee safety and health in the workplace. In accordance with some member states' previously established national health and safety laws, this directive comprises preventive measures for implementing standards and procedures, monitoring the work environment, and establishing preventive activities through information, consultation, balanced participation, and the training of employees and their representatives. The directive is a framework document that leaves much room for national interpretations and recognizes the importance of national traditions. Simultaneously, being a minimum directive it only has implications for some member countries, such as Italy. In particular the directive's emphasis on the participatory principles as a way of fulfilling employees' fundamental social rights has underlined the regulatory importance of participative principles – here within the realm of health and safety.

As mentioned, the document's status as a framework directive means that the intensity of employee participation, the improvement of preventive activities, and the degree to which different work dimensions are included in local health and safety activities will vary between countries, depending on traditions and the nature of national health and safety regulations. This may hold particular importance for shift work since, as demonstrated above, working time is regulated through agreements as well as legislation. One part of the regulation concerns the implementation of shift work in organizations under the heading of "considering conditions for production", while another part concerns the consideration of health and safety issues. One could reasonably speculate that this could increase differences in managing health and safety at a local level, not only between countries but also between companies. In 1999 (the time of data collection), Denmark, the Netherlands, Sweden, and Norway had framework laws, while France had codified laws, and Germany and Italy had fragmented laws (Gill 1993). The differences in health and safety statutes imply variations in which working conditions are covered by the applicable national legislation, and how. In the Danish framework, for instance, all working conditions that may cause health and safety problems are, in principle, included, whereas in reality they are regulated by a mixture of agreements and legislation (Jeppesen & Bøggild 1998). Where shift work is concerned, the handling of health and safety in the workplace is linked with participative bodies in individual organizations, and with the prevailing approaches to shift work and traditions for cooperation. Another aspect that differentiates the countries in this area is the legislation on employee representatives' rights to information and consultation with the employers on matters affecting health and safety. Yet another difference lies in the legislation that stipulates which participative rights fall to which bodies. These dimensions are shown, for the countries studied, in Table 2 below (based on Gill 1993).

Content of information and consultation rights Rights are granted to employee representatives on:	No statutory unambiguous right to information and consultation on health and safety matters	General and non-specific rights in health and safety matters	Specific information and consultation on certain issues as well
Health and Safety Committees		*Denmark* *Norway* *Sweden*	*France*
Works councils		*Germany*	*The Netherlands*
Bodies to be triggered at the workplace	*Italy*		

TABLE 2 *Institutional arrangements and information and consultation rights in health and safety for the participating countries in 1999.* (Based on Gill 1993; for Germany and the Netherlands the arrangements are acts of codetermination.)

These differences in coverage and participatory bodies following framework legislation and the attendant possible differences in local activ-

PARTICIPATION AND PREVENTION

ities offer exceptional opportunities for estimating the importance of participation. This can be done by investigating the different local processes for considering health and safety when using shift work, and by analysing their respective strengths and weaknesses.

It can be stated conclusively that the overall development in work regulations, including those on shift work, corresponds to the general labour-market trends towards increased local influence. Concurrently, health and safety strategies have moved from detailed technical legislative standards to framework regulations emphasizing building-up systems, outlining programmes and conditions conducive to health and safety, and stipulating the involved actors' rights and obligations. The framework regulations at national and international level therefore echo demands from organizations that allow adjustment to particular local conditions, and reflect the emergence of participatory systems and joint committees that ensure employees' rights to influence company matters, including working-time conditions and health and safety at work (European Directive 89/391). The participatory principles and operations, as determined in the health and safety regulations, imply that engaging in shift work issues at different levels should help companies monitor the work environment to prevent strain and make sure prescriptions are observed. They also imply that employees can contribute to changing work conditions and influence how work is organized. Presumably the frequency of such activities will also vary depending on national regulations, information given, and local traditions for cooperating at an organizational level.

2.2.2 SHIFT-SCHEDULE DESIGN

A shift schedule determines how employees' working time is organized so that the given work can be performed. A shift schedule designates the working-time periods (the applied shifts) and their location, as well as the successive sequence of employees handling the work during the shifts. This means that shift schedules can be designed using ergonomic principles to take health and safety into account. Shift schedules can also be designed to acknowledge situations where production requirements, compensation levels, and social conditions may impair health and safety. A shift schedule's design can be said to reflect existing regulations, the degree of regulatory compliance, and the employer's attitude to considering employee interests relative to company interests.

As noted, the essential shift schedule dimensions recognized in describing, analysing, or identifying possibilities for alterations include: a) Extent of continuity in production, b) Extent of rotation, c) Speed of rotation, d) Length of rotation/shift cycle, e) Level of regularity, f) Length of shifts, g) Location of shifts, including start and end times, h) Level of individual flexibility, and i) Direction of rotation between different shifts. The number of characteristics within a single dimension and the many combinations of rota features set the stage for considerable disparities in applied shift schedules, and thousands of different schedules are indeed possible. On the other hand, all schedules are constructed with an inherent interdependence between the different characteristics. This does limit the combinations somewhat, yet it also means that altering one aspect of the schedule will impact other parts of the schedule as well. It is generally accepted (Wedderburn 1994, Kogi 1995, Knauth 1996) that in shift-schedule design there is no ultimate, universal, or ideal, solution. This also means that, at least theoretically, any process of designing or altering a schedule within the confines of the organizational context and regulations will be open-ended. This allows local actors to select among, and seek to integrate, different options according to the established priorities of local needs and attitudes.

Studies on the importance of the various schedule dimensions have mainly been concerned with the speed of rotation (Williamson & Sanderson 1986, Knauth & Kiesewetter 1987, Knauth & Hornberger 1998), the direction of rotation (Orth-Gomér 1983, Barton et al. 1994), regularity (Kandolin & Huida 1996), and the length of different shifts (Kundi et al. 1995, Paley et al. 1998, Lowden et al. 1998). The results across studies have not been unequivocal, which may reflect variations in work characteristics, schedule features beyond the examined dimensions, level of employee influence, and the studies' designs and applied methods. In some studies, for example, several changes have been introduced simultaneously. Generally speaking, more often than not these studies have found reduced social problems, improved sleep, and increased well-being and satisfaction. Only rarely have studies reported a reduction in symptoms, but some have found that altering the shift schedule may reduce the risk factors for heart disease (Orth-Gomér 1983, Bøggild & Jeppesen 2001).

Based on research into the effects of shift work – more specifically, results observed after intervention, and experimental studies on redesigning shift schedules and implementing shift work – a set of ergonomic recommendations for designing shift schedules have been outlined (Knauth 1993, 1996, Wedderburn 1994, recommendations enclosed in the Appendix of this report). Changing the way work is organized and the temporal distribution of tasks and other work activities within the 24-hour day-and-night cycle may have preventive benefits, such as reducing the number of employees working at night, or during certain hours of the night (Knauth 1983). Moreover, the importance of taking a participatory approach when designing shift schedules has been emphasized (Corlett *et al.* 1988, Knauth 1996, Jeppesen, Kleiven & Bøggild 2004). The crucial aims are to reconcile potentially conflicting schedule-design interests, and to improve the working and living conditions of the shift workers involved.

Finally, it must be underlined that while there are certain limits to applying shift work, there are few recommendations on how shift-work conditions must be improved. One possible implication is that designing shift schedules is still a managerial prerogative. This, in turn, leaves local management responsible for determining how employees can participate, how much influence they are offered, and which design dimensions receive priority.

2.2.3 PARTICIPATION

Although important, the concept of participation does not have an unambiguous meaning. The term has nevertheless been used to define employee involvement in organizational processes and activities associated with managing working organizations. *Participation* can refer to activities such as QWL (Quality of Working Life) systems, works councils, and organizational processes like teamwork, health and safety committees and quality circles.

Participatory practices can rest on different foundations, assume different forms, take place at different organizational levels, have different intensity, and include different issues. This means that the applications of participation can be distinguished in terms of constitution, form, extent of influence, and objectives. However, an internal logical correlation between these different dimensions can often be found. The participation's constitution can either be formal, as set out in regulations, or inform and based on managerial initiatives. The form can be direct, representative, or financial, and the intensity may vary from a consultative role to decision-making authority resting with employees.

The objectives can be task-centred, revolving around daily operational work situations, or power-centred, concerning more fundamental managerial authority (Salamon 1987). In the latter case the schedule design is typically formal and representative. It is clear that the intentions behind introducing participative measures are determining for the design (Dachler & Wilpert 1978). Participative practices can express democratic rights or an organizational applications of the employees' resources, or both, and they can improve the organization's development and operations as well as the quality of the employees' working lives. Based on this approach, incorporating democratic rights and employee influence in decision-making processes, participation is defined as follows: "Participation is the combination of the different dimensions by which the employees take part in organizational decision-making processes in such ways that they are able to secure their interests in these processes" (cf. Wilpert 1998). From this point of view, one could similarly argue that formal participation, according to regulatory principles based on either legislation or agreements, constitutes a democratic restriction of the management's right to manage.

To sum up, participation may contribute to establishing preventive activities aimed at reducing the shift-work exposures, either as part of a regulatory framework or through managerial initiatives. Such activities fall within the following areas:

a) Securing the implementation of regulatory provisions and, accordingly, contributing to discussions about local agreements concerning working-time issues and about derogations from the provisions.

b) Strengthening the role and functioning of health and safety bodies, and thereby asserting the importance of considering health and safety in the organization of work.

c) Monitoring shift work and the shift-work environment.

d) Developing and exploring opportunities to initiate prevention activities granted in Council Directive L 183/1, 1989 and the various national provisions on health and safety activities in organizations.

e) Incorporating health and safety issues in the design of the shift schedules applied, based on the ergonomic criteria.

f) Organizing work processes so that as few tasks as possible are performed at night.

Typically, such initiatives either presuppose a participatory practice or are facilitated through participatory approaches. As an organizational process, the significance and impact of participatory prevention will depend not only on the foundations of the process, but also on its organizational context. Furthermore, the interaction of the many factors involved may increase the potentials and barriers encountered, due to the dynamics that inevitably unfold in such participatory processes.

3. DEVELOPING THE RESEARCH PROJECT

This project can be seen as an extension of the collaboration between Norsk Hydro and the researchers, aimed at investigating shift-work problems. It began with a study on the interplay between shift work and sick-leave. The comprehensive and essential basic material collected and registered by the Health Service Department at Norsk Hydro Norway, recording sick days over a 10-year period, was utilized to take a research approach. Contributors to the initial study included a member of the Health and Safety Service at Norsk Hydro Norway, as well as HB and HJJ, based at the time at the Centre for Working Time Research, Occupational Medical Department, Aalborg Regional Hospital. The study found that the documented increased risk of impaired health and of illness in shift workers was not manifested through a larger number of sick days for shift workers. The resulting article argued that a number of other organizational factors influenced the occurrence of sick days in the groups analysed (Kleiven, Bøggild & Jeppesen 1998).

The cornerstone for our extended study consisted of two components: first, the researchers' experience in shift-work research and interests in prevention and participation issues, and second, the unique opportunity that a continued cooperation with Norsk Hydro offered. Colin Gill from the University of Cambridge later joined the research team, motivated by his interest in industrial relations and regulations in Europe. During our work with the project proposal and our further activities, other colleagues throughout the Norsk Hydro organization expressed an interest in the project and supported its aims and completion. Employee representatives were particularly interested in the examination of preventive shift-work strategies in light of the actual working conditions. Representatives additionally expressed a need for clarifying the employees' attitudes to shift work and the applied schedules. At the same time, the participation of Norsk Hydro in the research project provided us with the sort of on-site and cross-national variations that are invaluable when establishing proper scientific conditions for investigating the themes and questions under scrutiny in this study.

Once the Research Foundation at Norsk Hydro had approved our application, a steering group was established following the normal procedures for Research Foundation grants. This steering group subsequently took part in the elaboration of the final project protocol and helped outline strategic time frames for data collection and contact with the individual companies.

The members of the steering group and the researchers agreed that the steering group's main tasks were to promote cooperation between the researchers and participating companies and to supervise the use of the resources granted. The steering group would also coordinate and advise on the project, determining the general strategies for cooperation between Norsk Hydro and the researchers and regularly discussing the progress made. It was further established that the steering group had no intention whatsoever of interfering with the research activities, nor would this group have any access to the data. The sole responsibility for communicating the results of the study in scientific journals would rest with the researchers, whereas the steering group would help determine how and when the results would be communicated to the participating companies and groups.

3.1   THE RESEARCH MODEL

As argued in the previous section, it is possible to prevent or reduce the adverse effects of shift work through the way shift work is organized at company level, and also to help offset these adverse effects either through the company's own initiatives or through national and international level regulations. However, the impact of these strategies to promote health and safety in shift work depends on how the different types of initiatives are transformed from international to national level, and ultimately to company level, interacting with both company-related and national conditions set out in regulatory frameworks. Thus, there is a need to determine what factors are decisive to the progress of these processes and their dynamics. At the time we were developing our research model, the obstacles to and potentials for improving health and safety in shift work remained unclear, and no empirical results were available on the nature of these processes for the field of working time seen in a cross-national perspective. The same paucity of results applies for the impact that participatory strategies and practices have on the processes, and for their significance to managing health and safety concerns when organizing working time and designing shift schedules, and when assessing the effects on employee health and safety.

In order to have a framework applicable to the design and methods of the project, we created the following general research model to illustrate the interaction between the variables of regulation, prevention, and participation in shift work (Figure 1):

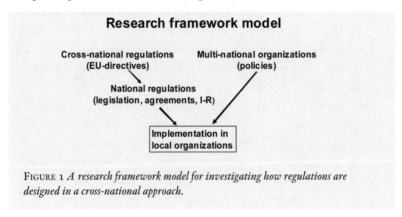

FIGURE 1 *A research framework model for investigating how regulations are designed in a cross-national approach.*

This model illustrates the context in which cross-national regulations are made and the processes of local implementation, and also local conditions are affected by the policies of a multi-national company. The model additionally shows that local design variations can spring from local and national differences. It also indicates how local variations may be linked to differences at both local and national level.

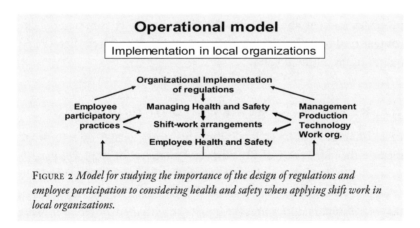

FIGURE 2 *Model for studying the importance of the design of regulations and employee participation to considering health and safety when applying shift work in local organizations.*

Figure 2 is the project's operational model. From a research point of view, our intention is to investigate the interplay between employee participation, regulations, and shift-work health and safety in local organizations. In this sense the model is specific, but it could also be regarded as a more general model in which shift work could be replaced with another organizational hazard. Depending on the shift-work design applied, the model also offers opportunities for examining the status of the variables in different ways, either as independent or dependent variables or as intermediary (mediating or moderating) variables. In this project, the figure designates the interactions between the variables involved in the application of shift work in local organizations. The variable shift work arrangements represent the design and operation of dissimilar shift schedules.

Thus the figure illustrates the organizational implementation of regulations, as well as the actors and conditions involved, the implications for employee participation in health and safety management, and the consideration given to health and safety issues when shift work is designed and operated. In the context of the general theoretical framework, the model also suggests that there may well be variations in the effects of cross-national regulations (for example EU Directive 93 or 2003 "on certain aspects of the organization of working time") between countries, depending on the existing national regulations and on local variations between companies in the same country. Cross-national variation may also depend on organizational conditions, including the degree of employee participation in each company. The model can accommodate different approaches to analysing variables, levels, and effects. This allows us to assess the importance of different dynamic processes and variables involved in different effect parameters. The context of this analysis gives rise to a number of research themes and questions, as outlined below.

3.2 RESEARCH THEMES AND QUESTIONS

In accordance with its general aims, this study focuses on two broad themes: the importance of different configurations for employee participation when designing and operating shift work, and the consideration of employee health and safety in these processes. This implies a design that offers opportunities to apply and work with these differences while keeping other variables (such as production, technology, and work organization) as comparable as possible across sites. Such underlying comparability improves the researchers' ability to analyse the variances in regulations and the levels of existing participation. For further details, see section 4 on design and methods.

Having presented the above reasoning, and our two models, we should like to note that our study did not examine how, or to what extent, local participatory practices complied with the national regulatory framework. Investigating, as it did, the interplay between differences in regulations, participation, shift-schedule design and operation, and employee health and safety, this study was more preoccupied with the processes and the importance of the investigated process variables. In accordance with our stated main purposes, research models, and research terms, and our cooperation with Norsk Hydro, this project deals with the following themes and research questions.

General questions:
- Do local employee participation practices influence the health and safety management in the organization of shift work?
- Do local employee participation practices in health and safety management influence the design and operation of shift-work arrangements?
- Does the application of different shift-work arrangements lead to differences in health and safety, and in organizational behaviour?

Particular objectives:
- Identify how the participatory practices relating to shift work are displayed at local levels, and clarify their participatory form and intensity.
- Identify potentials for and obstacles to considering health and safety issues in shift work arrangements.
- Investigate the existing knowledge about the health effects of shift work, and clarify how this knowledge is integrated into shift arrangements.

Anticipated benefits: Over and above the scientific merits of the project, we anticipated that our findings would benefit the participating companies and Norsk Hydro divisions by virtue of (a) contributing to the development of guidelines and methods for managing health and safety in shift work, and (b) strengthening the mutual utilization and application of each company's experiences with health and safety management in connection with designing and operating shift work schedules.

4. PROJECT DESIGN

The participation of the Norsk Hydro Agri Europe Division enabled the inclusion of companies based in Norway, Sweden, France, former East Germany, former West Germany, the Netherlands, and Italy. Because of Norsk Hydro Agri division's structure, the companies shared a common corporate culture but simultaneously had independent organizations. With employee groups ranging between 200 and 700, the participating companies would be roughly the same size. Companies situated in different countries belonged to the same production sector and operated a similar production technology and organization, which meant that the scientific demands to comparability of conditions and strategies for analytical purposes were acceptably fulfilled. In addition, a company located in Denmark, and forming part of the Norsk Hydro Aluminium Rolling Products division, was also selected for participation. Differences between this company and those from the Agri Division would therefore occur (regarding production sector, technology, and work organization), but all companies would still belong to the same multinational organization and share its general culture and policies (cf. comparable and detailed information on the participating companies in section 5). The remainder of this report only refers to the companies by their country name, and those located in formerly divided Germany are designated E Germany and W Germany, respectively.

As concerns the participation of a Danish company, we found that this could provide the study with improved opportunities for analysing differences in work conditions and operations of regulatory systems. Our interest lay in including the particular Danish system of "cooperation committees" at organizational level, as well as Denmark's tradition for negotiating labour market regulations in general, working-time issues in particular.

A cross-national project of this kind posed considerable demands, not only in terms of the scientific design and applied research methods, but also in terms of the cooperation between the researchers and companies involved. The chosen research design (which can best be characterized as a multiple-case study) offered opportunities for performing qualitative analyses of interview data and quantitative analyses of questionnaire data, as well as the integration of both. As for the collaboration between the individual companies and the research group, day-to-day contact, data collection, and planning to presenting the study's results were handled by local project groups, each consisting of representatives from the company and the research group. The local participants were representatives of the management, employees, and the human resources group. Thus, the project groups' role also included discussing the researchers' contacts with management and employee representatives in each participating company.

After the framework of the project had been decided in late 1998, each company was asked to select members for the local project group. The group's task at company level, besides coordinating project activities between the company and the research group, was to acquaint the company with the project, and to organize how to achieve the project activities. Initial meetings with the different local project groups were held at each company during 1998/99. Here the project was presented in greater detail and discussed in preparation for establishing an activity plan for each company, which could be gradually supplemented over time. Each company plan consisted of a specific project time schedule, a specification of how factual data and documentary material could and should be collected, a list of key persons selected for the interviews, and a proposal for handling subsequent communication.

4.1 DATA COLLECTION

According to the research model, data and material were only collected at the local organizational level. The information consisted of factual data based on existing documentary material and supplementary material compiled especially for this project. The documentary material embraced technology, participation, shift-work arrangements, distribution of employees, and other factors. Data obtained through interviews covered the function and operation of the involved organizational bodies and their influence on the examined processes, such as the management of health and safety, the design and operation of working-time arrangements, and the consideration of health and safety. The questionnaire data covered attitudes to shift work and the applied schedules, organizational working conditions, job satisfaction, social consequences, and the health effects of shift work. The contents of the data, the collection processes, the involved participants, and the specific analyses are clarified and further developed in the respective main sections of the report following this section.

4.2 GENERAL ANALYSIS STRATEGIES

The methods applied depended on the type of available data and the nature of the problem analysed. Qualitative methods were used analysing the examined processes (participatory practices in managing health and safety, organizing working arrangements, and considering employee health and safety) in order to identify the important variables and dynamics in the processes at company level, as well as any similarities and divergences between companies. The statistical methods included different types of analyses of employee health and safety effects, and they aimed to estimate the relative influence of the different applied variables. Further analyses were carried out to evaluate the importance of the differences in working-time arrangements and the local effects of regulations. In the different analyses the examined variables changed status from dependent to independent variables according to whether the analyses focused on causes, intermediary factors, or effects.

The results also provided information on the influence of participatory practices in managing health and safety and organizing working time. They additionally provided opportunities for discussing the terms for improving these practices, which are fundamental for managing health and safety in shift-work arrangements. Moreover, the analyses imparted knowledge about different conditions for employee participation and about considering health and safety when designing and operating shift schedules in the individual companies.

4.3 PROJECT ORGANIZATION

The following researchers participated:
- Hans Jeppe Jeppesen, Associate Professor, Department of Psychology, University of Aarhus, Denmark (former chief psychologist, Centre for Working Time Research, Department of Occupational Medicine, Aalborg Regional Hospital, Denmark), project manager and coordinator.
- Henrik Bøggild, Medical Officer of Health, the County of North Jutland, Denmark (former research physician, Centre for Work-

ing Time Research, Department of Occupational Medicine, Aalborg Regional Hospital, Denmark).

- Colin Gill, Senior Lecturer, Management Studies Group, Engineering Department, University of Cambridge, Cambridge, UK.
- Magnar Kleiven, Self-employed independent consultant, Vivilja A/S, Norway (former Chief Medical Doctor, Department of Occupational Health and Safety, Hydro Porsgrunn, Porsgrunn, Norway, and Chief Physician at The Federation of Norwegian Employers (NHO), Norway), administrative and financial accounts.

A central steering committee was set up to manage and develop the strategies for the cooperation between Norsk Hydro and the researchers, and to follow the project's progress. This committee originally comprised the following five members:

- Tor Geir Engebretsen, Corporate HR, chairman
- Fred Guldager, HAE, Porsgrunn
- Arthur Frank Bakke, European and Porsgrunn Workers Council, senior shop steward
- Magnar Kleiven
- Hans Jeppe Jeppesen

4.4 FINANCING AND RESOURCES

The Research Foundation of Norsk Hydro generously approved a grant of NOK 1.5m towards the accomplishment of this study. The Work Environment Fund of the Confederation of Norwegian Business and Industry later granted a further NOK 500,000 in additional resources for the project. The total financing corresponds to approximately EUR 275,000 at 2005 exchange rates.

5. BASIC INFORMATION

The documentary material we collected dealt with company characteristics, the local participatory bodies, and shift systems in operation. Although in principle this information existed independently of the actual
research, it served several purposes in the context of the project:

1. First, and most importantly, the documentary information was
   used as the basis for evaluating whether the necessary prerequisites for the relevant scientific analyses and assessments were
   present, in terms of common features and differences between the
   participating companies.
2. The information also constituted the framework and underlying
   documentation for our interpretation of the analyses and results
   derived from the questionnaire and interview data. As such, it
   also plays a role in our conclusions on the impacts the existing
   differences in organizational participation have on shift schedule
   design and operation and on the consideration given to health
   and safety.
3. It further provided the basis for categorizing the questionnaire
   and interview data in different units of analysis, enabling us to
   estimate the importance of variations in shift-schedule design for
   the shift workers involved.
4. Finally the material served as a starting point and framework for
   collecting additional information through our interviews.

The following sub-sections give a brief account of the information
gathered, which falls under three general headings: (a) company features, (b) participatory bodies, and (c) dimensions of the main shift
schedules in operation. Subsequent sections will give more details on
the function and significance of the bodies, based on the participants'
experience and interpretation.

The material was collected using two different forms, dealing with
information about company features and the participatory bodies, and
the shift systems being worked. These forms were forwarded to the
responsible officer in the HR department of each individual company,
and the responses returned to the research group. We found that for

some themes and questions no information existed, while for others the information was only available electronically at a few companies. In some cases, for example sick days and turnover during the last 5 years, the responses were based on estimates. It would have been particularly desirable for this project to have had the information on turnover and sick days separated into groups of day workers and shift workers, respectively, but most companies did not have these figures for an extended period of time. Not all company responses were sufficiently precise on all of the questions. Where adequate information was lacking, the responses were omitted from further collation, as was the case for union density at company level.

5.1 COMPANY FEATURES

Table 3 presents the general company features (besides cooperation and working-time issues) that form the basis for comparison and establish the framework we use to group the results. These features cover dimensions related to employment, organizational behaviour, production, and sense of belonging to Norsk Hydro.

Despite its dissimilar production process, the Danish company has been included in Table 3, as it has in the remaining figures for documentary material. This was done to illustrate the comparability of other dimensions. Table 3 shows that all companies but the Danish one belong to the same chemical sector, producing fertilizers or substances linked to fertilizer production. The plants had approximate revenues of ECU 75-400m. The total number of employees varied between 145 and 729. However, production employees alone varied between 96 and 564, and production was estimated to be the most adequate indicator for this investigation.

Figures for employee turnover and rate of illness concern all plant employees, and figures are not necessarily from the same year, but rather from each company's last computed year. A few companies gave estimated turnover rates. Generally the figures for both factors were concluded to be rather low, at 0.5-4.5% for turnover, and 2.2-5.0% for rate of illness. The companies had been part of Norsk Hydro for varying numbers of years before data collection; some for only 2-3 years and other for nearly 80 (see Table 3). The Norwegian company differed significantly from the others, in that it was the original company on which the later multinational company was founded. The other companies had been part of Norsk Hydro for around 24 years or less, calculated from the time of data collection. Five of the fertilizer-producing companies had been part of Norsk Hydro for 13 years or less.

PLANT	1. Products of the plant/core business	2. Total revenue of the plant (approx. in EUR)	3. Total number of em-ployees	4. Num-ber of em-ployees in production	5. Turn over among employ-ees (%)	7. Part of Norsk Hydro since	8. Rate of illness at the plant (%)
E Germany	Calcium ammo-nium nitrate, Ammonium nitrate, Liquid nitric acid	140m	250	164	0.5	1991	2.2
France	Nitric acid, Ammonium nitrate, NPK	100m	200	96	Very low	1986	4.8
Italy	Ammonia, Urea	130m	145	101	3-4	1996	3.5
Denmark	Extrusion of aluminium sections	75m	286	201	45	1975	2.9
The Netherlands	Nitrogen fertilizers	300m	729	564	1	1979	4.0
Sweden	Fertilizer, Tech-nical nitrates, Nitric acid	80m	233	140	2	1992	3.9
W Germany	Ammonia, Urea	135m	258	179	–	1997	3.0
Norway	NPK, Nitric acid, Ammonia	400m	550	300	< 1	1928	5.0

TABLE 3 *Information on company features.*

Comments:
1. The information was obtained in 1998/99. Revenue figures, number of employees, etc., therefore stem from these years, or the previous year.
2. The term "production" (column 4) covers laboratories, packing departments, etc. In practice, this figure therefore includes all employees except those in administration.

5.2 PARTICIPATORY BODIES

Regulations governing working time, which influence factors such as length, payment, compensation, and holidays, can theoretically be adopted (a) at national level via legislation, (b) at sector or trade level via collective agreements, (c) at company level via local agreements, and (d) at individual level via employment contracts (Anxo & Lundström 1998). Furthermore, negotiations at local level can allow possible deviations from the regulations, or lay down framework conditions for working time. The current study focuses on how employees at the local organizational level were involved in local shift-work organization and design, and in its health and safety aspects. Factual data was therefore gathered to clarify the institutionalized frameworks and bodies ensuring employee participation and employer–employee interaction.

The information on participation encompasses data showing features of the established participatory bodies at company level, divided into type of body, formal membership categories and basis of membership, and the basis for introducing the body. Data on other issues (such as the bodies' objectives and role in relation to shift work, and the influence of employee participation on the bodies' functioning) were not accessible as documentary material. Such information was gathered through the interview process. Hence, the description and grouping of the actual bodies as shown in Table 4 is primarily based on information obtained from the HR representative in each company's project group, supplemented with interview data. Consequently, there may be differences in national regulations that reflect sectoral variations, differences in implementation, the scope allowed in interpreting the provisions, deviations through local negotiations, and/or an absence of preconditions for employee participation. We have not aimed to identify deviations or non-compliance with national provisions, but rather to identify how certain types of employee participation interact with the organization, and impact the designing of shift work, and the attention paid to health and safety issues.

The columns in Table 4 are arranged to reflect the bodies' roles and objectives. The column on work organization shows that based on a structural dimension, the participatory bodies can be grouped in three different categories. The first is "works councils" (as found in E and W Germany and the Netherlands), in which all members are elected by, and from, all employees, and management is not ensured a place *a priori*. In this shape, the works council becomes a forum for external discussions and negotiations with management. The second category consists of forums we refer to as "cooperation bodies", in which both management and employee representatives, typically shop stewards, are ensured membership. This category includes Norway, Denmark, and

France (the works council in France has designated management seats and therefore falls into this category).

PLANT	WORK ORGANIZA- TION ISSUES	HEALTH AND SAFETY ISSUES	SAFETY GROUP
E Germany	Works council. Representatives elected by, and from, all employees. Legislation.	H&S committee. Representatives from management, works council and elected H&S representatives. Legislation.	
France	Works council. Representatives elected by, and from, employees, plus management representatives Legislation.	H&S committee. Representatives from management and elected H&S representatives. Legislation.	
Italy	Local collective negotiations. Local representatives from the company and unions, and from management. Legislation / agreement		Safety group. Members appointed by management. Company initiative.
Denmark	Cooperation body. Representatives from management and from employees (shop stewards). Collective agreement.	H&S committee. Representatives from management and elected H&S representatives. Legislation.	
The Netherlands	Works council. Representatives elected by, and from, all employees. Legislation.	Safety, Health & Environment (SH&E) committee. Advisory to works council. Members are appointed by, and/or are, works council members. Legislation.	Safety group. Advisory to management. Members appointed by management. Company initiative.
Sweden	Local collective negotiations. Local representatives from unions (shop stewards) and from management. Legislation.	H&S committee. Representatives from management and elected H&S representatives. Legislation.	
			Cont. next page

W Germany	Works council. Representatives elected by, and from, all employees. Legislation.	H&S committee. Representatives from management, works council and elected H&S representatives. Legislation.	
Norway	Cooperation body. Representatives from management and from employees (shop stewards). Legislation.	H&S committee. Representatives from management and elected H&S representatives. Legislation.	Safety group. Advisory to management. Members appointed by management. Company initiative.

TABLE 4 *The status of the established participatory bodies at organizational level, for work organization, health and safety, and safety. Function, membership, and basis (data collected in 1998/99).*

In a cooperation body, the debates, exchanges of opinions, and decision-making processes take place at an internal level, or as internal discussions. The third category, in which employee influence on work organization is based on local negotiations within the framework of provisions, sectoral agreements, and employers' prerogatives, includes Italy and Sweden. Here, employees are ensured influence via their right to negotiate with management through union or workplace representatives. However, they do not have formal influence on certain issues that can be allocated to a body like a works council or a cooperation body.

Table 4 also shows that in all the countries investigated, employee influence is handled through representative or indirect participatory forums. None of the countries have bodies for direct participation on working-time issues. In all countries except Denmark, the bodies dealing with work organization have a legislative basis, whereas the Danish body is based on a collective agreement between the parties. The main categories derived above for employee participation in work organization will later be applied as analytical units when we examine the interview data. It must also be emphasized that these categories represent only one dimension in our analytical categories; remember that employee influence varies in ways not necessarily connected to the shape of the bodies, and also varies with the level of formal and informal influence granted to the employees on the diverse issues at stake.

In four of the countries (Denmark, France, Norway, and Sweden), the participating companies have Health & Safety Committees (HSCs) that are based on legislation. These committees comprise both employee and management representatives. Thus, one can interpret an HSC as a "cooperation committee" combining representatives from the employee and management groups, and which is meant to operate as the local participatory body for finding solutions and pointing to preventive activities that address health and safety problems. The minimum-level tasks for HSCs are described in the various EU directives and corresponding national legislations, and can thus vary from one HSC to another. Germany (both E and W Germany) has "Work Safety Committees" (WSCs) with representatives from management, representatives from works councils (with a certain number of permanent seats are reserved for the latter), and employee representatives appointed by management. One question raised by the differences in council composition concerns the significance of having management-appointed employee members and works council representatives as mandatory members of these bodies. A categorical distinction can also be made for Italy and the Netherlands, which have no HSCs. In the Netherlands, the SH&E group is a supplement to the works council and functions as its advisory group, as opposed to safety groups, which are advisory to management. In Italy, the safety group is the only body for health and safety issues. As Table 4 shows, three companies (Italy, the Netherlands, and Norway) have established safety groups. They have no legal basis, their members are appointed by management, and the safety groups operate as advisory groups for management. The presence of safety groups may constitute, or imply, a different basis for the function of the HSCs as compared to the companies without safety groups, which means they may actually constitute another category for later analysis.

5.3 SHIFT SYSTEMS IN OPERATION

We gained information on the shift-work arrangements by examining the schedules used for the different shift systems, and from responses to a special questionnaire distributed only to the HR employee responsible for these issues at each company. This questionnaire was designed to enable us to classify the different systems according to the ergonomic criteria used for designing and describing shift systems (Knauth 1996, EU directives 93 and 03). These include the speed of shift rotation, direction of shift rotation, length of shift cycle, length of shift, number of weekends off, number of consecutive shifts, number of consecutive days off, and number of days off following night shifts. The questionnaire also elicited information on the number of teams working under each shift arrangement, the distribution of employees and, in particular, the numbers of shift workers on each shift system. These data were collected in 1999. Tables 5(a, b, c) deal only with the schedules from each company that included most shift workers, and which subjected employees to continuous shift work.

While comparing and assessing the schedules it is important to bear in mind that the schedule dimensions are internally connected, such that changes in one dimension have a knock-on effect on changes in other dimensions. The shift schedule from Denmark was not comparable with the others, as it operates with permanent shifts on weekdays for all three types of shifts, and with a special weekend shift. Here, although production is continuous, the schedules are non-continuous.

| | 1. Overlap time | 2. Duration of shifts in hours | | | | 3. Maximum consecutive shifts | | 4. Present schedule used since | 5. Rotation |
		2a. Morning shift	2b. After-noon shift	2c. Night shift	2d. Weekends	3a. Shifts	3b. Nights		
E Germany	15 min	8	8	8	12	7	7	1984	Clockwise
France	0	8	8	8	8	2	2	1995	Clockwise
Italy	0	8	8	8	8	2	2	1992	Counter-clockwise
Denmark	0	8 h 30 min	8	7 h 45 min	12	5	5	1978	Perman-ent shift systems
The Netherlands	0	8	8	8	8	4	4	1990	Counter-clockwise
Sweden	0	8	8	8	12	5	4	1996	Clockwise
W Germany	0	7	7	10	12	2	2	1998	Clockwise
Norway	15 min	8	8	8	12	5	2	1992	Clockwise

TABLE 5A *The ergonomic criteria of the applied shift schedules (1999/2000).*

Comments:
1. Some plants operate with multiple shift schedules, but the schedules presented above are the most common and cover the largest groups of employees. They are all continuous shift systems.
2. "Overlap time" is the time after the arriving team begins working and until the previous team leaves work.

PARTICIPATION AND PREVENTION

3. Most packaging departments, and some other departments, work in two-shift systems. These are not described in the table.
4. Rotation: Clockwise = night – morning – afternoon, counter-clockwise = morning – night – afternoon.
5. W Germany has 12-hour shifts only on Sundays.

Because the Danish shift system is not comparable, it will neither be mentioned nor included in the further comparisons, and the groupings will only encompass the other seven schedules. The similarities across the different schedules are reflected in the fact that individual flexibility is not a formal part of any of the included schedules. The number of schedules that are similar, or dissimilar, varies considerably across the applied criteria. The length of weekday shifts, irrespective of type, is 8 hours for six companies, with W Germany diverging.

| | 6. Number of weekends off duty | 7. Number of teams used in the shift system | 8. Longest work period (number of days) | 9. Longest off-duty period (number of days) | 10. Individual flexibility in the shift system | 11. Shift workers | | |
						11a. Percentage of shift workers with night work	11b. Percentage of day workers	11c. Percentage of day-and-evening workers
E Germany	3 of 6	4	7	5	No	52	48	0
France	2 of 5	5	6	7	No	36	53	11
Italy	2 of 5	5	2	2	No	60	30	10
Denmark	See comments	See comments	See comments	See comments	No	12	13.5	21.7
The Netherlands	2 of 5	5	4	3	No	50	50	0
Sweden	4 of 6	6	5	7	No	49	43	8
W Germany	1 of 3	5	6	4	No	47	53	0
Norway	4 of 6	6	7	7	No	60	35	5

TABLE 5B *The ergonomic criteria of the applied shift schedules (1999/2000).*

Comments:
6. We define "weekend off duty" as no work from the afternoon shift on Friday till the morning shift on Monday.
7. In counting the longest work period, we count only days of duty in production, not days off and days spent on education and training.

8. The number of shift workers with night shifts includes fixed night workers.

Four of the schedules operated with 12-hour shifts on weekends, and by extension varied the number of weekends off, but this is also connected to the number of teams applied in the schedules (Table 5a).

	12. *Start time of each shift*			
	12a. *Morning shift*	*12b.* *Afternoon shift*	*12c.* *Night shift*	*12d.* *Weekend shifts*
E Germany	05.15	13.15	21.15	05.30-17.30
France	05.00	13.00	21.00	As weekdays
Italy	06.00	14.00	22.00	As weekdays
Denmark	See comments	See comments	See comments	See comments
The Netherlands	06.00	14.00	22.00	As weekdays
Sweden	06.00	14.00	22.00	06.00-18.00
W Germany	05.30	12.30	19.30	06.00-18.00
Norway	07.00	15.00	23.00	07.00-19.00

TABLE 5C *The ergonomic criteria of the applied shift schedules (1999/2000).*

Comments:

9. We have also registered breaks on each shift. Across the board, there are one or two breaks per shift varying in length between 20 and 40 minutes in total.
10. Denmark has a special system that does not fully fit into Table 5c, as for instance, there are differences in the same shift over the week, and weekend work is done by employees who only work weekends on 2 x 12-hour shifts.

This varied picture seems to be replaced by greater consistency when comparisons are made within a category looking at other criteria. Thus we found that schedules with six teams (Norway and Sweden) are identical as to the length of the different shifts applied, clockwise rotation, maximum number of consecutive shifts, and length of off-duty periods (see Table 5b). They differ as to the number of days in the longest

PARTICIPATION AND PREVENTION

work period, and the number of consecutive nights. Three of the four countries that have schedules with five teams (Italy, France, and the Netherlands, with W Germany the exception) have 8-hours shift length irrespective of shift type. They also have the same number of weekends off duty, while differences occur in the number of consecutive shifts, and longest work and duty-off periods. Despite certain variations, we considered it reasonable to make further comparisons between shift schedules based on grouping them according to the number of teams applied.

The percentages of production employees in the companies show – once again with the exception of Denmark – that the employees working a schedule with two shifts (day and evening shift) only make up 11%, at most, whereas the proportion of day workers ranges between 30% and 53%. The proportion of shift workers with night shifts and continuous schedules is between 36% and 60%. In order to elucidate the effects of continuous shift work, we deemed it appropriate to compare day workers with continuous shift workers in various ways.

In conclusion, the documentary material showed that the differences in the way the participatory bodies and the applied shift schedules are designed constituted a valid foundation for our project, which would investigate and analyse these major themes: Whether the nature of employee participation is significant to the organization and design of shift work, and to the attention paid to health and safety. Furthermore, the possibility of grouping the participatory bodies in different categories, with more than one body in each, offered better opportunities to analyse, compare, and assess the dynamics of the processes involved in designing shift work. The similar possibility of categorizing employees according to type of working-time schedule also offered good opportunities to compare between shift workers and day workers, and also between groups of shift workers who worked under different shift schedules.

6. THE INTERVIEW PHASE

Our aims in using interview methods in this study were to exploit their ability to provide rich information, and to use the responses for exploring the processual dynamics that underlie the organization and design of shift work at an organizational level. The interviews also enabled us to further identify the actors involved, and to assess their relative importance. Our analyses focused especially on employee participation, on the participatory bodies, on how health and safety was ensured, and on the improvement of prevention strategies. Moreover, the results our interview-data analyses, when combined with the factual data and results from the project's questionnaire phase, facilitated the final integrative analyses and assessments relating to the study's operational research model.

This section of the report is structured to first offer information about the participants, the structure of the interview guidelines, the measures used, and the data collection procedure. We then comment on the different analysis strategies pursued, along with the concepts applied in the analytical processes. The results of the analyses are subsequently described separately for each participating company, under three general headings: organizing shift work, employee participation, and managing health and safety. The company-specific sections conclude with thematic interpretations, discussing results that represent a particular characteristic associated with the analysis categories and their interaction. Finally, we describe the integrating analyses conducted across the individual companies, which served to identify specific and general results, and to highlight characteristic features of the participatory processes.

6.1 DESIGN AND METHODS

6.1.1. INTERVIEWEE POPULATION

The interview phase was based on all eight participating companies, in France, E Germany and W Germany, Italy, Denmark, the Netherlands, Norway, and Sweden. Separating the two participating German companies into former East and West Germany, respectively, was crucial to understanding the similarities and differences in their basis for developing employee participation, and for regulatory and other conditions – and thus for their organization and design of shift work. To ensure as representative and as adequate an interviewee population as possible, five types of key positions, or key persons, from each company were selected to participate in the interviews. In choosing these individuals, we assumed that they would be active participants in the processes targeted in this study. We further assumed they should represent both sides of industry. The group of five key interviewees at each company was composed as follows: one person from management, representing the cooperation committee or works council (at companies where management was represented in these bodies; alternatively, we selected a management person who attended discussions and negotiations with the works council or union representatives); one management person from the Health and Safety Committee (HSC); two employee representatives from the cooperation committee or works council and the HSC; and one person from the company's HR function. This fifth type of interviewee, from HR, was chosen because this employee group was assumed to play a key role not only in the distribution of employees on different shifts and tasks, but also in decisions and negotiations concerning shift-work compensation, and in the designing of schedules. Despite the implication that more of the interviewees were from management than from production, this was considered appropriate in the interest of achieving the overall aims of the study. The various local project groups, established according to the study's protocol, were consulted on the choice of their company's five key persons – and the interviewee group could include members of the project groups if these persons were deemed to be the most appropriate choices.

6.1.2 INTERVIEW FOCUS

The design of the interview guidelines and the selected topics were primarily derived from the study's aims and the research model. Furthermore, the design drew heavily on the researchers' experience from previous research into working time and shift work, and into employee participation.

The interviews were based on the semi-structured methodology, which allows the interviewer to pursue further interesting issues and identify specific characteristics and dynamics, even while ensuring that all interviewees are asked about the same topics. The interview guidelines fell into four main sections: the organization of shift work, the management of health and safety, the management of health and safety in shift work, and the actual schedules in operation.

Each of these four main themes held a variety of sub-themes dealing with items such as responsibility, type and level of employee participation and participatory bodies, interaction between the staff involved, determining conditions, and future development. There were also more specific questions probing into the nature of the main theme, such as obstacles and factors for considering and promoting health and safety in shift work.

In addition, the four main themes were supplemented with rudimentary information on position, seniority, and representative functions, and with a small section at the end inquiring about how the interviewee experienced the importance of cross-national regulations, such as EU directives on working time and health and safety, as well as internal Hydro directives. The final versions of the interview guidelines were drawn up after discussions with the local company project groups, allowing them to incorporate special local features significant to the data analyses.

6.1.3 DATA COLLECTION

The interviews were all carried out as originally planned, with five people participating from each of the eight companies. As outlined above, the interviewees represented management and employees and were members of works councils and HSCs, and each of the eight groups included one person from the HR department. The HR interviewees also belonged to the respective companies' management groups. The interviews at each company were conducted in the course of two or three consecutive days in 1999-2000. They were all carried out by the same two researchers, one of whom was a chief medical doctor and head of the internal health department in Norway. One cannot ignore that this may have influenced some of the answers from some of the participants. Nonetheless, the research group chose to capitalize on company knowledge in order to achieve the most informative interviews. The interview conditions were also consistent, in that the same two researchers conducted all the interviews. Interview duration was around one-and-a-half to two hours, and the modus operandi had the two researchers be alternately responsible for interviewing and writing down answers. Simultaneous interpreting was used in all countries except Norway, Sweden, and Denmark. The interviews were conducted separately, except in a small number of cases where the researchers spoke to multiple interviewees concurrently. In these cases, the latter always belonged to the same group (either employees or management). Participants were assured anonymity and confidentiality as the basis of each individual interview. Moreover, participants were guaranteed that they would not be referred to in any way that might directly identify them.

6.1.4 ANALYSES

The data collected were processed in the following order:
- First they were treated at company level to identify the conditions underlying the development in shift work, the employees and staff involved, their interaction in the organization, and the designing of shift work at company level. The data were processed to elucidate the dynamics of these processes and the implementation of the applied shift systems and schedules, and to determine how changes were introduced.
- Second, to shed light on employee participation, participatory practices were identified and analysed from the perspectives of *formal* and *informal*, and *representative* and *direct* dimensions of participation were examined. We also investigated the importance of the employee's influence and the possible development of participatory activities.
- Third, the same strategies as described above were applied to analyses of health and safety in relation to how health and safety was ensured, what kind of knowledge existed as to the health effects of shift work, how extensively health and safety was considered when designing schedules, how important employee participation was, and which prevention activities were in place.
- Finally, integrative analyses were carried out to ascertain the dynamics of each company, the aim being to investigate whether particular common characteristics were manifested in the processes. We also analysed whether differences in findings could be observed from one company to the next or whether they were context-dependent, and also sought to identify any differences between management and employee representatives. In our final

discussions, we also investigated the extent to which health and safety issues were considered a *health* problem or a *work organization* problem.

6.2 FINDINGS

This section presents our findings for each participating company, according to the above-mentioned analytical strategies. The individual company sub-sections first describe the findings derived from substantive facts about how that company has organized its shift work, including the development of, and conditions for, its choice of shift system, schedule design, and implementation. Second, we deal with employee participation, including its form and influence on the shift system, and with how employee influence is experienced. The third issue treated is the management of health and safety issues, including responsible staff and employees, promoting and inhibiting factors, and future prospects for development. Fourth, we give thematic interpretations of characteristic features of employee participation and health and safety management in the actual organization of the company's shift work, and discuss features assumed to be of general significance.

Note that after this treatment of the specific companies, the summary in section 6.3 outlines our discussions and interpretations of the identified themes across the companies. These summary findings are not necessarily valid for all of the companies, however. They were selected either because they represented a dominant trend at one of the levels of analysis, or because they represented special characteristic features linked to the interaction of the parties involved (relative to employee participation or health and safety management). It should also be noted that the nature of the data, results, and findings in both section 6.2 and 6.3 necessitated a concise and focused descriptions throughout.

6.2.1 FORMER WEST GERMANY

Organizing shift work
The company's shift system with five teams was introduced in 1998. Local management stated that the company experienced a growing need for greater functional flexibility, where the individual employee would be able to perform a greater variety of tasks than before, and would

be more able to work both inside and outside the control room. This called for the introduction of a new system with increased opportunities for education, better operational flexibility in relation to fluctuating productivity demands, and new requirements for replacements in case of illness and holidays. The demands for flexibility in more recent years were also linked to company information concerning a workforce reduction. The source of inspiration for designing a new system was a company located in the vicinity.

Legislation emphasized that changes in working time must be discussed and negotiated between the company's management and works council – *Betriebsrat* (BR). Statements from the interviewees indicated that such negotiations also had to be conducted within a framework that safeguarded the interests of the company and the employees. Management and BR jointly appointed a group with representatives from the BR and the HR group to elaborate proposals for a new system that would comply with the above-mentioned demands. This group designed a system that had five teams instead of four, but drew on the same number of people. This led to a reduced number of shifts outside day work for each individual shift worker, which in turn meant a reduction in compensations and thus in wages. According to the interviewees, the new system and schedule could imply an increased number of unforeseen changes in an individual shift worker's schedule because of the replacement demands. At the same time, however, they stated that the system would enhance their social life and well-being, with only two consecutive night shifts compared to six in the previous system (more detailed schedule information is found in Tables 5a, 5b, and 5c). Management and BR were in agreement about the new schedule, but because of anticipated, and encountered, resistance from shift workers to the wage reduction, the BR did not present the proposal to the employees for a vote, as the BR feared that the improved health conditions (associated with the new work schedule) would be rejected in favour of monetary compensation. This approach was supported by the knowledge that a neighbouring company had experienced this problem.

Employee participation
The employees had an indirect influence on the design of the actual shift system by virtue of representative participation through the elected employee representatives on the BR. Based on the framework requirements

and considerations concerning functional flexibility and replacement, management had entrusted a working group under the BR with the task of proposing new schedules designs. The BR utilized the opportunity to elaborate a design that focused more on the employees' social and health benefits than their financial benefits. To ensure introduction of the new schedule, and to avoid its rejection – after a vote whose outcome the BR would have had to accept – the BR refrained from sending the design proposal for a vote. The involved shift workers therefore did not directly influence the schedule by participatory voting. No employee participation was possible through the Work Safety Committee (WSC), as this committee was not involved in working-time issues unless they had a bearing on safety. At the same time, here the nature and the principles behind the employee participation should be viewed as a matter for discussion, given that the employee representatives were appointed by management.

No direct formal participation existed in the possible shape of autonomous working-time groups. The interviewees rated the level of employee influence on shift scheduling as follows on a scale from 1 to 7, with 1 signifying the greatest influence: 1.5 / 2.0 / 2.5 / 2.5 / -5.0. (As for the last rating, it became apparent later in the interview that here the interviewee was contemplate rating the level of employee influence not on scheduling, but on shift work overall, and that this person therefore perceived that management had the final decision-making authority.) No substantive differences between the parties could be identified from the average rating of the other four estimations.

Managing health and safety
Concerning the management of health and safety in shift work, the interviewees unanimously stated that shift work had not been a subject of discussion for the WSC, and that the WSC had not been involved at any previous time. The WSC had received some information, but the new system had not been on its agenda. As one interviewee put it, "Shift work is not discussed at WSC meetings; the WC will have to attend to it." However, as one employee indicated, even if health and safety had not previously been an issue for the WSC, perhaps it might be in the future. Similarly, questions related to work organization and psycho-social factors had not been discussed by the WSC either. Furthermore, BR discussions did not deal with long-term health effects or with possible derived prevention strategies.

Thematic interpretations and discussions

Through the BR, the employees did have indirect or representative participation and had an influence on the design of the new schedule that was introduced. The influence and activities of the BR suggested that social and health considerations were taken into account when the new schedule was designed. Management had informed the BR that the company needed a new shift system that would permit the necessary increased level of operational flexibility while attending to educational demands and covering replacements. Within the operational framework of the new system, defining factors like the number of teams operating and the number of employees (factors that could still be considered mainly as managerial prerogatives), the BR was given the authority to influence the schedule design. In this way, advantages were established on both sides through a combination of influencing different dimensions and levels during the organization of the company's shift work.

At the same time, it became apparent that the role of the BR – as the body involved in the schedule-design process, granted certain rights through legislation, and also empowered by management – was subject to particular demands by virtue of the preliminary conditions for its functioning. In the given situation, ideas for a new system originated in the shift schedule of another company nearby. According to the interviews, knowledge about long-term health effects was not considered, nor were illness risks or prevention strategies. One would expect that gaining improved knowledge about health effects and risks through systematic information, and preventing them in shift work, would be crucial in helping the BR to improve its activities in accordance with the intentions laid down in the legislation. It is reasonable to suggest that without improved levels of systematic information, the BR might be prone to act on more incidental, less valid, or less supported information.

Furthermore, the process by which the new shift system was introduced revealed potential conflicts between representative and direct employee participation, and between health and financial considerations. As explained, the BR found it necessary to limit employees' direct participation in order to ensure the implementation of the new work schedule with its concern for employee's social life, due to conflicting prioritization of health and financial benefits. These contradictions highlighted how employee participation in shift-work organization must be developed pursuant to regulations that take employees' health and social life into account. Such regulatory considerations can be said to combine societal responsibilities, ensuring employee participation as well as health and safety – both fundamental social rights of workers, as set out in the labour market regulations (see Commission of the European Communities 1990). Finally, the process of introducing the new schedule also highlighted the importance of the choices made in the BR, and the BR's role as an influential body in which different responsibilities and interests converge.

6.2.2 FORMER EAST GERMANY

Organizing shift work

The dominant shift system operating in production was introduced at the company in 1985 while the GDR still existed, and it was retained after Norsk Hydro took over in 1991. Initially the system had 5 consecutive day, evening, or night shifts, in conjunction with various weekend combinations. As a majority of shift workers wanted 12-hour shifts in order to increase their number of weekends off. Within the limits of the regulatory framework, the company therefore designed a schedule with 8-hour shifts on weekdays and 12-hour shifts at weekends. According to this schedule, a shift-worker on the night-shift sequence would have to work seven consecutive night shifts, ending with two 12-hour weekend shifts. In the early 1990s, some shift workers experienced problems and suggested changes, but the majority of shift workers were in favour of the old schedule. Only minor changes in shift start times had taken place. One interviewee mentioned that the employees could continue using the system because dispensation from the regulations was granted to shift systems that had been applied under the GDR. As one person emphasized, *"The employees know that the schedule is not optimal, but the employees want it, as they have got accustomed to it. They have longer continuous periods with days off, and save extra days off, and it provides better earnings"*. Changes in the form of production fluctuations and a gradual, continuous reduction in the number of employees had clearly created a need for greater operational flexibility. As one interviewee put it: *"Flexibility implies that schedule plans will be normative and that the scheduled plans will have exceptions, and that the workday can be extended according to requirement and that overstaffing in periods with low production demands can be applied to cover being understaffed in periods with high production demands – and flexibility means reduction in costs."* Neither individual flexibility nor group autonomy were discussed.

Employee participation

The interviewees stated that the company's employees exert real influence through the works council – *Betriebsrat* (BR) on the areas defined by legislation. Thus, management cannot introduce changes in working-time conditions without first having consulted the BR. Relevant issues include the start and end time of shifts, the length of shifts, flexibility and overtime – themes typically associated with the designing of schedules. The influence of the BR was also clear from the fact that although regulatory limits set the maximum shift length at 10 hours, management and the BR can agree to deviate from these limits. Further, it was mentioned that the BR was basically involved in all issues significant to the health and social lives of the employees. Even so, as one employee representative said, "*The BR is interested in improvements concerning the health of the employees, but if the BR does not get employee acceptance then action is not possible.*"

Regarding the conditions underlying the operating shift schedule, it was found that the shift workers had direct participation at a collective level through voting on the schedule's design. Moreover, it was due to management's and the BR's interpretation of the shift workers' overall opinion that had kept the existing schedule in force up until the time of our interviews, at which time it was under pressure, particularly in the face of new production demands. No direct participation was found in the form of individual schedule flexibility or autonomous working-time groups. The employee influence on working-time issues was rated by the participants as 2.0 / 3.0 / 2.0 / 2.0 / 3.0, and without substantive differences between management and employee representatives.

Managing health and safety

As for health and safety in shift work, all interviewees indicated that the Work Safety Committee (WSC) did not deal with shift work, and that it had not been on the agenda. One person said that it might be a topic for the WSC, as this body also deals with health issues. Another mentioned that if one had health problems linked to shift work, one would go to see the doctor. The interviewees did not have any information about relationships between shift work and illness, and possible prevention strategies. The pressure to change the actual shift system had arisen primarily out of a need for greater operational flexibility, with some integration of social issues. At the same time it was suggested that, at least for some employees, the shift schedule had adverse effects on well-being and social life and ought to be improved. There was no mention of illness or risk of illness. Medical examinations were carried out every second year, but the interviewees were uncertain of the implications, and of the possibilities for being transferred to day work.

Thematic interpretations and discussions
The discussion about the design of shift schedules revealed a particular interaction between representative and direct participation, and between the BR and the employed shift workers. It points to the general problem of whether or not the BR should take initiatives out of consideration for employees' well-being and social life, even if these go against a majority of employees, or whether to act when a group of employees experiences problems but are insufficient in number to have schedule alterations introduced via voting. It is fair to suppose that this second problem may have been underestimated, in that it was reduced through a secondary selection of healthy workers – since those dismissed during the gradual reduction in the workforce were mainly older workers. Different studies have demonstrated that problems in handling the demands of shift work intensify with increasing age (Härmä *et al.* 1994, Folkard 1996).

The implementation process accentuates questions about how and when a BR should act, and what type of responsibilities a BR has towards the employees. By the same token, a crucial question arises about the BR's responsibility towards employee participation: Should a BR follow a majority simply because they constitute a majority, accepting this majority's priorities, or should it implement changes to improve health? Although this complex set of problems about responsibility, and about whether to act from a participatory approach or not, has been discussed in relation to the BR, arguably the ultimate responsibility for ensuring employee health and safety according to regulations lies with the company. This once again stimulates discussion about specific ergonomic framework provisions, such as the number of consecutive night shifts worked. As conditions for the designing of shift schedules, such framework provisions could be integrated with operational demands.

Another issue illustrated by the development in the design of the applied schedule, or rather by the lack of development, was the attachment to the existing shift system and schedule. One pressing question is whether the prevailing wish to stick with the existing system was to be understood based solely on the prioritizations mentioned earlier, relating especially to extra income, or whether this attachment was combined with other important reasons. This query was prompted by some of the statements taken down during the interviews and also supported by the fact that an alternative schedule could have been designed that would roughly fulfil the prioritizations stated. Furthermore, as the interviews revealed, *"it was these kinds of systems we knew. The schedule showed regard for the employees that had a long commute, and it included every second weekend off."* To this one can add traditions, living habits, and a possible negative adaptation, under which reduced well-being is regarded as a natural cost of being a shift worker. It is likely that the lack of alterations or trial adjustments was also related to insufficient information about risks, and about the potential for designing preventive shift-work schedules. Another contributory factor would have been that other nearby companies had similar schedules. These arguments underscore the importance of continuously providing information on shift work, and of taking a directly participative approach in order to involve employees as much as possible in schedule alterations, as has been demonstrated in previous studies (Jeppesen & Bøggild 2000, Jeppesen 2003).

The interviews highlighted that contradictions and differences in attitudes to working time can exist not only between management and employees, but also between employee groups and individuals. This may contribute to inhibiting a company's innovation dynamic. Finally, the ways in which management and employees interact with the participatory bodies point to an uncertainty as to the functions and tasks related to working time and shift work.

6.2.3 THE NETHERLANDS

Organizing shift work

In the company's organization of shift work, management had the responsibility and the right to determine the shift system and its framework, such as the amount of day and night production, the number of employees on the different teams, the functions of the shifts, and the number of teams. The interviewees described the tasks of the Dutch works council – *Samenwerkingscomité* (SC) – as falling within different dimensions. The SC was the body responsible for monitoring tasks aimed at ensuring that the company's organization of shift work, including its schedule designs, complied with prevailing regulations. In relation to the unions, the SC worked with the regulatory, safety-related, and health-related aspects of shift work organization, while the unions attended to issues like compensation for working shifts, including financial aspects and any deviation from regulations. The interviewees said although management had the authority, the SC had to agree before changes could be made. One participant stated that *"If management want to change the existing schedule, the SC has to be asked. Management can change the frames for the applied shift system, but has to agree on design of the schedules"*. It was also mentioned that the SC could only reject a design, or a certain dimension of it, if the body could argue and substantiate its case based on proven documentation of effects on safety and health. As clarified below in the section on employee participation, a practice had developed at this company whereby, subject to certain voting criteria, the employees had decision-making authority in the area of schedule design.

Until 1990, the company had a shift system with four teams and, for example, seven consecutive working nights. In 1990, however, the five-team system existing at the time of this study was introduced. The schedule design using the five-team system had only undergone minor changes since then. A number of different conditions were found to have influenced the introduction of the new five-team system and the designing of schedules, and we found some variation among interviewees in their assessment of how important different factors were. However, their general perception was that the system had to be changed in 1990 after a general reduction in the weekly working hours from 40 to 38. Management wished to achieve greater functional flexibility, even while the employees were finding it difficult to satisfactorily place their earned compensation days. The employees expressed a strong desire for shorter shift sequences to improve their sleep, well-being, and social conditions, particularly in relation to the 7 consecutive night shifts. Some interviewees emphasized that the changes did not take place because of health considerations *per se*, but rather that the changes, taking the employees' wishes into account, took place because the system and schedules had to be changed anyway. It was through the unions that the SC received information on, and inspiration for, the new design using new schedules with 5 teams and 3-4 consecutive night shifts. An agreement was reached about the new system and its design, and management and unions made the necessary formal agreements.

The interviewees from the employee group mentioned that the problems in the existing system and schedule related to manning levels, as the number of employees was too small. The operational flexibility was manifested as part of the shift schedule in the shape of a 7-day period with on-call duty, during which the relevant employees had to be available to fulfil potential production needs. We also learned that there were great personal differences as to who would agree to substitute for an absent colleague when phoned. The interviewees indicated that the potential extra days' work was experienced as very disrupting. Examples emerged of employees sometimes having to work six consecutive nights because they were called in to substitute for others. All employees had roughly 10-15 extra days per year. The company's situation at the time of the interview was also influenced by a reduction in the workforce of about 100.

Employee participation

It was emphasized that the employees' influence was determined by the legislation governing the SC's functions, tasks, and influence. At the same time, a prevalent practice had been established by which the employees could decide themselves if they wanted to see a change in the work-schedule design. In such instances the employees had to contact the SC, which would subsequently discuss the case with management. Before a proposal could be put to a vote, at least 50% had to be in favour of voting. If the proposal was to be approved, and later implemented, two-thirds had to vote for the change, and voting rate had to be at least 75% of the employees involved. In this way, as stated by a management representative, the employees could decide themselves whether changes should be introduced to an existing schedule, and further, *"The most important thing for management is that production runs as planned."* As for employee influence on the design of shift schedules, integrated frameworks had been established encompassing both direct and representative participation. Participants rated employee influence as follows: 1.0 / 1.0 / 2.0 / 2.0 / 5.0. Regarding the last answer, which differs significantly from the others, it was apparent from later statements that the interviewee's assessment had also included influence on the shift system itself and the existing conditions. Appraised solely from the answers of the other four ratings, the employees were estimated to have a considerable influence, and no substantive differences between the interviewees were identified.

Managing health and safety

The company had a Health, Safety and Environment Committee (HSEC), which, by virtue of legislative provisions, served as an advisory committee to the DC. Up until 20 years ago, HSEC members were appointed by management, shifting to half of members being appointed by management and employees, respectively. Then, around 10 years ago, the appointment of members was transferred to the SC, and then to a sub-committee under the SC. Management, on the other hand, had its own safety group that was advisory to management. The HSCE considered health and environment issues, and could discuss relevant cases with management. If no agreement could be reached on a case, it was transferred to the SC, which would subsequently negotiate with management. To clarify: The function of the HSCE was to give advice to the WC about prevailing rules that dealt with health and safety, and stress in the workplace was discussed as well. Generally, the interviewees did not perceive shift work to be a theme for the HSEC, but no specific arguments for this were offered. This perception might be somewhat related to the fact that the SC, according to legislation, also had influence on working conditions that affected health. It did not appear from the interviews that any knowledge existed about shift work and the risk of illness, or its long-term effects, in such a way that it had informed or influenced shift-work organization. The company had an internal health department that was established about two years prior to this study. This department attended to four particular fields, one of which was organizational and human-resource conditions. However, it did not appear from the interviews that the department had been involved in questions relating to working time, beyond performing health examinations according to EU regulations (EU Directive 93/104/EC). The parties held different views on the tasks and manning of the department, which might have influenced its function.

Thematic interpretations and discussions

Regarding the nature and influence of employee participation, the interview findings revealed that a special integration had been established of employees' direct influence and their influence via the SC, and between direct and representative participation. The SC was empowered, pursuant to the legislation, to agree to shift-schedule changes before they could be implemented. The employees had been empowered, primarily by management but also, under certain preconditions, by the SC, to demand changes to the existing schedules. The features of this integration provided opportunities for preventing internal disparities between two forms of participation, and possibly stimulated their interaction, and in doing so encouraged the development of employee participation in the organization of shift work.

The way the voting was organized, with groupings in work functions or departments, suggested possibilities for reducing potential disparities between employees regarding shift-system design, regardless of the actual dispersion of the voting that took place. In fact, the interviews did not clarify how closely the schedule variations were linked to the different shift systems or to the variability within a single system. However, all things being equal, one could expect that discussions and decisions about schedules would be closer to the individual employee. Furthermore, interesting insights into the development of direct participation or autonomy might be gained by studying the levels at which it would be possible to have voting take place, and thereby increasing the differentiation in the options for working on different schedules based on which schedule can produce the greatest congruity between working life and social life. Such autonomy would also express another form of shift-work flexibility for the individual employee, with flexibility no longer being connected to daily administration or planning, but to a variety of design options.

It should also be recognized that health and social questions raised in 1990 had influenced the discussion of new schedules, reflected in the employees' wish to break down the blocks of 7 consecutive nights into a maximum of 3-4 night shifts. According to employee representatives, the ideas for schedule design and information on avoiding the 7 consecutive nights for health reasons primarily came from the unions. However, the schedules were not altered because of health and social problems, but because they were to be changed to achieve increased operational flexibility.

6.2.4 FRANCE

Organizing shift work
The transition from a shift system with 4 teams to the company's existing system with 5 teams and a 2+2+2 schedule was implemented in 1983. The system change was initiated in response to a need for greater functional flexibility proposed by management, and in response to needs

expressed by employees. The latter group wanted change because they experienced fatigue and reduced quality of family life while working under the previous system, which applied a 6+6+6 schedule. In 1994 the schedule was altered with regard to the distribution and position of days off. Management had also proposed changes in organizing and manning. The shift workers wished for longer periods with 3-4 consecutive days off distributed periodically throughout the year. As a result, 16 of the employees' days off, in addition to their permanent days off, were now scheduled by management – which effectively transferred the desired operational flexibility to management. The employees were given longer periods with days off, but at the same time they had their individual flexibility reduced. One of the participants stated that previously, the placing of days off was mainly up to the individual shift worker, and that the company had a person employed to organize the placing of days off. According to one interviewee, the employees also received a pay rise to help reach a mutual understanding and agreement.

One interviewee noted that the larger financial compensation for working on Sundays and holidays was standardized in such a way that employees received the same compensation irrespective of the actual weekday worked. The interviewees indicated that there was general satisfaction with the schedule, except for disagreement among the employees as to when the morning shift should start. This internal disagreement split the group into older and younger shift workers, with the older employees wanting to keep the existing start time at 05.00 while the younger employees wanted to start later. An early start time also meant a shorter evening when employees were working the night-shift sequence. The interviewees expressed that *"The average age is past 50, so the younger shift workers will have to wait until they can have alterations introduced."* Regarding flexibility in the future, it was generally stated that individual flexibility was not possible in continuous production, and it was more likely that demands for operational flexibility might result in reduced flexibility for employees where holidays and days off were concerned.

Employee participation
The interviewees unanimously explained that no legislation or regulations prescribed employee influence on shift-schedule planning and design. Thus, it was through managerial initiatives that the employees were involved. We did learn, however, that the regulatory basis did

grant employees influence in different ways, for instance on other conditions through the works council – *Comité d'Entreprise* (CE). In 1983, when the 5-team shift system was introduced, management asked the employees about their opinions on the new system using a kind of voting procedure. One of the management interviewees argued that it was inconceivable that management would not have listened to employees who were in favour of the new system by a 60-40% majority. This made the procedure seem more like a hearing than an actual vote. In 1994, management entered into an agreement with the unions. It came out in the interviews that employee influence, or consultation, was a management initiative, and that deciding how much influence the employees should be offered was a management prerogative. The interviewees rated the intensity of employee influence on the design of shift schedules as 5.0 / 2.5 / 2.0 / 7.0 / 3.0, showing considerable variation between interviewees. The influence was rated higher by management than by employee interviewees. At the same time, both sides of the company acknowledged that, compared to most companies in France, the cooperation between employees and management at this company was good.

Managing health and safety
The interviewees all said that the Health & Safety Committee (HSC) was not, and had not been, involved in shift work. Some thought that the HSC might become involved in the future, as shift work could come to fall under work organization problems. The HSC attended primarily to safety problems, but theoretically also handled health problems, typically upon request from the company physician. In this respect the HSC was concerned with the individual employee's health. It was explicitly stated that the health problems of the individual employee were dealt with by the company physician. Some attention was paid to the effects of shift work, and one of the employee interviewees mentioned having proposed that shift workers should be able to retire one month earlier for every year they spent in continuous shift work, due to the strain and, most importantly to the fatigue that increases with age.

Thematic interpretations and discussions
According to the interviewees' information, no regulations determined employee participation in, and influence on, the planning and design of shift work. The involvement of the employees, or employee participa-

tion in shift-work design, occurred on the basis of managerial initiatives and thus under informal conditions. The company's history of developing shift systems and designing schedules revealed that the employees had been consulted. Furthermore, the statements of those interviewed about the introduction of the new shift system in 1983 also portrayed a situation that allowed the employees to express their attitudes, although they could not be sure of the result, as the process was a hearing, not a vote. The uncertainty that might have accompanied informal participation may have had some bearing on the interviewees' rating of employee influence, and on our understanding of the divergences in the interviewed group. Their assessments and statements during the interviews showed that when the employees evaluated the level of employee influence, they seemed to weight the actual administration of informal participation less than the conditions that ensured employee influence. This difference may also help explain the considerable differences in the perception of employee influence that existed between management and employee participants. The diverging perceptions may also rest on the fact that employee influence could be experienced differently – differently, that is, because of the differences related to whether one is sacrificing influence (whereby one may experience a reduction in one's own influence); or whether one is receiving influence (but without knowing how often, or whether, the influence will change depending on one's reaction, and without knowing what effects one's influence will have). These aspects accentuate the ambiguity of informal participation, the manifold implications connected to participation, and, in particular, the differences between formal and informal participation.

The French company also highlighted the type and origin of the information underlying schedule alterations. Once again, the information did not arrive through methodical communication about regulation activities, but was incidental and came from a neighbouring company that had introduced the 2+2+2 system. While discussing the background of the experiences at the French company, the interviewees explained that other Hydro companies in the sector had similarly introduced the 2+2+2 system. However, none of the interviewees had experienced or heard of any cross-national knowledge-sharing concerning shift work within the Norsk Hydro group. The importance of sharing knowledge and experiences was underscored here at local-community, or sector, level but also, for a multinational company, at cross-national level, in that such sharing may facilitate a dynamics of innovative development when creating shift schedules and selecting and planning shift systems. This emphasis on sharing was not to be perceived as a replacement for regulatory-derived initiatives, but as a set of parallel activities.

Another aspect of understanding the dynamic behind designing or altering shift schedules was plainly elucidated by the example of varying attitudes to the day shift's start time. The difference ran along age lines, between two groups that split at around 40 years. This example illustrated some of the possible internal contradictions within the employee group relating to shift-schedule designs. It also shows that there was a general acceptance of the employee majority's right to decide, and of the minority group having to wait for change until they achieved a majority. In the given situation this would be realistic, as those dissenting tended to be younger employees – unless, of course, their attitude changed because of adaptation as their age increased. In this case, the younger newcomers wishing for a later start time would still be a minority. Such a gap might also have run along other demarcation lines with no prospect of change because of age development or other factors. This raises the very important issue of investing resources in trying to solve the problem through some sort of rescheduling, trials with individual or group flexibility, or a third approach, to stimulate the dynamic of innovative shift scheduling.

Finally, the problem of dealing with health, or rather illness, was similar to that experienced in other participating Norsk Hydro companies, illustrated here in the role of the company physician and health staff. The interviewees mentioned that it was the company physician who took care of the health problems of individual employees. For those health problems that might be connected to working conditions, such as the organization of shift work, this practice could increase the likelihood of linking work-related health (or illness) problems to individual problems rather than to work-environment problems. In other words, the focus would be on the individual workers and not on the working conditions.

6.2.5. NORWAY

Organizing shift work
Initially it should be noted that one of the researchers was chief medical doctor and head of the internal health department in Norwegian company. Naturally we recognize that this may have influenced some

of the answers from some interviewees. Even so, the research group chose to capitalize on company knowledge in order to achieve the most informative interviews, and to keep interview conditions consistent by having the same two researchers conduct all the interviews.

All interviewees agreed that management had the responsibility for, and made decisions on, conditions and frameworks relating to the existing shift systems. In addition, the company traditionally involved employee representatives in drawing up proposals for shift-schedule design, sometimes jointly with management representatives. Activities in the field of shift work were found to be determined less by certain established criteria than by informally determined traditions within the organization.

Regarding the implementation of the existing six-team shift system in 1991/92, a special working group was set up with a management representative as chairperson and with shop stewards representing the employees. This group was to prepare proposals for new schedule designs, so the company's Health Department was invited to contribute information about health and the long-term effects of shift work. Important arguments for a new shift system came from management, who noted that the need for substitutes had changed, as had the demands for competence development. These demands had increased, meaning external substitutes would no longer be adequate replacements. Furthermore, a system with 6 teams would also increase the operational flexibility of working time. This was a result of the continuously available shift, which would allow the system to respond to fluctuations in production. Employees would have fewer shifts outside daytime than before, and easier access to counterbalancing overtime. In addition to 6 teams, the system framework required that all employees working under the new system must adhere to the same schedule, and that the shift succession times in the schedule would be 07.00-15.00-23.00. The working group presented two alternative proposals along with the schedule that was actually applied. The employees had made suggestions that included 12-hour shifts at the weekends. Moreover, the new system reduced the required number of substitutes from two to one for the shift normally used for competence development and training, as the transition was to be introduced without increasing the number of employees.

This involves a potential risk of increased unpredictability in the schedule, following a possible increased in the number of changes to individual shift workers' shift plans, as well as a possible need for more overtime work until substitutes could take over. The three proposals for new schedules within the new system framework were put to a vote among the employees. Here employee influence and choices were limited, not only by the framework set out for the new system, but also by certain conditions in the schedule itself, such as start times. It was mentioned that at a later stage, some employees wanted another schedule implemented, but those contacted did not wish to proceed, and so the matter went no further.

Regarding flexibility in the future, it was indicated that a high level of operational flexibility already existed, with possibilities for using overtime and changes in plans. It was also mentioned that flexibility ought to be more reciprocal than was the case. Some wished for greater responsiveness from management on this point. As one said, *"Individual flexibility is not part of the company's flexibility and has not been put into practice, but there is a wish for that among employees."*

Employee participation

It was difficult to precisely describe the structure and framework for employee participation in shift work, since what we did identify were more informal initiatives determined by company traditions and culture. These initiatives involved employee representatives and shop stewards in an interplay with management, but also included direct forms of employee participation within delimited frameworks of schedule-design choices. As mentioned, in 1991, a group comprising shop stewards and management representatives was set up, and its proposals were put to the vote among the employees. We learned during the interviews that *"The voting was about the new plans; it was not possible to oppose changes."* In several instances the interviewees also referred to health and safety regulations as the foundation for employee participation and company traditions.

At the same time, employees participated mainly through the shop stewards. Furthermore, the interviews showed that in practice, employee participation took place as cooperation with management, and that practices had to be established for each particular case or situation. Case-specific decisions were also made as to when, and whether, cases could be most appropriately presented to, and resolved by, certain relevant company bodies. The interviewees did not mention the works council (*samarbeidsutvalg*) or Cooperation Committee (CC) as an involved actor. On the contrary, they indicated that activities typically went on at a sub-company level and at meetings with employee representatives. It appeared that a definite structure for dealing with shift work based on applicable legislation was neither determined nor existing. Activities could take place at different levels, or different activities could take place at the same level in different departments. The interviewee assessments rated employee influence on shift-schedule design at 2.5 / 2.0 / 3.0 / 2.0 / 2.0, with no appreciable difference between the parties.

Managing health and safety
A central Health and Safety Committee (HSC) had been established to cover the entire the Norwegian company. This was supplemented by local subsidiary-based HSCs representing the interested parties and based on legislation. On addition, the Norwegian company had a management-appointed Safety Group that acted as an advisory body to management. Health issues and long-term effects from shift work had been part of the considerations when the new schedules were designed in 1991, brought up by the employee representatives in the established working group. They asked the company's Health Department (HD) to give a presentation about shift work and health, as they the HD had been interested in the topic. Health and sickness risks had not been brought up by the central HSC or the local subsidiary HSCs. The interviewees had no knowledge that these bodies had been involved in questions about shift systems, or in designing shift schedules.

This was also the case for the Safety Group. To clarify the company HD's involvement, note that a determining factor here was that some of the HD people were interested in shift work and health, and that the HD had consequently gathered knowledge and documentation – which was the reason for involving the HD. No practice had been established, or agreement made, about integrating the HD, or about HD being particularly entrusted with handling shift work. From this perspective, the involvement of the HD can best be described as incidental. It was mentioned that individual shift workers experiencing shift-work-related problems address their problem to one of various contact points. Some would contact the HD, others the employee representatives, and yet others their supervisor or manager. Interestingly, it was mentioned that "... *more employees would not address anyone in particular, but just grit their teeth.*"

Thematic interpretations and discussions

To a substantial degree, the developed organizational culture regarding work schedules, health, and safety, with its mixture of formal and informal participation, along with direct and representative forms of participation, was context dependent. Furthermore, it was carried forward by traditions in the organization and by the attitudes of the actors involved. The informal aspect was further underlined by the fact that the level of influence, or intensity, in employee participation was not clear, and by its capacity to diverge from case to case depending on the attitudes of management. This was because choosing shift systems and schedule designs, and related issues, were mainly managerial prerogatives. The interviewees indicated a general satisfaction with the existing potential for cooperation. At the same time, however, one could assumed that this organizational culture might contain an inherent ambiguity. On the one hand, the structure of the involved actors and processes revealed that specific forms and conditions for employee participation could be developed that offered employees influence within the special structural framework. Because of the context dependency here, the potential for generalizing and transforming such a structure to fit other organizations will certainly be limited, and a similar structure elsewhere for dealing with shift work, health, and safety would have to develop in its own context. Nevertheless, the approach taken here can offer guidance. On the other hand, the informal dimension might reflect an uncertainty as to the structure's robustness, or as to how tenable it is in response to market fluctuations, possible conflicts of interest, organizational changes, and so on. Thus, what may be the structure's greatest strength may also be its gravest weakness.

The structure's informal aspects are further highlighted by the fact that the interviewees did not mention the Cooperation Committee (CC) as an actor in organizing shift work. On the contrary, they explained that much of the cooperation between the parties (the employee representatives and management) took place *ad hoc*, and was mainly informal where shift work was concerned, but that it perpetuated a tradition whereby management in some areas could assign influence to employees. As concerns employee influence in general, the interviewees reported that this approach was a Hydro Agri tradition, and that the legislation was just a framework.

The informal and *ad hoc* practice may further imply an uncertainty with regard to detecting problems and implementing strategies to resolve them. This may reflect the description of variations in whom individuals address when they experience problems, and when they do so. Moreover, the informal procedures might also make it more difficult for individual employees, or groups of employees, not only to have work problems (for instance about changes) raised, but also to determine how they can follow up on their issues of concern.

The consideration given to organizing and designing work schedules illustrated that if a documentary knowledge existed about risk and illness, it would be integrated into future planning. One interviewee indicated that employee representatives depended on the existence of available research results.

The development in the application of flexibility showed a clear tendency to reduce individual or employee group flexibility and to increase operational flexibility.

6.2.6 DENMARK

Organizing shift work

Note that at this company, 11 people participated in the interviews. There were 5 representatives from management and 5 from the employee group, plus the HR manager, who also belonged to the management group. All 11 interviewees were encouraged by the company's research group to participate. They were divided into 5 interview groups according to position, work tasks, and representative function. This yielded 3 groups from management and 2 from the employees, and 5 interviews were therefore conducted.

It must also be emphasized that the Danish company was part of Hydro's aluminium sector and was not subject to the same conditions and demands for continuous production as the other 7 participating companies. In Denmark, market fluctuations were reflected in production by having some periods when production was suspended during the weekends, so strictly speaking the company had discontinuous production supplemented with weekend production most of the year. These circumstances naturally had an affect on the shift system and schedule designs.

The company had agreements according to which the responsibility and authority for shift systems and schedules lay with management – but according to the same agreements, the employees had a right to be consulted on working-time issues. In practice, the shift schedules were designed by means of meetings and discussions between the representatives for the company's interested parties.

The history of the shift system in force went back to the 1970s and the founding of the factory. At first the company had only day work, introducing a rotating day-and-evening shift system in some areas after about 6 months. Then, after about a year, night work was implemented, and because only very few of the employees wanted to have night work, new employees were assigned to work permanent night shifts. Later still, when the company planned to expand production and begin weekend operations, the employees were again consulted about these changes. Because the employees did not wish to have weekend work, permanent weekend work with 12-hour shifts was introduced. This meant that certain employees would work two 12-hour weekend shifts, then be off for the rest of the week while receiving nearly the same wages as the other employees, due to the weekend compensation pay. Excepting minor adjustments, such as the length of the Friday shift and start time on Fridays, this system had been preserved up to the time of the interview. It can be suggested that the actors involved experienced the course of development to have been a fair and democratic process connected to the gradual expansion of production. The interviewees reported that those already employed had been consulted and had rejected the 12-hour weekend shifts, whereas new employees had been informed in advance about the special conditions for their shift work and had accepted the weekend shifts. There had been no deliberations about health and safety.

With regard to the shift system and schedules in force, it was noted – by management representatives in particular – that the employees had got the working time that they wanted, and that the system provided no special production advantages. The employee representatives also expressed that the existing system and schedules were an advantage compared to a rotating schedule, and also that the employees who exclusively worked nights or weekends did not want to change. Furthermore, it was noted that these attitudes were based not on health considerations, but rather on social and financial reasons. The interviewees reported that many of those who worked permanent night and weekend shifts were owner-operators of farms or other small businesses, and were allowed by legislation to have extra jobs. We also learned that some were part of a couple were one partner worked day-evening shift and the other worked nights to accommodate childcare needs. The employee representatives believed that some would change to day work if the wages were the same. Both management and employee representatives asserted several times, in different contexts, that it was better from a health perspective to have permanent shifts rather than to rotate, and that they did not understand how employees at neighbouring companies could handle rotating systems. Regarding social interaction among the employees, it was stressed that weekday workers had no contact with weekend employees, and had only limited contact with night workers. The interviewees deemed that permanent shifts resulted in more pronounced splitting of the company's employees into separate groups.

The management interviewees emphasized that there was a growing need for flexibility, and that one possible initiative to meet this need could be a 'time bank', which would allow for better adjustment to market demands. In one area of the company, the employees had individual flexibility around a fixed time (08.00-14.00), but they had only day work and particular tasks. It had not been possible for other employee groups to begin discussing individual flexibility. According to the representatives, management had simply said that it was not possible.

Employee participation
The employees had an influence on shift-schedule design through both representative and direct participation. The conditions for employee participation were based on company tradition and on informal procedures arising out of a practice developed in a mutual understanding between the parties. At the same time, initiatives for schedule changes could come from employees or from management. Whoever took the initiative, representatives from management and employees would meet in a special forum established to solve working-time issues and problems. The representatives from the parties would discuss the situation, negotiate about compensation conditions if necessary, and draw up new schedule plans. The schedule-change proposals would then be put to a vote among the employees involved using either a written ballot or a show of hands, and the proposal with the most votes would be implemented. The interviewees noted that they had never experienced a situation where a proposal with majority support had not been introduced.

The special forum group was informal. Existing outside the works council (*samarbejdsudvalg*) or Cooperation Committee (CC), it had no predetermined interaction with these bodies or with the Health and Safety Committee. Further, this group was organized *ad hoc*, so it could meet quickly and only when necessary. The employee interviewees also expressed that schedule design tended not to be a subject for negotiation, so the influence employees were offered by management was informal, and as one interviewee said, *"when the schedule corresponds to production, management are easy to discuss with."* Management interviewees stated that the *ad hoc* group's composition ensured the participation of the relevant representatives, facilitating and speeding up the negotiation process.

The interviewees assessed employee influence on the shift-schedule design as follows: 2.0 / 2.0 / 2.0 / 3.0 / 3.5. The results suggested that, in general, the management representatives tended to rate employee influence higher than the employees did.

Managing health and safety
The company had a Health and Safety Committee (HSC) composed of management representatives and elected employee health and safety representatives. The interviewees stated that the HSC was primarily involved in accidents, safety issues, protection, and so on, but that shift work was not a topic in that body. At one point, shift work had been mentioned in relation to safety, and questions raised about 12-hour shifts, but otherwise the HSC did not discuss shift-work issues. Some interviewees said that it could potentially be a topic, and that if information appeared about health effects it would be relevant to discuss shift work in the HSC. All interviewees agreed that health aspects had not played a role in determining the shift system or designing the schedules, and that because of the perception that adverse health effects were connected to rotating schedules, the subject was not discussed.

Thematic interpretations and discussions
In accordance with applicable regulations, the Danish company had established a Cooperation Committee and a Health and Safety Committee with equal representation from both sides of the company, and elected separately by the parties. Neither body was involved in shift-work matters. Soon after company started operating, in the 1970s, the employees were offered influence on the fundamental dimension of having schedules with permanent or rotating shifts. They had maintained such influence ever since then, and only minor changes had subsequently been introduced. An informal participatory system, integrating direct

PARTICIPATION AND PREVENTION

and representative participation, had developed, based on company traditions and management attitudes and on the parties' mutual understanding of its advantages. For management, this system was a way to strengthen employee involvement, to offer influence for both forms of participation, and to ensure a smoother and quicker handling of shift-work issues. For the employees, the system provided a way to gain influence on matters that, in principle, were management prerogatives. At the same time, one can argue that the handling of shift work was moved from formal participatory bodies, with only broad provisions about influence on work organization and employee health and safety, to informal processes with increased influence. Nevertheless, potential adverse health and long-term effects were not taken into account when designing shift schedules.

However, the company's practice also showed its limits when employee representatives tried to raise the question of individual flexibility and further discussions were refused. Even so, the traditional practice still appeared to be a 'win-win' situation for both parties – but because no conditions had been determined, the robustness of this practice may become a key issue in future. The lower level of influence experienced by the employee representatives interviewed might be connected to its informal character, and also to the fact that the established participatory practices had been related to minor changes in the schedules. This naturally raises the question for employee representatives: What of future influence and practices in the event of major changes or more conflict-ridden issues? The existing shift system and its accompanying schedules were introduced at a certain period, during the company's early years and in response to the market conditions at the time. However, the system's historical standing in the company may also mean that it will be fairly hard to change if the need arises due to production and market changes. This may, in turn, constitute a potential for new internal conflict. Moreover, the schedule's permanent shifts illustrated a shift system's importance, and potentially limiting effects, on the nature of the social interaction among the employees group as a whole, including management. This could also create some unevenness in how the company develops its work organization and employee competencies.

The schedules with permanent night shifts highlight a sort of ambivalence: On the one hand, it was beneficial for the other employees as they would not have to work at nights (or weekends). On the other hand, however, it led to an explicit primary selection among job applicants, who were offered permanent night work with all its implications. One could similarly argue that on the one hand, the problems connected to night work (see section 2.1) would be isolated to a smaller group of employees, while on the other hand they might constitute a higher risk among permanent night workers than would otherwise be the case. However, the rigorous and explicit selection process might have influenced that risk. The interviewees also revealed that working nights was associated with a higher income, and that day workers had a working-time system consistent with their original wishes, so nobody seemed to want to make changes. Characteristically, we learned that there was a strong adherence to one's own shift schedule as the best solution, justified by arguments regarding the difficulties associated with other schedules.

6.2.7 ITALY

Organizing shift work
In a formal sense, management at the Italian company had the responsibility and the decision-making authority regarding the organization of shift work. This included such system choices as manning, tasks, number of teams, competencies, and employees assigned to the various teams and schedules. The employees' influence was manifested through local negotiations between the parties. Company-based negotiations had gained increasing importance throughout the 1980s, and the practice was institutionalized by a national agreement reached in 1993 between the state and the labour-market parties, which also included the foundation on which employee representatives were to be elected. Besides the elected employee representatives, it was also usual for representatives from the unions to participate. Even though the local negotiations had gained importance, they took place continually within the frameworks set out in the central negotiations. Besides wage conditions linked to increased productivity, typical negotiation themes would include the distribution of working hours, flexibility bonuses, and overtime (Pelligrini 1998).

As for developments in the way shift work was organized in the Italian company, since 1968 it had applied a rapidly rotating schedule with a maximum of 2+2 shifts in a sequence. Until 1968 management had determined how schedules were designed, but subsequently schedule designing took place in cooperation with unions and employee representatives. Later a tradition developed whereby the task of designing schedules within the agreed frameworks was transferred to the unions. Beyond the negotiated conditions, management had the ultimate formal decision-making authority. According to the interviewees, it was the union that had identified the new system in 1968, arguing in favour of its implementation that it was less harmful to employee well-being and social life. The schedule was later changed to have fewer shifts between days off. This was in 1974 following the general reduction in weekly working hours in Italy, but the principle of rapid rotation was maintained, and the new schedule was also designed by the union. The schedule used at the time of this study, which operated over most of the year, was introduced in 1992 following a resolution from the employees.

The interviews indicated that the union had improved the new schedule-design proposals based on requests and suggestions from the employees. The process of altering the schedule ran as follows: Initially, management and the union, including employee representatives, met and laid down a basic framework,, which was later approved by the employees in a show-of-hands vote. There were several follow-up meetings between representatives and employees before the final proposal for the new schedule design had been elaborated, incorporating the various employee wishes that were practically possible. The employees the voted on the final proposal, also by a show of hands. One interviewee stated that he had never heard of a situation where management did not accept the final schedule proposal. The process itself was rooted in tradition rather than in a formal agreement, with the framework established as the first step.

The existing system was applied 6-7 months a year. In order to fully cover all 24 hours, including illness and other absence, the existing schedule called for 5.5 persons, whereas the previous work schedule (now applied during the rest of the year) only called for 4.5 persons. One main difference was that the new schedule had 6 more days off per year. These days, along with other accumulated hours, had been incorporated into the schedule to result in fewer consecutive shifts before days off. Compared to the old system, the 6 days represented a special reduction in working hours for shift workers, combined with compensation and a general reduction in weekly working hours. Accumulated hours were spread more randomly in the old system, depending on the combined employee needs and production demands, whereas such hours in the new system were permanently integrated in the shift schedule. The employees wanted the present system, used for 6-7 months each year, to be extended to encompass the whole year, but this would also require more people, and the employees' wishes were refused with reference to central agreements. This case illustrated the importance of the schedule-design frameworks as well as the influence of management's decision-making authority.

Some interviewees also indicated that a six-team system had been discussed, and there had also be talk of closing down part of the factory, which would cause a reduction in the number of employees. We also learned that management had tried to introduce something called "the Shell system", but the employees had preferred the existing system and returned to it. Ongoing topics for discussion were start times and the location of days off, as well as financial compensation for plan changes and overtime. Some interviewees further mentioned that a new regulation had been introduced stating that employees should have greater influence on their schedule, in collaboration with unions and management. It would be interesting to find out how this was to be implemented and put into practice.

With a view to increasing functional flexibility, the company had developed a 'joker' function, whereby a person possessing multiple competencies or skills could substitute in a number of different tasks. Management representatives also pointed out the need to strengthen such functional flexibility in order to also increase operational flexibility. Individual flexibility was not found to have been a topic for discussions, or an issue when drawing up proposals, and this was apparently also the case for the employees.

Employee participation
Employee participation in designing shift schedules had formally taken place via employee representatives, elected by all employees since the 1993 Italian collective agreement regarding employee workplace representation. Jointly with union representatives, the company's employee representatives formed a group authorized to handle negotiations with management on certain work-related issues. These included issues relevant to the shift system and to shift-schedule design, such as the distribution of hours and days during the week and flexibility compensation. Meanwhile, as noted earlier, other issues significant to schedule design fell under management's decision-making authority. This gave em-

ployees greater potential influence, through local negotiations, on the conditions applying to schedules, and on the way they were designed.

We could deduce from the interviews that the ultimate decision lay with management, although a variety of issues had to be negotiated. A tradition had developed in the sector and the region that, within the established frameworks, employees had the right to decide on the design of their schedules. The combination of company negotiations and employee decision-making on schedule design had led to the establishment of a particular forum that ensured an ongoing interaction between representative and direct participation, and between the formal and informal conditions.

The company had only one elected workplace employee representative. This was because, according to the established criteria, only one representative per full 100 employees could be elected, and the Italian company had between 100 and 200 employees overall. Hence, no local group of workplace employee representatives, corresponding to a works council, could be established. Besides this one employee, there were no participatory bodies elected by the employees, or elected jointly by the management and the employees. The company had a management-appointed safety group or committee, which acted as the management's advisory group.

The interviewees assessed the level of employee influence on the designing of shift schedules as 1.5 / 3.0 / 3.0 / 3.0 / 6.0. Those who gave the two extreme ratings were interviewed in greater depth, in order to ensure that the conditions for their answers were the same. After this was confirmed, both answers were included in the analysis. The assessment ratings illustrated a considerable divergence, with representatives from the two sides at either end of the rating scale. When grouped, the answers showed that the management representatives estimated employee influence to be greater than the employees perceived it to be.

Managing health and safety
The company had no elected Health and Safety Committee (HSC) with equal representation, and according to the interviewees there was no foundation for such an HSC in Italian legislation. The company established a safety group around 1987. The members were appointed by management, and the group played a consultative role to management. The safety group was primarily involved in preventing accidents,

accident risks, and "near misses", and in analysing accidents, and its efforts were stepped up after Norsk Hydro took over. None of the interviewees believed, or had heard, that the safety group was concerned with shift-work issues. One explicitly asserted that "*Shift work has never been a theme for the safety group. It has not been estimated that a need existed for discussing a connection between accidents and shift work in general, or between accidents and night work or schedules. Nothing in that relation has been investigated.*" The company had no health department, but did call in external assistance to comply with the demands of the EU Directive regarding health examinations. However, this had not influenced the design of the company' schedules. No special information had been given about risks of illness or long-term effects.

The health aspects contained in the 1972 proposal from the union about schedule design was found to have been primarily concerned with social life, sleep, and well-being. Further, it was evident from the interviews that as far as schedules were concerned, social considerations were the main topic of discussion. Illness risks and long-term effects did not emerge as issues in the interviews.

Thematic interpretations and discussions

It was difficult to estimate and unequivocally interpret the size and scope of employee influence on schedule design, within the framework of the applied shift system, as the premises for doing so were not sufficiently explicit – in that our information about the conditions governing local negotiations on the schedule-design frameworks was inadequate and unclear. We also realized that the foundation could constantly vary, according to the wishes, needs, and demands of both parties. In addition, the influence employees were given was effected through local negotiations and traditions. Furthermore, considerable variations could exist in the application and content of local negotiations within companies, regions, and sectors (cf. Regalia & Regini 1998, Ponzellini 2003).

The interviewees' assessments of employee influence, and the widely diverging ratings, were found to depend on how such influence was rated relative to the actual process of designing new schedules. The parties agreed at the initial meeting, within the already established shift-system framework, which particular specifications and conditions should apply when schedules were designed. One interviewee indicated that the employer or management had the right to distribute hours and days across the week, based on the regulatory framework. It had become increasingly prevalent in Italian working-time regulation, and organization, that a number of issues such as flexibility, wage conditions, and compensation could be linked, even while linking these issues to productivity increases. Furthermore, these issues would have to be developed within the framework of any existing local agreements, and in accordance with the national agreement in 1993 and other current central agreements and legislation. This process had made the Italian system highly complex, but also given it a potential local flexibility within the regulatory frameworks (Ponzellini 2003), depending on local conditions for cooperation and local tradition.

In our estimation, variations that were particularly significance to the schedules were related to the initial discussion, which set out the framework for the schedule within the established system. At this stage, demands for functional flexibility (such as minimum skills required in each team, and operational flexibility) would narrow the design framework, and the flexibility would have to be achieved through financial compensation or extra hours off, which might in turn be subject to productivity considerations. Finally, the compensation paid to fulfil demands for functional flexibility would be put into practice at individual or group level (being paid only to those who had the desired skills), and not collectively. However, this would still be the case for the schedule frameworks derived from these conditions. Within the given frameworks, employee influence on the schedules was considerable, in keeping with the sector tradition of leaving schedule designing to the employees, their representatives, and the unions.

The Italian company had no participatory bodies where employee representatives could organize in a sort of works council or *Rappresentanza Sindicale Aziendale* (RSA), although this was potentially supported in the legislation. The company only allowed employees to have one employee representative, based on the size of the workforce. The company did not have a participatory body to ensure health and safety. One could reasonably expect that the absence of employee representative groups and participatory councils or committees would affect the development of local cooperation, consequently augmenting the role that local attitudes, cooperation experience, local negotiations, and traditions play in employee participation in shift-work organization.

According to the interviewees, social conditions and well-being were the factors that had influenced schedule design of schedules, and not the risk of illness or the prospect of long-term effects. Moreover, health problems and symptoms were found to be predominantly treated as individual problems, and health examinations were not used as a prevention strategy.

Despite the absence of participatory bodies, the process of implementing new schedules showed a remarkably high level of ongoing interaction between direct and representative participation. This is a significant feature for the company's internal participatory dynamics, but could also spur the growth of direct employee influence or participation in shift work matters. Based on the evidence obtained, we advance the conclusion that by virtue of direct and representative participation and local negotiations, the Italian regulatory system provides special opportunities for developing working-time flexibility that are guided by a 'bottom-up' process (Ponzellini 2003).

We also found another interesting feature of implementing employee influence via local negotiations, which was associated with the employees' interactions with actors outside the company. It is worth noting the impact that such external interaction had on the parties' level of specific and general knowledge of work issues, over and above the information existing in the company.

6.2.8 SWEDEN

Organizing shift work
The management had the formal and final responsibility and authority for organizing the company's shift work, including its shift system and schedule design. This responsibility also involves the health and safety aspects of shift work. Any practical improvements were implemented through the Spokesmen's Council (SC), a body established according to Swedish legislation on employee co-determination. This legislation specified a management obligation to inform employees about issues that concerned them, and called for discussions and negotiations to be opened on these issues. The SC consisted of the spokesmen from the three unions present at the company, plus the human resources manager and occasionally the managing director (the chief executive officer). It was this group that put the legislative intentions into practice, and the SC itself was an example of this. According to the interviewees, although the Swedish legislation on co-determination stated that negotiations had to be initiated, management still made the final decisions.

The SC could set up sub-groups or committees to handle specific tasks. Earlier, when the company had several subsidiaries, this was the case for shift work, which was handled by a permanent shift committee. Its function had been taken over by the SC, which sought assistance from *ad hoc* advisers on shift-work issues. The practice of the shift committee and employee voting was an old tradition established before Hydro took over the company, and had nothing to do with the takeover. Most of the interviewees mentioned that the old approach had been developed based on the positive interaction between management and employees. We were also told that employee influence was determined by the Swedish legislation on co-decision, but that the company, in a mutual understanding with its employees, had developed a particular practice and tradition that offered employees a special influence on shift work compared to other companies.

According to most of the employees interviewed, the existing shift system with 6 teams was introduced around 1980. Originally, the 6-team system was introduced during holiday periods in the summer, then discontinued during the winter. Later, in the 1980s, the sixth team was implemented permanently, as the need grew to have a team continuously devoting time to competence development, project work, and so on.

The development in the company's shift schedules had been characterized by ongoing adjustments within the framework determined by management, which called for the same schedule for all employees in production, and no 12-hour shifts on weekdays. The interviewees stated it was the unions that had exerted pressure to have 12-hour shifts introduced at the weekends, resulting in more weekends off. Because the system had changed to a six-team shift system, the SC members agreed that an employee vote on the shift-schedule design should be arranged every six years. They reasoned that during that time period, all employees would have experienced the different rotation plans in the schedule, including holidays on duty, and thus experienced the various advantages and disadvantages of the shift system. The shift schedule in operation at the time of the interview had been chosen by a vote in 1996, with the next vote scheduled to take place in 2002.

As for the existing schedule, different points of view and desired alterations could be identified for the next vote in 2002, but very few concrete proposals had been advanced. The interviews showed that employee wishes mainly centred on changes to shift start times, and on the location of shifts after a sequence of night shifts and a day off.

As for flexibility in the future, the interviewees stated that extended operational flexibility had not been discussed, but that the topic could be brought up in relation to individual flexibility. Flexi-time for shift workers had been discussed, and further to this point, some interviewees mentioned that extensive opportunities for exchanging shifts internally already existed, as most employees were highly skilled. As expressed by one management representative, "... *the company does not interfere when agreements are made in the teams – the employees are allowed to exchange shifts as much as they want, as long as the teams have the number of employees and the necessary competencies*".

Employee participation

As noted, Swedish legislation on co-determination required that there be information, discussions, and negotiations concerning issues with a bearing on employees. However, the legislation determined the principle of negotiation itself, not its manifestation, so the establishment of the local *ordföranderåd*, or Spokesmen's Council (SC), was company or context dependent. The SC was composed of the spokesmen or heads of the three unions that organized the company's employees according to profession, as well as the HR manager and sometimes the CEO. On issues like choosing a shift system and designing schedules, the regulatory principles of co-determination had to be followed, but the company retained the ultimate right to decide. At the participating Swedish company, the right to decide on schedule design fell within the framework set up by the conditions from the shift system and two specific company-determined dimensions: first through the schedule being handed over to the employees in practice, and second through a combined informal process of representative and direct participation.

The employees had representative participation through their union spokesmen with regard to any special conditions on working-time issues directly negotiated between the local parties, such as exemption from legislation. This representation was reflected in the SC as well. The council worked out proposals for voting on the design of shift schedules, and here the employees' rights of co-determination were fulfilled. A permanent shift committee had existed at one time, but its tasks had been taken over by the SC. The SC would sometimes call in advisers, who would contribute to the process according to their knowledge and interests, and the SC could also establish *ad hoc* sub-groups.

The process of direct and representative participation became more intense and dynamic every six years as the periodic vote on shift work approached, but as an interviewee stated, *"discussion about shift schedules is an ongoing process, and it does not only have relations to the period before the voting."* The employees discussed and made suggestions on certain aspects of new schedules, or proposed new designs and modifications. The SC collected the proposals and co-opted persons with special knowledge in the area to help combine and draw up the proposals that would be put to the vote. The employees could normally choose among three to four proposals. In 1996, there were six different proposals to vote on, and the two that received the most votes passed on to a second round, in which the proposal with the most votes won. Before being submitted for the vote, the proposals were scrutinized by the SC to ensure their compliance with the frameworks determined by the company and the regulations. As stated in an interview, *". . . it has never happened that the company had objected to a voting result."* One employee representative indicated that after the tradition was established during the 1980s, people seemed to be more satisfied, and the discussions had become calmer.

The interviewees rated the level of employee influence on the design of shift schedules as follows: 2.0 / 2.0 / 1.5 / 2.5 / 2.25. The assessment of this type of influence was lower for the employee representatives than it was for the management representatives.

Managing health and safety
The Health and Safety Committee (HSC) primarily dealt with issues like accidents, co-ordinating activities with the company health service, individual health problems, rehabilitation, and, if necessary, follow-up activities based on general individual health examinations or workplace surveys. Shift work was not a topic for discussion or an independent item on the agenda. The HSC focused on individual cases and not on the shift system or schedules. The SC or its *ad hoc* shift group only dealt with shift-schedule design and not with risks of illness or long-term effects. The company did not have its own health department, but did obtain services from an external health organization that had not been involved in shift-work organization. However, all the interviewees stated that shift work ought to be a topic of discussion for the HSC, and as one interviewee emphasized, *"It is important to bring up health effects from shift work as a point [on the agenda], but I do not experience that we have a formal system that attends to health risks in shift work."*

At the same time the interviewees reported, to various degrees, that discussions among the employees concerning the effects shift work might have on health and accident risks, and concerning its possible long-term effects. These discussions dealt not only with voting on future schedules, but also more generally with the impacts of shift work. This emerging interest and understanding had grown, and been further stimulated through a company/employee initiative that invited an external capacity to give a presentation about shift work and its health effects. Some interviewees expressed uncertainty about how to proceed.

Thematic interpretations and discussions
The most characteristic feature of participation in the Swedish company was its practice as a product of a more complex and informal, ongoing process that reflected the integration of direct and representative participation in an interplay with management. The informal aspects of the process were described by the interviewees as not being written down or agreed upon in a traditional, formal fashion and recorded in a book of minutes.

This company was also another example of how much the tradition and attitudes of an individual company could influence its implementation of regulatory provisions concerning employee participation. Gradually, as part of the cooperative tradition, a practice had developed that, according to the interviewees, went further than the legislation as for special representative forums combined with, and with particular emphasis on, frameworks for direct participation.

As part of the employees' direct influence. a practice had developed whereby voting was arranged at predetermined intervals, corresponding to the number of teams in the shift system. This procedure seemed to have created better conditions for stimulating continuous, active, direct participation. This was particularly noticeable during the period prior to and around the voting (with extensive talks and discussions of design proposals and possible schedule modifications). According to the interviewees, however, activity in these areas was also stimulated in general. The initiatives were believed to have added an innovative quality to participation when giving consideration to shift work. Another interesting aspect, described indirectly by the interviewees, was the importance of the temporal association between voting and increased satisfaction with the schedules. This aspect also covers the ensuing question of how closely the increased satisfaction could be seen as being linked to the assurance of periodic votes on shift-work changes. Having such voting as an established practice may give employees an experience of fairness, and confidence in the knowledge that later changes are a real possibility – and make it easier for them to accept the schedule voted in by a majority of their colleagues. A further implication may be that this knowledge of a future vote might provide an extra opportunity to gather dissatisfaction and disagreements, and to have them put to the test in a majority vote.

The informal nature of the employee influence can additionally be explained by the fact that, subject to the conditions of the shift system and the delimited framework of the schedule, management had given the employees influence on the schedule design. The participatory principles developed in the company can also be viewed as an extended implementation of the co-determination provisions on information and negotiations, which the law stipulates must be carried out through cooperation.

In continuation of this, we were able to identify an open discussion about flexibility, including individual flexibility. The parties cited a readiness to also discuss individual flexibility and put it into practice, provided it was possible to work out a design that ensured the constant presence of the necessary competencies and number of employees.

As was also the case in other companies, the Swedish HSC had not been involved in questions about health, risks of illness, and long-term effects associated with the work-schedule design. However, the parties and the interviewed participants expressed the view that shift work could be a theme for the HSC, especially with a view to obtaining more information on health effects. As for attending to the health and long-term effects of shift work, the company was found to stand midway between, on the one hand, a growing understanding of health risks, including long-term effects, and, on the other hand, uncertainties as to how to proceed. Finally, it is also worth mentioning here that both the company and its employees had been active in collecting relevant information.

6.3 SUMMARY

In this section the company results and interpretations are appraised, taking a cross-national approach aimed at identifying the central features or trends in the results across the participating companies. It should also be noted that we will present specific results whose characteristics allow us to suppose that they are of general importance to the area – their merit being that they contribute important information about particular dynamics or possible developmental perspectives that could be applied in other contexts. In the following we consider:

- Particular aspects in the organization of shift work, and the way they are linked to the structure of employee participation and its formal and informal dimensions.
- The various dynamics between representative and direct participation, health, and safety strategies.
- The implications of having different decision levels when organizing shift work.

These findings will later be a part of our final integrating analyses, along with results from the questionnaire phase and the factual data. Ultimately, the section on conclusions and perspectives is aimed at presenting our deductions and summarizing our findings in relation to the general problems of the project, as well as presenting considerations about participation and prevention strategies that can be applied when organizing shift work.

The interviews we conducted at the participating companies highlighted the fact that by virtue of the managerial rights, management tended to have decision-making authority over the application of employees' working hours in relation to production demands and company development within the regulatory frameworks. This suggested that management held the formal authority in decisions concerning the organization of shift work, including laying down specific conditions for shift-system choices, such as manning, tasks, the number of teams, and employee skills development. It also included – albeit with some variations – the distribution of employees according to task type and functional demands. In addition, it included assigning employees to the different teams and schedules within the operational framework to accomplish the shift work – and thus, choosing the type of shift system also fell under managerial responsibility. Simultaneously, we established that management had granted the employees the right to decide on schedule design within certain limitations. These were related to issues like additional compensations, whether the new schedule would trigger additional hiring, and how to meet fluctuations in productivity. Therefore, as part of the decision-making process, frameworks had been determined for the designing of new schedules. This was done through negotiations and discussions at the beginning of the process (Italy), after the collection of proposals for new schedules (Sweden), or through the delimitation of specific premises for the design (the Netherlands and Norway). These frameworks and conditions could vary, and be more or less rigid, implying that employees' wishes for certain design features in a schedule might not be met, as this could counteract flexibility considerations. At the same time, the designated shift-system type and schedule design might suggest that conditions governing the administration of employees' working hours would potentially allow frequent changes in the shift plan through the introduction of new shifts or overtime. In our reasoning, it was in these areas that organizational tension manifested itself in relation to the organization of shift work. We further reasoned that this was what caused employee participation to be displayed in its various forms, and with different intensities and internal dynamics. It was also in these areas that the parties' attention to particular interests, and their desire to obtain and utilize control, manifested itself. A further field of tension was identified relative to the conditions for making decisions that would influence work-schedule design – where the company might present demands that were at odds with employee wishes, such as how many employees the schedule was to encompass (see Sweden, the Netherlands, W Germany, and Italy).

The way the individual companies handled organizational tensions and conflicts of interest were very different, depending on their various traditions, attitudes, and regulations. A company's attitude towards employee participation, and the conditions for such participation, had a particularly great impact, since deciding schedule design was a managerial prerogative. This was, however, less pronounced in W Germany and E Germany, the Netherlands, and Sweden, where the parties had to discuss schedule design. It was in shift schedule design, too, that the interviewees assessed employee influence as being established and expressed.

By grouping the companies according to the employees' mode of formal representative participation to influence working and organizational conditions, as described in the section presenting factual data, different characteristics were revealed in how representative participation was managed. At companies in Former West Germany, Former East Germany and the Netherlands where representative participation was practically implemented in the form of works-council-like bodies (WCBs) composed of representatives elected by, and among, all employees (excluding top management), we found that with the formal power they held through working-time regulations, these WCBs were met with contradictory demands to deal with potential conflicts that arising from the interaction with direct participation.

In W Germany, the WCB chose to refrain from putting a proposal for a new schedule design to the vote among the employees, subsequently igniting internal conflicts among them. The WCB assumed the responsibility of giving well-being and social considerations priority over financial benefits. The new schedule design was also chosen to protect employees who may have had difficulty coping with the demands of the previous schedule. The WCB's prioritization meant, however, that it did not opt for an employee vote for fear that the proposal would fall (because the WCB believed the employees had other priorities). In doing this, the WCB positioned itself in a conflict, not only in relation to the type of schedule designed, but also in relation to the employees by limiting the democratic rights that were understood to exist, and which employees saw as their opportunity to participate in choosing their own schedule.

At the company in E Germany, the WCB saw itself more as a mediator of employee interests. The interviewees stated that the company's employees did not want to alter the existing schedule to avoid a sequence of seven night shifts finishing with two 12-hour shifts, asserting that a WCB could do nothing without the support of the employees. It must be remembered that although the WCB knew about the effects of shift work on well-being and social life, it knew nothing about the risk of illness and long-term effects. These effects may have remained hidden from the WCB (and others) due to the company's drastic reduction in the number of employees. Furthermore, earlier regulations and traditions may also have exerted an influence.

In the Netherlands, where the regulations also ensured the WCB the same functional conditions as in Former E and W Germany, a practice had developed whereby management and the WCB had granted employees the power to decide whether they wanted a new schedule or not (the schedule being subject to design and voting conditions). The employees had thus been given an authority, by management and the WCB, that held the potential to prevent internal disparities between two forms of participation, to stimulate their interaction, and to thereby help develop employee participation in the organization of shift work.

For these three companies, as far as shift work was concerned, strengthening employee participation created special demands to managing indirect participatory responsibilities (which, along with health issues, had been assigned to the WCB) and their interaction with direct participation, aiming overall to stimulate participatory practices. The above cases also highlighted that, without a framework, employees could not simply be assigned the task of complying with regulatory health and safety responsibilities as part of the direct participation process. This was especially true when internal conflicts existed between giving priority to employees' financial, social, and health concerns – as was also the case for other actors. The societal and organizational obligations ensuring fundamental social rights also had to do with health and safety in the workplace, a right encompassing all employees and not just certain groups of employees (compare, for example, recent Danish Parliament legislation on the Danish work environment act, 2004).

The group of companies with joint committees (JCs), France, Norway, and Denmark, revealed two characteristic problems: first, the application, or rather non-application, of the participatory bodies in relation to shift work, and second, the conflict-ridden interaction between the formal and informal conditions for participation.

None of these three countries had clear provisions governing employee influence on the designing of shift schedules; only broad, general descriptions about work conditions (potentially including shift work) that were to be discussed before action was taken. At any rate, the organization of shift work within existing regulations was still a managerial prerogative. As in other countries, this must be differentiated from such conditions as compensation, deviations from regulations, and certain issues related to flexibility, which were to be negotiated between the parties. A change took place in the way Norway and Denmark handled issues relating to shift-work organization. These two companies shifted from formal, organizational, participatory bodies or JCs to an informal *ad hoc* body, composed of management representatives and shop stewards (the latter representing the employees). This enabled the body to respond faster to demands and, if necessary, to include negotiation (as observed in Sweden, albeit partly on a formal basis). Thus, in reality the formal joint bodies were made redundant as far as shift work was concerned, while at the same time the employees were ensured an influence not found in regulations, which was handed to them by management (though now on an informal basis). In addition, a tradition existed of the employees having influence on the shift schedule via voting, within the framework and design conditions set up by the shift system itself and by management. The informal system also indicated that management could more readily specify the agenda of topics for discussion. Compare this with the Danish management's refusal to discuss individual flexibility.

In France, employee participation was based on informal cooperation. Apparently, no legislation or regulations determined employee influence on the planning and designing of shift schedules, and thus it was managerial initiatives that involved the employees in consultations, directly and through representatives. This also made the expression of employees' views and positions seem more like a hearing than a real vote. In 1994 management entered into an agreement with the unions. As described in section 6.2.4, besides the actual amount of influence exercised, the informal basis of the influence may have contributed to the widely diverging perceptions of employee influence that were held by employee and management representatives, respectively. In general, employee influence was rated lower than in any of the other participating countries.

Clearly, informal influence can be experienced differently, regardless of the actual level of influence exerted: Differences can arise in relation to determining for oneself whether one wishes to exercise influence (thereby potentially experiencing a reduction in one's own influence), or in relation to receiving unspecified influence (without knowing how often it will be offered, or whether one's influence might change depending on one's reaction, or which effects one's exercising of influence will bring about). This was reflected in the interviewee's statements about how they experienced employee influence. These viewpoints accentuated not only the ambivalence of informal participation, but also its vulnerability to different attitudes and dissimilar interests. This could unintentionally generate undesirable organizational effects, like a weaker foundation for developing employee participation within shift work – an area where employee participation increases the possibilities for developing schedules that satisfy employees' needs and wishes (Jeppesen 2003). The possibilities for creating mutual win-win solutions could also suffer. Moreover, such informal influence might also erode the use of the formal participatory bodies or JCs, interfering with the interaction between representative and direct participation and thereby disrupting the potential stimulation of an innovative employee participatory process. On the other hand, the employees did receive a type of ongoing influence they would not have been able to obtain based on the existing formal regulations.

The companies in Sweden and Italy had no formal representative body, such as a WCB, and the employees' participatory role in organizing shift work was formalized as a management obligation to discuss and negotiate work and organizational issues with employee representatives and unions. Regarding health and safety, the Swedish company had a JC, whereas the Italian did not. Even if the conditions for, and extent of, influence varied, in both companies we found a considerably greater continuous dynamic going on between representative and direct participation in relation to schedule design. Employee influence on the design was informal in both cases. The influence given to employees by management was based on a tradition that the new owners had accepted. The influence was found to vary, however, in that (according to the interviewees) there also seemed to be differences in employee influence on schedule-design condition, differences in cooperation, and variability in attitudes to the importance of employee participation. In spite of these differences, both cases (Sweden and Italy) represented an ongoing dialogue between representatives and employees, including feed-back about options and views, which appeared to give the process an innovative quality. This interaction while developing the design was found to help reduce tensions and potential conflicts between employees, and to help establish modes of participation that embodied a higher degree of involvement of employees' views in the process. Compare here Ponzellini's reflections on the Italian way of handling working-time issues and the potentials for developing a more bottom-up-oriented arrangement of flexibility (Ponzellini 2003). In Sweden this interactive process was found to be stimulated in advance by the predetermined, regular intervals for employee voting on shift-schedule design. At the same time, we were able to identify how in Sweden, and even more distinctly in Italy, the informal basis of influence affected the reported experience of influence.

We found strengths and weaknesses reflected in the companies' various processes for having employees participate in designing their schedules. They suggested that in the area of shift work, good results were achieved by combining A) an ongoing innovative process resting on a regulatory framework that ensured health and safety, and B) a formal foundation that ensured employee influence. This combination would not only be able to consolidate employee participation and create a schedule design that could integrate production requirements, social life, and health concerns, but would also establish win-win situations as a result.

In addition to this, a number of other characteristic features that appeared to influence the organization of shift work also merit special mention. First, we identified a general feature that falls under the theme of flexibility and was reflected by the fact that all companies, with some variation, experienced a continuous need for developing operational flexibility. The companies made a great effort, hatched many ideas, and displayed great creativity in seeking to fulfil this operational demand and develop its interaction with functional flexibility. However, when it came to individual or group-based flexibility, the companies seemed to be much poorer on ideas, and have a less pronounced sense of experimentation. Very often the answers focused on such flexibility being impossible because production was continuous. This would, of course, depend on manning levels as well – which could, however, partly be evened out by developing group-based autonomy in administrating shift plans. This sort of autonomy would offer employees a better chance of balancing their working life and private life, and the company's operational flexibility, with development sustained so as to bring mutual benefits to company and employees. We identified a second additional theme of significant interest: the sources of inspiration for developing new schedules. Based on the interview statements, inspiration was not found to be the result of any formalized, systematic promotion of information arising out of regulation-derived initiatives. Nor was it found to be shared through systematic exchanges of experiences, even though it was moving within the same multinational company. On the contrary, the companies' inspiration arrived in the form of incidental information in many different guises. In certain cases, as when provided by the unions, it may have been provided by a more systematic information source. Whatever the case, sharing information about designing shift systems, the processes concerned with schedule alterations, and the implementation of new schedules would have offered mutual inspiration to all the companies involved.

In none of the participating companies were the health and safety bodies, irrespective of form or foundation, involved in organizing shift work or designing schedules. Shift work issues had been mentioned in a few HSCs, but it had not been an item on the agenda when prevention strategies were discussed. In those companies where well-being and social conditions had been considered, this had been done by the involved bodies within the works councils, and primarily presented in these forums by the employee representatives. The interviews suggested that the bodies had little or no information about shift-work-related illness risks or long-term effects and only modest information about accident risks. The notable exception here was Norway, where initiatives had been launched because the company's Health Department had taken a special interest in shift work, although there were no differences in relation to health and safety bodies. The knowledge companies had put to practical use has to do with well-being, sleep, fatigue, and social conditions, and these issues had been taken into account in several companies' schedule designs. In this way most of the companies, with a few exceptions, operated a rapidly rotating schedule corresponding to the prevailing ergonomic recommendations enclosed as a supplement to this report.

The activities of the health departments dealt mainly with the illnesses of individual employees', and not in relation to shift work as such, but in relation to transferring these employees to another work schedule because of their illness. Health examinations were not used for preventive purposes, or in strategies that analysed problems and symptoms in connection with schedule design. This suggested a tendency to individualize symptoms in shift workers, and not to understand them as work-environment problems. Finally, it should be noted that interviewees from some companies (mostly those where the HSC was a joint committees) reported that if a connection between shift work and illness could be documented, it would be a relevant area of attention for the HSC.

Regarding the statements from interviewees about how they experienced employee influence on the designing of schedules, it should briefly be mentioned that originally there were five statements for each company, even though more than one person had participated in a given interview. In two instances the statements were omitted because further questioning revealed that the responses were given on a different basis than we presumed. Each interviewee assessment of employee influence was rated on a scale from one (extreme influence) to seven (no influence). An analysis of the 38 statements that found an average between the participants at each company, then grouped responses into employee and management parties, revealed that management representatives at seven out of the eight participating companies estimated the employees to have more influence than did the employee representatives. If only differences of 0.5 or higher were considered, the above was no longer the case for the Norwegian company or for the three companies that had works councils composed of employee representatives elected by and among the employees. This mainly applied to companies where employee influence rested on a formal foundation. Across the companies, it was also at these four companies and in Sweden that the assessed employee influence was rated highest. The lowest ratings company were found in France, followed by Italy.

In an analysis of all interview statements grouped into management and employee participants, respectively, we found a group difference of one. The management group's total rating corresponded to 'much influence', and the employee group's to 'quite a lot' of influence, but the greatest internal differences were found within the employee group. It might reasonably be assumed from the results that beyond the actual level of influence in the workplace, employees' experiences of influence were mainly connected to the basis of the influence and its structural form, while management's experiences were, to a much higher degree, independent of these factors. These analyses must be appraised in light of the uncertainties associated with potential linguistic inaccuracy or incomparability across countries. On the other hand, our results correspond to other data about employee influence, and our findings are coherent enough to argue that there is adequate substance and validity in the statements gathered and the interpretations made.

7. THE QUESTIONNAIRE PHASE

7.1 DESIGN AND METHODS

We begin with a brief account of the methodology employed in the project's questionnaire survey. We describe the results and analytical findings based on the responses, continually attempting to interpret the meaning and significance of the results as they are presented. The concluding section sums up the most important findings from the questionnaire process. The questionnaire phase was designed as a cross-sectional study encompassing data from employees at comparable companies in different European countries (cf. the general description of the project methodology in sections 3 and 4).

All the companies participating in the project had accepted that a self-report questionnaire should be included as part of the research project. Approval was given through the local project groups, and all companies agreed to participate in the survey using the questionnaire designed by the research group. The intention was that all participants in the questionnaire survey should be employees who were part of the production process at the individual companies (at the sites in W Germany, Italy, Sweden, France, Norway, E Germany, the Netherlands, and Denmark), regardless of their function.

7.1.1 QUESTIONNAIRE FOCUS

The questionnaire was designed to reflect our original intention: that the data collected, and our subsequent analyses, should shed light on certain specific areas we had targeted for investigation based on self-reporting. The questionnaire focused on the following areas:
- The employee's attitude to shift work
- The employee's influence on, and preferences regarding, shift-system design
- The influence of working hours on social life
- Aspects of health and well-being
- Job satisfaction

Focusing on these areas enabled us to obtain data that would be useful for taking informed, preventive steps while designing shift schedules, and could indicate ways to improve the work situation. Moreover, the data would provide a basis for comparing satisfaction, organizational behaviour, social effects, and some health aspects between day and shift workers, and between shift workers with different schedules. The survey would also yield some information about the importance of cultural factors. Our project was not initiated to identity health factors or health risks related to shift work, since such information is already available (cf. our introductory remarks on shift work in section 2).

The questionnaire design built on experience from the contributing researchers' participation in previous research projects carried out at the Centre for Working Time Research, and on information from other research literature dealing with working time. Questions were formulated to gather general information about personal, social and employment issues, and about the respondent's influence and satisfaction, experience of advantages and disadvantages with the applied working-time schedules, and wishes for change, as well as the interaction between the respondent's working hours and social life. Moreover, rating scales were used to investigate sleep quality in connection with different working hours (from the Standard Shiftwork Index described in Barton *et al.* 1995), vitality, and mental health (which are both sub-scales from the Short Form SF 36 described by Bjørner *et al.* 1997). We finally included a scale of 20 questions about overall job satisfaction (derived from the Overall Job Satisfaction measure presented in Cook *et al.* 1981).

We had originally designed a larger questionnaire with more variables concerning health, fatigue, and actions or coping strategies. When it was tested in a pilot project at the Danish company, the response rate and interviews with respondents indicated that this questionnaire too long, and that it contained too many similar questions. It was consequently abbreviated into the version described above. This version, written in Danish, was the basic questionnaire, which was then translated into the national languages used in the participating companies. A 'back translation' was done in all languages in an effort to minimize possible linguistic variations in the translations. In other words, the questionnaire was first translated from Danish into the other language, then back into Danish again (by a translator not acquainted with the original Danish version). Finally, we compared and evaluated these translations before settling on the final versions of the questionnaire.

Nevertheless, possible influences from minor, linguistically based differences between the individual countries cannot be completely ruled out.

7.1.2 PROCEDURE AND SAMPLE

It was agreed that the local project group at each individual company would distribute the questionnaires to the company respondents, who were to be found exclusively among employees in production. Each project group would then report back with the number of questionnaires distributed to day workers and to shift workers. The questionnaires were filled out anonymously and, when completed, were handed back to an employee representative in a sealed envelope. These envelopes were then sent to the research group.

The questionnaires were sent to all participating companies and, with some variation, handed out in May and June 2000. The completed questionnaires were collected during the summer, then returned to us late in the summer of 2000. To avoid colliding with other surveys, the questionnaires were distributed later in the Netherlands, and were returned to the research group in March 2001. In Norway, the project group did not adhere to the planned procedure, as questionnaire distribution, collection, and forwarding to the research group was handed over to individuals who were not part of the original research agreement. This circumstance, combined with personnel changes, means there is no exact, total overview of the questionnaires handed out in Norway – and, in the interest of veracity, it must be conceded that such a figure cannot be precisely reconstructed, but must be approximated.

At the company in France, both the employee representatives and management had expressed a great interest in participating. Before the questionnaire study was carried out, however, the company received word from the division headquarters that cutbacks had to be made in France by reducing the number of employees. This being the case, the employee representatives informed us that, understandably, this had created such insecurity among the employees that they no longer wished to participate in the questionnaire survey. In W Germany, representatives from both management and employees had likewise confirmed their desire to participate in the questionnaire survey, but informed us that they would probably put off distributing the questionnaires for a couple of months. After this, the research group neither heard news nor received any responses from W Germany. As a result, only the companies in Italy, Sweden, Norway, E Germany, the Netherlands, and Denmark participated in the study's questionnaire phase. Only questionnaires where the question about "working-time schedule in operation" was filled out were included in the response rate for the relevant company. Table 6 shows the number of questionnaires handed out, the number returned with information on working-time systems, and the response rates at company level.

Company	Italy	Swe-den	Nor-way	E Ger-many	The Neth-erlands	Den-mark	France	W Ger-many
Distribu-tion (number)	86	171	300	178	564	160		
Respon-dents (number)	51	108	74	88	202	100	-	-
Response rate (%)	59	59	25	49	36	63	-	-

TABLE 6 *Details of distribution, respondents, and response rate.*

The number of questionnaires distributed in Norway is not based on information from the local project group, as in the other companies, but rather on factual information about the number of employees involved in production. In total, there were 623 respondents in the survey.

Looking at participation among the central working-time group in this project, namely shift workers who work night shifts, we get a varied picture. A calculation of the response rate for this group – based on employees' specifications of their own actual working-time system, supplemented with factual data – shows a different level of participation (see Table 7). This is especially true of Norway and the Netherlands, where the shift workers with night shifts constitute a proportionally larger part of respondents than in the other countries. At the same time the response rate now shows a smaller variation of 40-59%. Denmark is not included in these figures, as the company has no employees working a continuous shift system, but uses fixed night shifts. In total, the group working night shifts counts 369 individuals. Details for the five countries are illustrated in Table 7.

Company	Italy	Sweden	Norway	E Germany	The Neth-erlands
Shift workers with night shifts (number)	74	69	180	129	287
Respondents (number)	38	41	72	59	159
Response rate (%)	51	59	40	46	55

TABLE 7 *Details of distribution, respondents, and response rates for shift workers with night shifts.*

7.1.3 QUESTIONNAIRE ANALYSES

As we carried out the statistical analyses, we divided the respondents into different groups, based on the collected data, in order to make comparisons between, for instance, shift workers and day workers, and between shift systems with four, five, and six teams. In the analyses, the responses to the single-factor measures were compared between the chosen groups, and for questions that were answered using a rating scale, the responses to the individual single questions were combined to form the measure score for the analyses. As for the question about work satisfaction, which had 20 sub-questions, the responses were analysed both as a total-satisfaction measure (global satisfaction), and as a single-question measure (facets of job satisfaction). This was done because of the potential it offered to better evaluate areas in which initiative could be taken.

The following section begins with a description of the respondents in total, using a frequency distribution of the data. We then describe the results of the comparative analyses, first between day and shift workers, then between respondents with and without children living at home, and finally between shift workers working night shifts with and without children living at home. We then go through the results of our comparative analyses of respondents divided into two age groups divided along a median split (median=41), with one group being 41 years of age or less, and the other group 42 years or older. One part of the analyses focuses on the entire body of shift-worker data, while another part includes only shift workers with night shifts. Finally, we describe findings from our comparative analyses between participants in different shift systems divided according to the number of teams in the system. Furthermore, for the benefit of the individual participating companies, we have conducted analyses in which respondents at each company have been compared to the rest of the respondent group (which included all respondents from the other companies as a single group). Note, however, that these company-specific results are described in this section, but are treated separately, per company, in the Report Supplements appended to this document. Non-parametric statistical procedures were used for the analyses, as follows: in the comparative analyses of single question responses, Pearson's Chi^2 test; for comparisons between groups, the Mann-Whitney U test; and in analyses of trends, the Kruskal-Wallis test.

In the following account of our results and findings, the expression "significance" or "statistical significance" is used when referring to differences between groups. Significant differences are differences that will only occur with a certain minimal probability and therefore have a low probability value ("p-value"). Typically, a p-value of 0.05 is applied. What a 0.05 p-value indicates is that the probability of the observed differences being a result of chance is less than 5% (so conversely, we are 95% certain that the results are not a result of chance). Put more simply, the concept of statistical significance is a way of expressing how certain we are about whether there are differences between the analysed groups. If the significance was 1%, then the probability of differences existing would be less than 0.01. In the results reported here, a significance of 5% or less is indicated by one asterisk (*); of 1% or less by two (**); and of 0.1 % or less by three (***). In our account of the analysis results, we will focus on those findings that are significant as indicated in the analyses described in the supplementary reports for the individual companies. Exceptions are made when the results, independently of the comparisons, yield important information about areas such as age or attitudes to alterations in a shift system.

It must be emphasized that our questionnaire-based research is a cross-sectional study in which the statistical analyses investigate the strength of the association or link between the given variables. This means they give some indication of the degree of variation (change) seen in certain factors, or measures, in comparison with the variation in others. Note that such analyses do not identify the ways in which the examined variables may be causally linked. However, we do include various reflections on such links, given the analyses and other pieces of information we have collected. Although some conclusions could be drawn from our examination in this study of differences between independent factors, the establishment of causal relations is typically explored in longitudinal studies, which allow one to follow, over time, the development in the examined variables and their interplay. Under such circumstances researchers can try to take into account other variables that may form part of a complex interaction with the independent and dependent variables, and be important for the causal sequences and for their dependency on the given context.

An interpretation of the various analysis results relies on the certainty – the statistical significance (see above) – of the differences between the groups investigated. It also hinges on the question of whether or not the data, on which the analyses are based, are evenly distributed for the given variables. This reflects the extent to which the respondents can be said to represent the groups in the population being investigated. Such difficulties in evaluating the results of research analyses, also called "bias problems", can increase the uncertainty in the interpretations and lessen the generalizability of the findings. In a questionnaire survey, for example, there could be a bias related to the drop-out rate among potential respondents, and the risk of such a bias increases as the drop-out rate rises, since this increases the chances of a skewed distribution. The reason is that one cannot know how the drop-outs would have answered the questions. The most significant bias problem is linked to generalizability, meaning the degree to which the results can be extended from the analysed groups and applied to a broader shift-working population (say within Norsk Hydro, or beyond). Another source of error when investigating relations between variables can be "confounding variables". This term refers to the potential for connections between exposure and effect being clouded by extraneous variables that have not been accounted for in the research design. Such confounding variables can have the same effect as the other risks discussed, and can independently lead researchers to observe effects that could lead to incorrect conclusions. Problems with confounding variables typically arise in longitudinal studies of causal factors, and researchers always include checks aimed at revealing such problems in the statistical analyses. In cross-sectional studies like this project, uncertainty in the results could arise because the link between exposure and effect was impacted by intermediate variables, which can weaken or strengthen the link, or sometimes be necessary for the link to exist. In a project like this one, such variables could be age or family status. In this context, note once again that the aim of this project is not to investigate the frequency of illness and its possible causes among shift workers. Rather, it aims to throw light on attitudes and actions among shift workers, and on possible links with different types of shift systems (see the introduction).

In this study, bias problems are related to the relatively large drop-out rate among the respondents, which in some of the individual companies was more than 50%. Drop-out was generally most significant among day workers. If drop-out is coincidental, it is less important than if it is systematic. This means that certain experiences of effects could be represented in a specific group, say day workers, as less pronounced than they would have been if the entire day-worker group had responded. In this study we have not clarified the significance of drop-out. There was no information available to assess whether an imbalance existed or not, and a potential imbalance may have differed in nature from one participating company to another, or among the examined groups. Conversely, there is no basis for assuming that the nature of a potential imbalance should differ among the participating companies, so if one existed, it would possibly affect comparisons between companies with different shift systems to a lesser degree. Moreover, bias can be relate to staff redundancies and rationalizations over the years, occurring in the individual companies to varying degrees. Another problem of bias can be related to the self-selection arising because employees who experience problems with shift work are more likely to leave the workplace of their own accord. One can consequently assume that such self-selection will reduce the possibility of finding effects and differences relating to the examined influences, since those employees experiencing effects will be the ones who have left. Conversely, when a study tends towards not finding differences between the examined groups, it will indicate with greater certainty that any differences found are related to the themes examined.

7.2 FINDINGS

7.2.1 FREQUENCY DISTRIBUTION FOR ALL PARTICIPATING COMPANIES

This sub-section offers information about the general characteristics of the respondents. It describes the distribution of attitudes, work, and socio-demographic data. It does not contain analyses as such, since there are no norms of reference for the working population examined. Comparative analyses are presented where the material is segmented into sub-groups, such as day workers versus shift workers, companies versus other companies, participants with children versus those without, and so on. Only certain selected figures and schedules showing the applied variables are presented here. The majority of variables can be presented more meaningfully at company level, since the responses were related to specific company features.

As for the distribution of demographic data, 89% of respondents were men, while only 11% were women. Most of the women were employed in Denmark. This probably relates mainly to differences in production: Denmark is the only non-chemical factory among the companies. However, social and cultural differences between the countries may also play a role. The age distribution shows that 9% were under 30 years of age; 30% were 30-39 years; 41% were 40-49 years; 18% were 50-59 years; and only 2% were over 60. As for seniority in the company, 21% had up to 4 years of seniority; 14% had 5-9 years; 36% had 10-19 years; 22% had 20-29 years; and 7% had 30 years or more. The data distribution shows that 80% were married or had a cohabiting partner, while 20% were single. Most respondents had one, or several, children living at home. It must be stressed, however, that these numbers showed great variation, both internally within the individual companies and between the companies, and therefore the stated averages can hide large divergences.

Table 8 shows the distribution of employees on work functions, or roles. The table is arranged so that the roles in Denmark (which differ because Denmark is an aluminium unit and the others fertilizer companies) are shown in the last four rows.

Role at work	No	%
Operator inside control room	21	3
Operator outside control room	67	11
Operator both inside and outside control room	213	67
Maintenance	84	14
Shipments/stores	18	3
Laboratory	17	3
Other	78	13
More than one role	32	5
Package operator (Denmark)	27	4
Press/tool operator (Denmark)	34	5
Processing (Denmark)	24	4
Maintenance and stores (Denmark)	6	1

TABLE 8 *Distribution of respondents according to work functions or roles*

The largest group by far is the operator group, which represents nearly half of all participating respondents. Within this broad group, operators working both inside and outside the control room had the work role with the highest number of respondents. The two groups 'maintenance' and 'other' are nearly equal in size. The role termed 'other' may conceal employees who handle different management tasks that are not strictly covered by the work roles indicated.

One third (33%) stated that they had management tasks, while two thirds (67%) indicated they did not. As concerns union-related tasks as company steward (representative), almost one fourth (22%) stated they had such tasks, while a good three fourths (78%) indicated they did not.

The distribution of the 623 respondents on different work schedules is shown in Table 9. The vast majority were employees on shift work that included night shifts, followed by employees with day work. Then came the groups with shift work without night shifts, and with on-call work, respectively. Regular or fixed night and weekend work occurred only in Denmark.

Current working hours	Number of respondents	%
Day work only	108	17
Shift work without night shifts	43	7
Shift work with night shifts	358	57
Evening work only	3	–
Night work only	29	5
Day work with on-call work	44	7
Weekend work only	9	1
Other / missing data	29	5
Total	623	100

TABLE 9 *Distribution of participants according to work schedules.*

To the questions about changes in working hours, 49% replied that they had extra hours during the last four weeks, and 27% stated that they had 10 or more extra hours during that period. As for changes in the work schedule due to individual preferences and company needs, 37% replied that this has happened once or several times. The table below shows the influence of respondents on the arrangement of current working hour.

Influence at the individual level on working-hour arrangements (distribution in %)	None	Not much	Some	A good deal	Complete
All respondents	39	29	18	11	2

TABLE 10 *Perceptions of individual influence on working-hour arrangements.*

Here the majority, 68%, stated that they experienced little or no influence on the arrangement of their working hours, and just 13% indicated they had a good deal of influence or complete influence. Looking further at the influence as experienced by the employees considered as a group within the companies, the distribution of employee perceptions is as follows in Table 11.

Influence of the employees as a group on working-hour arrangements (distribution in %)	None	Not much	Some	A good deal	Complete
All respondents	26	32	27	14	2

TABLE 11 *Perceptions of influence as a group on working-hour arrangements.*

The answers demonstrate that respondents experienced slightly more influence as a group than as individuals, but there was still a majority of 58% who reported having little or no influence. The shift in the response pattern compared to personal influence is mainly confined to the category 'some'. We also posed the question "Who do you think should have most influence on the design of shift work in order to ensure health and safety?", and obtained the following distribution of answers.

Attitude to who should have most influence on shift work to ensure health and safety	All respondents (%)
You yourself	8
The employees as a group	51
Representatives / unions	8
Health and Safety Committees	10
Works councils	18
Management / supervisors	3

TABLE 12 *Preferred influence on shift work in relation to ensuring health and safety.*

This response distribution clearly shows that employees want the employees *as a group* to have the most influence, so neither individuals nor the different forms of representative systems were preferred overall. It must be stressed, however, that among the group-representation options, works councils stand out as the second-most desirable approach to influencing health and safety on shift work.

On the other hand, as regards respondents' satisfaction with working hours, 50% stated that they were generally or extremely satisfied, whereas only 13% indicated they were generally or extremely dissatisfied. When asked about changing to work in normal daytime hours if the opportunity should arise, and changing to day work without it affecting pay or other working conditions, the distribution of answers was as shown in Table 13.

Shift workers only (distribution in %)	Yes	No	Don't know
If given the opportunity, would change to day work	36	39	25
If given the opportunity, would change to day work if pay or working conditions were not affected	64	22	14

TABLE 13 *Responses on changing to day work.*

Posing these two questions adjacent to one another illustrated that a group of just over one third (36%) would like to quit shift work in any case, but responses also suggested there was a group of slightly over a third (39%) for whom continuing in shift work seemed to be related to having other pay and working conditions than applied for daytime work. Furthermore, a group of just over one fifth (22%) would wish to maintain shift work, irrespective of being offered the same pay and conditions for day work.

The selected questions about social and health conditions were included to clarify effects relating to shift work by comparing shift workers and daytime workers. Therefore they are not part of the present section. On the other hand, it is appropriate to draw in all respondents' answers to the questions about satisfaction with their general working conditions, since this can give us an impression of whether there are any particular dimensions that diverge from the others in one direction or the other. The results are summarized in Table 14. Categories of replies expressing different levels of satisfaction and dissatisfaction were aggregated into one category on each side, plus one for the neutral category 'indifferent'. The questions were posed as shown below:

The following questions are about how content you are with your present work situation. (The response data is from participants at 6 companies, in %.)

	Very dis-satisfied	Dissat-isfied	Slightly dissatisfied	Indif-ferent	Slightly satisfied	Satisfied	Very satisfied
a. Your physical working conditions		32		11		58	
b. Freedom to carry out your work		19		11		70	
c. Your colleagues at work		14		7		79	
d. The recognition you get for your work		39		12		50	
e. Your immediate supervisor		31		15		55	
f. The amount of re-sponsibility you get		23		11		66	
g. Your pay conditions		41		11		48	
h. Opportunities to use your abilities		31		13		56	
i. Cooperation be-tween management and employees		48		10		42	
j. Your opportunities for promotion		41		24		35	
k. The manner in which the work-place is run		48		15		37	
l. The attention your suggestions receive		37		20		43	
m. Your working time		33		11		56	
n. Variety in your work		27		12		61	
o. Security in your employment		35		12		53	
p. Your influence on the arrangement of your work		28		23		49	
q. The extent of work tasks		23		17		59	
r. The pace of work		24		17		59	
s. Clarity of your tasks at work		26		11		63	
t. Your possibil-ities for personal development		37		14		49	

TABLE 14 *Respondents' satisfaction with their work situation.*

Generally, the answers show a variation between the individual facets of job satisfaction, which may be connected to differences in individual companies, although there is also some uniformity in conditions across the companies. We provide more details on these differences and similarities when reviewing and discussing the results of our analyses in the company-specific supplements. The distribution of 'satisfied' and 'dissatisfied' responses for the different sub-questions demonstrates a prevailing level of satisfaction, where in 13 out of 20 categories more than half of the responses fell within the three satisfaction categories. In the sub-question related to influence on one's work (p), it was notable that far more answers indicated satisfaction than dissatisfaction (49 versus 28), but here, in contrast to most other dimensions, there was also a proportionally larger number of responses indicating indifference. In 3 sub-questions (i, j, and k), the majority of answers fell within the dissatisfaction categories. For another 3 sub-questions (g, l, and t), dissatisfied responses made up 37-41%, though they had more responses (43-49%) within the satisfaction categories.

If we examine the contents of these last six questions (g, i, j, k, l, and t), and partly also question d (where dissatisfied responses were 39% against 50% satisfied), one deals with pay conditions. The other questions constitute the majority of sub-questions dealing with management and personnel policy, and we can suggest (at least taking the responses at face value) that the most pronounced dissatisfaction lies here. We cannot rule out the possibility that the drop-out rate may have influenced response distribution somewhat. However, the variation in the distribution of answers does not suggest that distribution is related to the drop-out rate, since the placing of answers is selective and does not reflect a general dissatisfaction. We are unable to specify which particular level of management dissatisfaction is directed against. All we can say is that it does not seem to encompass the supervisors or managers closest to the respondents, where a majority express satisfaction on this issue.

7.2.2 ANALYSING DAY WORKERS AND SHIFT WORKERS

We divided respondents into analytical categories in accordance with their own specifications of their actual work schedules. The category 'day workers' consisted of respondents who stated they only had daytime work. Likewise, the category 'shift workers' consisted of those who stated they worked shift work with night shifts. The groups came to consist, respectively, of 112 day workers and 369 shift workers. Here, as elsewhere, we only report on analytical findings where we found statistically significant differences between the groups.

Our analyses of the work-related and socio-demographic variables showed no difference in marital status. As for age, day workers were older, with proportionally more found in the group of 60 years and over, although seniority at the company was higher among shift workers. Regarding experience in working outside daytime hours, 32% of day workers had previously done shift work for 5-25 years, while 60% had never done shift work. Among shift workers, a majority of 64% had 10-25 years' experience doing shift work. There was also a difference in work functions, in that the greater part of shift workers were operators inside and outside control rooms, which applied to very few of the day workers. Most of the day workers, however, worked in storehouses, shipment and delivery, and laboratories. No differences existed between the groups with respect to management or union-representative tasks.

In relation to planning working hours, shift workers had more often worked extra hours during the last four weeks than day workers had, although there was no difference between the groups when it came to changes in working-hour schedules. As for influence on the organization of current working hours, however, there were considerable differences between the two groups. Tables 15 and 16 illustrate respondents' influence, experienced individually and as a group, for both shift workers and day workers.

Influence on the arrangement of one's own working hours (distribution in %)	None	Not much	Some	A good deal	Complete
Day workers	31	20	22	22	5
Shift workers	45	34	15	5	1

TABLE 15 *Personal influence on working hours.*

For both day workers and shift workers, the majority reported that they had little or no influence on the organization of their own working hours. However, far more shift workers than day workers experienced this, since 79% of shift workers indicated experiencing little or no influence, versus 51% for day workers.

Influence of the employees as a group on the arrangement of working hours (distribution in %)	None	Not-much	Some	A good deal	Com-plete
Day workers	23	32	31	14	1
Shift workers	26	32	27	13	2

TABLE 16 *Influence as a group on working hours.*

There appeared to be no major differences in the perception of employee influence on working hours when exerted by the employees as a group, although more than half of respondents still reported little or no influence here. However, a comparison of this table with the table on own influence (Table 15) reveals far more interesting displacements: The grouping of day-worker responses shows that slightly fewer day workers experienced some or complete influence for the employees as a group (46%) than experienced some or complete personal influence (49%). At the same time, fewer day workers experienced no group influence (23%) than experienced no personal influence (31%). On the other hand, for shift workers reporting on group influence, more responses fell within the categories 'some' to 'complete' and fewer in 'none' and 'not much' than in shift-worker reporting on personal/individual influence. These varying displacements between group influence and individual influence among the shift workers and the day workers suggest a genuine difference in perceived influence, with shift workers clearly perceiving a greater influence exerted by the employee group as a whole. However, the trends pointing in both directions – towards both more and less influence for the group – might suggest that the day-worker group comprised a more complex sample population that included personnel from different functions and working-hour systems with varying levels and forms of influence.

As for respondents' attitude to whom they would prefer had the greatest influence on designing shift systems in order to properly handle health and safety issues, the results were differently distributed (***) between the categories for the two groups (see Table 17). The preference for giving most influence to oneself and to union representatives was similar for day workers and shift workers. At the same time, these were the categories that fewest respondents preferred – with the exception of the 'management/supervisors' category. This latter category was particularly low among shift workers, while for day workers it was in line with the response category 'you yourself'. Variations are primarily found for the category 'employees as a group', which was chosen by a large proportion of day-worker and shift-workers respondents, though by rather more shift workers than day workers. On the other hand, proportionally more day workers than shift workers chose 'works councils' and 'Health and Safety Committees', but for both groups the 'works council' category was chosen by the second-largest percentage. The distribution of the responses suggest several interpretations; one being that shift workers more often believe they themselves are most knowledgeable about their working hours, and about what can and must be done in relation to safety and work-related strain. Another, complementary, interpretation could be that as a day worker, one has more contact with cooperation and management bodies, or representatives sitting in such bodies, and hence one places greater faith in their functions and opportunities for influence.

Attitude to who should have most influence on shift work to ensure health and safety (distribution %)	Day-workers	Shift-workers
You yourself	7	8
The employees as a group	40	57
Representatives / unions	7	8
Health and Safety Committees	15	11
Works councils	23	15
Management / supervisors	7	1

TABLE 17 *Preferred influence on shift work in relation to ensuring health and safety.*

As for the questions about reasons for having the current working-hour system, noteworthy differences in the distribution of responses (***) were displayed between the two groups – except on the question of personal freedom, where the difference was slightly less significant (*). As for the questions of "the only possibility if I wanted the job", "the only possibility of obtaining work at this workplace", and "the only possibility to continue at this workplace", between 56% and 66% of the day workers stated that this factor ("reasons for current working hours") had little or no impact. In comparison, only 25-37% of shift workers indicated little or no impact. As for the question of the influence of pay, the same distribution emerged, with 75% of day workers stating that it had little or no influence, while only 13% of shift workers stated the same. As for the question of fitting in better with family life, the distribution of answers was contrary, with 69% of shift workers stating that it had little or no influence on choosing/working the current work schedules, whereas 46% of day workers stated little or no influence. As for the question of personal freedom, the same tendency was found, but with a more uneven distribution in the response categories, since 48% of day workers indicated little or no influence, versus 40% of shift workers. At the same time, 34% of day workers said that this factor had 'much' or 'very much' influence, versus 33% of shift workers, which illustrates two different sets of attitudes to the question within both groups. In total, the answers to the above questions showed that generally the shift workers did not choose shift work for social reasons, but that this might be the case for individuals, depending on the design of the shift systems.

It should be noted that only the shift-worker group provided answers for some of the items evaluating the current shift system, and that no comparative analysis of the two groups was possible here because the day workers were not supposed to answer these questions. Regarding the times for reporting to work on day shifts, 45% stated that they found start time to be too early, and 51% that start time was appropriate. In addition, 56% stated that there were too few weekends off, and 34% stated that there were too many hours in the weekend shifts. Considerable differences were found for the question concerning satisfaction with working hours (***), with a higher degree of satisfaction among day workers: 86% replied that they were 'somewhat' or 'very satisfied', versus 35% of shift workers. Furthermore, 18% of shift workers said that they were 'somewhat' or 'very dissatisfied', versus just 2% of day workers. Among shift workers, the largest proportion, 47%, said that they were both satisfied and dissatisfied.

Table 18 shows the perceived adequacy, or sufficiency, of time that the individual day workers and shift workers experienced as having available for social activities in relation to their working hours.

Your experience of your available time as a consequence of your working hours (distribution in %)	Completely or somewhat sufficient	Neither sufficient nor insufficient	Completely or somewhat insufficient
Family (***)			
Day workers	65	26	9
Shift workers	26	38	36
Friends and acquaintances (***)			
Day workers	58	28	14
Shift workers	20	31	49
Hobbies you pursue on your own (***)			
Day workers	64	19	18
Shift workers	35	29	36
Hobbies you enjoy pursuing with others (***)			
Day workers	60	23	16
Shift workers	17	26	57
Cultural activities (cinema, concerts, education) (***)			
Day workers	62	21	18
Shift workers	22	26	51
Organized work (unions, community involvment) (***)			
Day workers	63	21	16
Shift workers	16	21	63
Yourself (***)			
Day workers	67	20	13
Shift workers	38	30	32

TABLE 18 *Sufficiency of available time as a consequence of working hours.*

The table shows that for all areas of social activities mentioned, shift workers reported that they did not have sufficient time available, and this illustrates the potential interaction of shift work with social life. Furthermore, the table suggests that limitations were experienced in organized activities involving other people, and to a lesser extent individual activities. The differences between day workers and shift workers appear as very significant and unambiguous, so it is a reasonable, though not conclusive, assumption that they apply across national borders and cultures. At the same time, we found that the shift workers were not a uniform group, but that smaller sub-groups could be identified, reflecting differences in the way respondents experienced the effects of shift work on social life, and thus also experienced opportunities and strains.

Where health conditions were concerned, there were no significant difference between day workers and shift workers on the question of general health status, where 86% of day workers reported 'good' to 'excellent' health, while this applied to 84% of shift workers. Health was additionally illuminated through 9 sub-questions about vitality, including facets such as energy and mood, which collectively formed a health-related scale. Our analyses demonstrated that shift workers had a lower score (*), indicating lower well-being in general for shift workers as measured using these specific questions.

The way day workers and shift workers experienced working conditions was investigated using a scale that indicated relations or involvement with colleagues. Here our analyses demonstrated a significant difference (**), where day workers scored higher than shift workers on relations with colleagues. Again, this could indicate that shift workers have narrower scopes for establishing and maintaining social relations. However, it must be emphasized here that we asked about colleagues at work in general, and not about the colleagues in one's primary social group – such as one's shift team. This could have resulted in a different distribution. We carried out analyses comparing the two groups in terms of how they experienced work satisfaction. Table 19 shows the analytical results relating to individual work satisfaction, which aimed to identify specific areas where differences might emerge. Moreover, we carried out analyses comparing the two groups based on a total satisfaction score (derived from combining all the items). This analysis showed that global work satisfaction was significantly higher (***) for day workers than for shift workers.

In some individual areas such as pay, opportunities for promotion, and colleagues, no differences were found. Lower satisfaction seemed to broadly relate to other dimensions such as management, influence, cooperation, working conditions, and work tasks. Given the fact that there was no difference in satisfaction between the two groups, this does not imply that there is greater dissatisfaction than satisfaction among the shift-worker group.

If we further investigate the internal distribution of satisfaction and dissatisfaction in the shift-worker group, we find that for 10 out of 20 sub-questions, more than half of shift workers have indicated satisfaction. If, on the other hand, we look at the facets where more respondents have indicated dissatisfaction than satisfaction – or where the figures are equal – we find that the questions revolve around the topics of management (d, i, k, and l) and personnel policy (j). The extent to which the responses reflect the "destabilisation hypothesis" – the tendency for dissatisfaction in some areas to make dissatisfaction in other areas more likely – in addition to showing real differences in employee experiences, is uncertain. As has been pointed out by others (Haider *et al.* 1981), this situation is more likely to be true of shift workers dissatisfied with their shift working hours than of day workers.

Questions about how content you are with your present work situation. Shift workers (S) with night work are compared with day workers (D), significant differences (p) are marked $* p \leq 0.05;$ $** p \leq 0.01;$ $*** p \leq 0.001$

		Very dissatis-fied, Dissatis-fied, Slightly dissatisfied	Indifferent	Slightly sat-isfied, Satis-fied, Very satisfied	
a. Your physical working conditions	D	21	7	73	**
	S	34	12	54	
b. Freedom to carry out your work.	D	11	4	85	***
	S	21	15	63	
c. Your colleagues at work	D	10	5	85	
	S	17	8	75	
d. The recognition you get for your work	D	25	8	67	***
	S	43	13	43	
e. Your immediate supervisor	D	18	10	72	***
	S	33	17	50	
f. The amount of respon-sibility you get	D	17	6	76	*
	S	25	12	63	
g. Your pay conditions	D	38	9	53	
	S	42	12	47	
h. Opportunities to use your abilities	D	25	7	68	**
	S	35	15	50	
i. Cooperation between management and employees.	D	35	7	58	***
	S	53	12	35	
j. Your opportunities for promotion	D	39	19	41	
	S	44	24	32	
				Cont. next page	

k. The manner in which the workplace is run	D	35	17	48	**
	S	52	17	32	
l. The attention your suggestions receive	D	23	20	56	**
	S	40	21	39	
m. Your working time	D	10	4	86	***
	S	41	13	46	
n. Variety in your work	D	13	9	78	***
	S	33	14	53	
o. Security in your employment	D	23	11	66	**
	S	40	12	48	
p. Your influence on the arrangement of your work	D	15	12	73	***
	S	32	28	40	
q. The extent of work tasks	D	16	10	74	***
	S	25	21	54	
r. The pace of work	D	15	8	77	***
	S	26	21	53	
s. Clarity of your tasks at work	D	23	3	75	***
	S	29	14	58	
t. Your possibilities for personal development	D	28	11	61	**
	S	41	15	45	

TABLE 19 *Perceived work satisfaction for day workers and shift workers.*

7.2.3 ANALYSING RESPONDENTS WITH AND WITHOUT CHILDREN

We analysed the questionnaire material to investigate whether children living at home made a difference to the respondents' attitudes to working conditions, in terms of working hours and how respondents experienced the effects of working hours. We found no coherent significant differences between the groups in the context of the research questions posed in this project. The analyses were carried out using the sample population reporting 'shift work with night shifts only', for those with and without children living at home. As indicated, no notable coherent differences between the groups were found.

7.2.4 ANALYSING RESPONDENTS IN RELATION TO AGE

The age groups were determined by using the median of 41 to split the sample (the younger group of respondents being 41 years or younger, while the older group were 42 years or more). This division and analysis was carried out in order to investigate whether age has an impact on the distribution of responses.

Regarding the work-related and socio-demographic conditions, we found that the respondent group contained more (*) younger than older women. More women in the younger group than in the older group lived alone, and fewer had children. More women in the older group had management tasks (***), whereas there were no differences between the two groups when it came to union-representative tasks. In terms of working-time schedule, we found differences between the older and younger groups (*), with more older workers having day work and on-call shifts, while rather fewer had steady night work. No difference emerged between the groups for shift-schedule alterations and extra hours worked. In addition, we found no differences between younger and older groups in their reported experience of personal influence or employee-group influence, nor were there any differences relating to whom respondents wanted to have most influence on the arrangement of shift work. No differences were apparent in the two group's reasons for having the current working-time system, except in their answers to the facet of 'personal freedom', which was found to be less important to older people (*). No differences were observed in satisfaction with working hours, or in wishes for changing to day work if possible. The analyses here also showed that the influence of pay and other working conditions on respondents' wish to change was the same regardless of age. As for opinions on the arrangement of working hours, we found that more younger people than older reported they felt there were too many evening (*) and night shifts (**). On the other hand, it was the older group who tended to feel there were too many night shifts in a row.

More often than the younger group, the older group also stated that they (* and **) had taken special initiatives to better adjust their own behaviour and social life to the particular conditions of their working hours. As for experiencing having available time, the analyses showed no differences between the groups, but for both groups we found more replies in the category not having sufficient time than having sufficient time. The older group more often felt (*) that their health was not so good. No differences were observed in the responses concerning vitality and well-being.

In terms of work-related variables, the analyses showed that older workers felt more attached to colleagues than younger workers (*). However, no differences existed between the age groups with respect to overall work satisfaction, suggesting that neither age nor seniority influenced the evaluation of one's satisfaction with working conditions.

Further analyses were carried out based on the same age groupings (41 or less, and 42 or more), but exclusively for shift workers with night shifts. In these analyses, almost all the age differences described above disappeared. There were no differences between the groups in terms of self-evaluated health, or vitality and well-being. Nor were any differences found in relation to work satisfaction or attachment to colleagues.

7.2.5 ANALYSING RESPONDENTS WORKING SHIFT SYSTEMS WITH FOUR, FIVE, AND SIX TEAMS

By combining factual data with questionnaire data, we identified the groups with continuous shift work in the individual companies. Note that this included all respondents who had indicated having shift work with night shifts (to the question about working-time systems). Data was omitted, however, for workers stating that the number of hours on weekend shifts was irrelevant, as that group could be assumed to have discontinuous shift work. At the same time, information was available from the individual companies about the number of teams operating on the continuous shift systems in production. E Germany had four teams, the Netherlands and Italy had five teams, and Sweden and Norway had six teams. Denmark was disregarded in these analyses, since the company did not have continuous shift systems, but rather fixed night and weekend shifts. This gave following distribution of respondents: 55 in E Germany, 29 in Italy, 145 in the Netherlands, 39 in Sweden, and 66 in Norway.

A further division of the material was carried out, based on the idea that if more homogenous or comparable groups could be established, one could reasonably assume that any emerging differences among the examined groups (based on the number of teams) would be more certain. In this division, all respondents who were not operators (either inside control rooms, outside control rooms, or both) were excluded. This meant that only employees with the work role and associated work functions of 'operator' in one of these three groups were included in the further analysis. Moreover, it should be noted that differences in the number of teams applied in the shift system indicate differences in shift-system design. Even so, this does not explain all variations since, for example, the start time of the shifts can be placed at different times independently of the number of teams in the system. On the other hand, the number of weekends off, variations in number of shifts in a row, and the possibility of negotiating the location of days off are typically related to the number of teams. This further adjustment of the respondent population gave the following final composition, with the following number of respondents in the groups distributed according to number of teams and participating companies as follows:

No of teams	E Germany	Italy	The Netherlands	Sweden	Norway	Total no of respondents
4	36	0	0	0	0	36
5	0	29	115	0	0	144
6	0	0	0	27	53	80
Total	36	29	115	27	53	260

TABLE 20 *Numbers of shift-working teams, and respondents, operating across countries.*

Respondents: Almost all (97%) of the operators with continuous shift work in the five participating companies were men. There were differences (***) in the age distribution among the three groups: The six-team group was the youngest, with 53% aged 30-39 years; 13% aged 20-29; 21% aged 40-49; and the rest (13%) 50 or over. Similarly, the four-team group had 50% of respondents aged 30-39; but only 3% aged 20-29; whereas 42% were aged 40-49; and just 6% were 50 or older. The eldest group overall was the five-teams group, but here the distribution was more equal, with 14% aged 20-29; 25% aged 30-39; 40% aged 40-49; and 21% aged 50 or older. The variations in age are also reflected in seniority, with the six-team group having the lowest seniority (*). Next came the five-team group with slightly higher seniority, followed closely by the four-team group, where seniority was highest. No differences in marital status were found among the groups, but there was an understandable tendency towards more single respondents in the six-team group. The groups did not differ with regard to the number of children living at home, either.

There were no differences among the groups regarding the distribution of employees working as operators inside control rooms, outside control rooms, or both inside and outside. Nor were there any group differences regarding the handling of representative tasks. Conversely, however, significant differences (**) were found in the handling of management tasks, where significantly fewer respondents were involved in such tasks in six-team companies than in four-team or five-team companies. This is not necessarily linked to the number of teams, since, for instance, there are no differences between four and five teams, but it could be related to cultural differences in the respondents' understanding of the question: whether certain types of tasks should be characterized as management tasks or not. The age of the six-team group may also have played a role here.

Management tasks	4 teams No in %	5 teams No in %	6 teams No in %	Total No in %
yes	40	37	17	32
no	60	63	83	68

TABLE 21 *Management tasks relative to number of teams.*

As for working hours, significant differences (***) among the groups were found in the reported number of extra hours worked within the four weeks prior to completing the questionnaires. There was an apparent connection between the number of teams used in the shift system and the number of extra hours worked in the preceding four-week period, where the number of extra hours could be interpreted as expressing the extent of company-based flexibility. Table 22 illustrates, in percentages, the number of extra hours worked by the individual respondents. (The sums in the individual rows in Tables 22 and 23 are not necessarily 100%, as decimals have been weighted and "no response" answers are included).

No of extra hours in 4 weeks	4 teams (% of respondents)	5 teams (% of respondents)	6 teams (% of respondents)
0	86	62	44
1-5	8	6	8
6-10	-	16	17
11-20	-	10	17
21-40	6	6	15

TABLE 22 *Number of extra hours worked relative to the number of teams.*

On the other hand, there were no statistical differences among the three groups concerning the frequency of changes in work schedules of more than one hour within the last four weeks, although a higher frequency did appear to be linked to the five-team and six-team groups.

Changes in planned workings hours (number of times)	4 teams (% of respondents)	5 teams (% of respondents)	6 teams (% of respondents)
0	86	62	59
1	6	12	17
2	3	8	9
3	0	5	10
≥ 4	6	12	4

TABLE 23 *Changes in working hours relative to the number of teams.*

How respondents experienced their individual influence on the working-hour system varied significantly among the three examined groups (**). Individual influence appeared to increase in line with an increase in the number of teams (as it was perceived as greatest in the six-team group). This does not necessarily indicate that a shift system with six teams offered better opportunities for individual influence. The respondents' perception could also be related to the process of shaping the schedule design, to culture, and to traditions for cooperating and involving employees in decision-making processes in the various companies and countries. Percentages for self-rated personal and group influence on the working-hour system are shown below.

Personal influence on working-hour arrangements (distribution in %)	None	Not much	Some	A good deal	Com-plete
4 teams	75	25	–	–	–
5 teams	41	37	17	5	–
6 teams	34	39	19	8	1

TABLE 24 *Personal influence on working hours relative to the number of teams.*

The reported influence of employees as a group on the working-hour system was found to increase in line with an increasing number of teams (***), and it was once again largest in the six-team group. All three team-based groups perceived influence as being larger for the employees as a group, but with a proportionally larger figure for the five-team group.

Group influence on working-hour arrangements (distribution in %)	None	Not much	Some	A good deal	Complete
4 teams	67	19	14	–	–
5 teams	19	36	26	15	4
6 teams	10	31	41	16	1

TABLE 25 *Group influence on working hours relative to the number of teams.*

The results regarding group influence suggested that the respondents' assessments of influence had to do with the shape or design of the shift system, rather than with opportunities for continuously being able to change and adapt a system. On that basis one might tentatively suggest that in companies with a more well-established tradition for employee influence in the form of involvement in organizational decision processes, such practices are also likely to extend to the area of working hours.

Attitude to who should have most influence on shift work to ensure health and safety (%)	4 teams	5 teams	6 teams
You yourself	8	7	4
The employees as a group	56	62	58
Representatives / unions	8	10	7
Health and safety Committees	6	11	12
Works councils	22	8	19
Management / supervisors	0	2	0

TABLE 26 *Preferred influence on shift work in relation to ensuring health and safety, relative to the number of teams.*

No significant differences were found among the groups in terms of respondents' attitudes to which forum they wanted to have most influence on health and safety when designing working hours. In all three groups, more than half of respondents wanted the employees as a group to have most influence. The second-most popular choice for two of the groups (those with four and six teams) was the works council, while the third group (with five teams) had a somewhat lower score here; almost in line with choice of union representatives and Health and Safety Committees. This suggests that national or specific, local conditions might influence the assessments, including, for example, traditions for using works councils and cooperation committees in the countries with four teams (Germany) and six teams (Norway and Sweden). It is actually striking to see the relatively low support, of around 10%, in all three groups for having Health and Safety Committees be most influential in shaping the working-hour system to ensure health and safety. Compared to the other response distributions, the answers to this question suggested that most respondents wished to have direct influence jointly with their shift-work colleagues (as a group), in contrast to having influence through representative systems to ensure health and safety in shift-work schedule design.

Significant differences were found, at varying levels, in the responses to the sub-questions about reasons for choosing/working the actual shift-work system (see Table 27).

To what degree have the following reasons led you to have your current working hours (distribution in %)	little or no importance	some importance	a good deal of, or great importance
The only possibility if I wanted a job (*)	23	17	60
4 teams	43	23	35
5 teams	32	29	39
6 teams			
The only possibility of obtaining work at this workplace	19	17	64
4 teams	25	23	52
5 teams	21	26	53
6 teams			
The only possibility to continue at this workplace (***)	14	3	83
4 teams	34	18	47
5 teams	21	17	62
6 teams			
			Cont. next page

Fits in better with my family life (***)			
4 teams	79	3	18
5 teams	76	19	5
6 teams	57	24	19
Pays better			
4 teams	14	19	67
5 teams	12	31	57
6 teams	14	24	62
Gives greater personal freedom (***)			
4 teams	43	31	26
5 teams	54	24	22
6 teams	23	29	48

TABLE 27 *Reasons for working the given shift schedule, relative to the number of teams.*

Employment and financial reasons appeared to be more important (to all three team-based groups) than family and personal reasons as far as having or choosing the current working schedule was concerned. There were significant variations among the three groups, with two exceptions: working the system being 'the only possibility for obtaining work at this workplace' (which, however, approached significance), and financial reasons. Where the latter was concerned, we found that besides showing a lack of differences among the groups, this facet was where fewest respondents, within all three team groups, reported having little or no influence. Employment conditions were most important for employees working in four teams (E Germany), which could be related to special production conditions due to the labour market there. Family life as a reason to work the particular shift schedule was reported as important by the smallest numbers of respondents. Of the three groups, those working in six teams regarded family reasons as most important, and regarded the workload and weekend work as less important than the other two groups. The perception of personal freedom as a reason also loomed largest for employees in shift systems with six teams, and the distribution shows that more of the six-team group stated this to hold a good deal of, or great importance. Whether or not this indicated a positive selection of their shift system over other systems, or an expectation of greater personal freedom, was not something we could determine in this research.

Table 28 deals with satisfaction levels, showing the distribution of responses to the question of how satisfied respondents are with their working hours. There was a difference (*) in the distribution of answers, in that satisfaction was highest among employees in shift systems with four teams and lowest in systems with six teams. This was particularly evident in the response categories indicating satisfaction (as opposed to dissatisfaction). The results can initially appear surprising, since the extent of shift work and weekend work increases as the number of teams decreases. At the same time, however, the responses to the questions about extra hours and changes to working hours, as an expression of irregularity in the system, indicate that irregularity increases with number of shifts. This could support the idea that, besides expressing satisfaction related to knowledge about possible alternatives, the responses might also reflect a correlation between the number of shifts and levels of regularity versus irregularity. Satisfaction with shift systems was further investigated in two questions about respondents' attitudes to hypothetically changing from shift work to day work only, with and without extra compensation, respectively.

How well are you satisfied with your working hours? (distribution in %)	Very satis- fied	Gener- ally satisfied	Neither satisfied nor dissatisfied	Gener- ally dis- satisfied	Very dissat- isfied
4 teams	8	39	39	3	11
5 teams	6	30	41	17	6
6 teams	1	20	60	14	5

TABLE 28 *Satisfaction with working hours, relative to the number of teams.*

The first question about changing to day work only without compensation showed a difference (**) among the groups examined. Far fewer employees in shift systems with six teams wished to change, and more of them were unsure about making such a change than the employees working systems with four or five teams. The responses for the two latter groups were largely similar.

If given the opportunity, would change to day work (distribution in %)	Yes	No	Don't know
4 teams	40	40	20
5 teams	43	36	22
6 teams	18	42	41

TABLE 29 *Would change to day work, relative to the number of teams.*

Where changing to day work with compensation was examined, differences between the groups (**) still emerged to a similar extent, but all three groups reported a relatively similar and large increase in the number of people who wished to change to day work under these conditions. Thus, about three quarters of employees in shift systems with four and five teams and a little more than half with six teams stated that they would wish to change, which was similar to the answers about the importance of salary as a reason for having shift work. Furthermore, there was still a group of employees – more for six teams – who did not wish to change their working hours. The smallest group was clearly made up of employees in doubt (i.e. most had a good idea about what they would do).

If given the opportunity, would change to day work only if pay or other working conditions were not affected (distribution in %)	Yes	No	Don't know
4 teams	72	22	6
5 teams	78	13	9
6 teams	54	29	16

TABLE 30 *Would change to day work with conditions maintained, relative to the number of teams.*

Respondents' satisfaction with their current work situation was examined using a total satisfaction score. We deemed it unsuitable to focus on the distribution of answers to the individual sub-questions, since, as shown in earlier analyses of answers among companies, any differences seemed to be connected to company-specific and probably also cultural conditions rather than the design of the shift system *per se*. Analysing the total satisfaction score revealed no differences among respondents in shift systems with four, five, and six teams, but as in earlier answers collated at company level, we found differing responses to several of the component questions.

The questionnaire also contained questions aimed at investigating the effects of the different shift systems employed as to demands to organizing activities, time structures in social life, quality of sleep, energy levels, and emotional and mental state. As emphasized earlier, the intention of the research project we designed was not to extensively investigate health consequences of shift work, since a substantial body of knowledge already exists in this field (cf. in this field as outlined in section 2.1 and its sub-sections.

Demands to the arrangement of one's life outside work reflected the extent to which shift workers, because of their working hours, had taken initiatives concerning their family life, contact with friends and family, spare-time activities, regular mode of life, ensuring sleep, and special attention to food. The distribution of responses and our findings are shown in Table 31. Regardless of the number of teams in their shift system, around half or more of the shift-worker respondents had taken initiatives, especially in relation to social activities. The results show there were differences (**, ***) among the groups depending on the number of teams employed in the system. For the first three questions, the need for taking initiatives decreases in line with the number of teams. The reasons for having shift work, and for choices made on this issue, could play a role in the response distribution for the individual systems and cannot be ruled out as an influence here. Around a third of respondents stated they had taken initiatives to ensure sleep, with no significant difference among the three groups. There was, however, a difference concerning eating habits, in that almost twice as many in the five-team systems stated that they paid attention to what they ate. What is more, this group was older and more experienced than the other two.

Have you taken special initiatives outside your work during the last five years because of your working hours? (distribution in %)	Agree strongly, or somewhat	Neither agree nor disagree	Disagree somewhat, or strongly
Arranged family life (***)			
4 teams	71	23	6
5 teams	65	17	18
6 teams	38	40	22
Contact with family and friends (**)	78	17	6
4 teams	75	10	15
5 teams	55	28	17
6 teams			
Arranged leisure activities (***)			
4 teams	72	25	3
5 teams	69	13	17
6 teams	46	31	23
			Cont. next page

Lived a more strictly ordered life			
4 teams	14	17	69
5 teams	25	21	54
6 teams	14	26	60
Ensured sleep			
4 teams	39	22	39
5 teams	42	18	40
6 teams	32	27	41
Taken special care with eating (*)			
4 teams	19	31	50
5 teams	39	31	29
6 teams	22	28	50

TABLE 31 *Initiatives taken because of working hours, relative to the number of teams.*

Social effects were further investigated in relation to shift workers having sufficient time available for different types of activity, covering a combination of family and social activities, as well as individual and collective or shared activities. Table 32 gives an overview of the results. Generally, respondents found that their available social time outside work was insufficient in those areas where activities were performed with others, such as 'hobby activities you enjoy pursuing with others' and more formal organizational activities.

Social, cultural activities and contact with friends and acquaintances made up the second-most problematic area, where around half experienced not having sufficient time. For activities with the family, there were also more respondents than not who experienced having insufficient time available. For respondents' individual activities, generally more respondents than not experienced having sufficient time available. By comparing between the number of teams in the shift system, we found differences in some of the areas to varying degrees (*, **, ***). In most cases, respondents in five-team systems seemed to report social time as insufficient to a relatively greater extent.

Your experience of your available time as a consequence of your working hours (distribution in %)	Completely or somewhat sufficient	Neither sufficient nor insufficient	Completely or somewhat insufficient
Family			
4 teams	19	31	50
5 teams	29	36	35
6 teams	26	33	41
Friends and acquaintances (*)			
4 teams	25	28	47
5 teams	24	24	53
6 teams	14	36	50
Hobbies you pursue on your own (**)			
4 teams	44	38	19
5 teams	35	21	44
6 teams	35	42	23
Hobbies you enjoy pursuing with others			
4 teams	19	26	55
5 teams	16	23	61
6 teams	18	35	47
Cultural activities (cinema, concerts, education) (**)			
4 teams	32	24	44
5 teams	23	23	54
6 teams	24	31	45
Organized work (unions, community involvement.) (***)			
4 teams	17	33	50
5 teams	13	16	70
6 teams	18	26	56
Yourself			
4 teams	42	30	27
5 teams	35	30	35
6 teams	38	29	33

TABLE 32 *Sufficiency of available time as a consequence of working hours, relative to the number of teams.*

In addition, for some of the activities, fewer respondents in the five-teams group were neutral about the sufficiency of time available.

Besides showing general features of the shift systems, the results apparently suggest that cultural differences, possibly enhanced by differences in geographical location, influence the response pattern. On the issue of taking initiatives, we cannot rule out that variations linked to the selection of employees and, possibly, the choice of applied system could have an influence.

The respondents' quality of sleep was investigated by asking about the quality of sleep attained when working the different shifts: sleep between day shifts, sleep between evening shifts, sleep between night shifts, and sleep between days off. The analyses revealed no differences in the quality of sleep attained by the different team groups in relation to working individual shifts. As for sleep on days off, however, the respondents working five-team systems stated a somewhat lower quality of sleep than those working other systems. How to interpret this difference, or what significance it might have, was not immediately clear.

The interplay between shift system and health was investigated on three different levels. No differences emerged between the team groups for the individual question concerning general health. Energy level or vitality ('in the last four weeks') was investigated, and we found that respondents in four-team shift systems reported having a higher energy level than those in systems with five or six teams.

Interpreted in connection with the fact that the shift schedules show more shifts outside daytime hours and on weekends for respondents in systems with four teams, these findings suggest possible effects of the actual administration of systems, where the systems with five and six teams reflected a company-based flexibility (expressed in the number of extra hours and changes in shift schedules), which increased in line with the number of teams in the shift systems. No significant differences between the team groups were found with respect to mental health.

7.3 SUMMARY

Bearing in mind the potential uncertainties in interpreting and generalizing the results, due to the possible bias problems described in earlier sections, the questionnaire investigation still offers some interesting findings in relation to shift work. However, it should be emphasized that the selection bias (the 'healthy-worker effect') – linked to the fact that people with shift-work-related problems leave the company – could reduce the possibility of finding effects, and consequently diminish the impact of the results found. For a more extensive discussion of the strength of our findings and their association with the results at company level, see the supplementary reports in the Appendices, as well as the results of our analyses of the interview data and factual information. The remainder of this section is a brief summary of the most significant findings from the questionnaire phase of our research.

In the comparative analyses of shift workers and day workers as to their reasons for having the current working time system, the results showed that for shift workers (as compared to day workers), salary conditions were especially important, but that working conditions also played a role, both in the form of having a job and in relation to the given workplace. Family life was a major reason for day workers choosing their schedule, but for a small group of shift workers (14%) family life was also a very important reason for them to work shifts. These results emphasize that shift workers cannot be considered as a homogenous group when it comes to the interplay between working time and social life. It is likely that small parts of shift workforces may choose shift work for social reasons. These findings are further supported by the result that 35% of the responding shift workers would like to change to day work, while 40% said they would not change should the opportunity arise. If, however, there was a chance for wage compensation and unchanged working conditions, 64% would like to change – but there was still a sizeable minority of 22% who said they would not. A similar pattern was found in the variables relating to time available for social activities. Far more shift workers than day workers experienced not having sufficient social time. These responses were most notable for activities with others outside the family (group activities).

On an individual level, shift workers experienced having less influence on the current working-time system than day workers did, whereas there was no difference at group level. Both shift workers and day workers would prefer the employees as a group to have the most influence on shift-work design to ensure health and safety, but shift workers expressed this to a greater extent (compare the issues concerning direct participation raised in section 6). Representative systems, including works councils and Health and Safety Committees, were, perhaps surprisingly, less preferred as options for influencing shift work scheduling, and the lower support was particularly noticeable for shift workers.

Satisfaction with working time was reported as lower among shift workers, but only about 18% stated they were 'generally' or 'extremely' dissatisfied – which, based on the response patterns described above, raises the problem of what the responses to the 'working-time satisfaction' question actually reveal. Given its interplay with social life, it is fair to assume that this question is connected to an assessment of one's current working-time schedule, but one's assessment of satisfaction could perhaps be influenced by an awareness that the schedule could be designed differently. This indicates a need for closer and more precise explanations in future studies. The shift workers reported less satisfaction than day workers in most of the specific work- satisfaction areas. However, only in a few questions (relating to themes of management and cooperation, and promotion possibilities) was the dissatisfied group larger than the satisfied group. This raises the problem of whether working conditions are worse for shift workers, or whether there is a tendency to transfer one's dissatisfaction with working time (which is greater for shift workers) to other conditions (cf. the destabilization theory of Haider *et al.* 1981), or whether the explanation may lie in a combination.

In the participating companies, shift work was operated by four, five, or six teams, with the number of shifts falling outside daytime hours and the amount of weekend work being reduced as the number of teams increased (see Table 5a, b, and c on the most commonly used shift systems at company level). At the same time, analyses among the three groups demonstrated that with more teams in the shift system, respondents reported proportionally more extra hours worked and a tendency to change the fixed schedule within an arbitrary four-week period, although the latter difference was not significant considering the levels used. All in all this seemed to reflect a trend toward less regularity in the schedules, due to changes related to company demands for increased organizational flexibility. An increase in irregularity has been found to increase social strains (Bohle and Tilley 1998). Influence on the working-time system varied among the respondents. The least influence on working time was reported by shift workers in four-team systems. This finding is likely to be related to cultural and organizational variations in participatory practices among the companies.

There were no differences among the three analysed groups as to which forum people would prefer had the most influence on designing shift work to ensure the handling of health and safety. For all three team groups, regardless of national variations and local participatory practices, shift workers wanted to see this influence exerted by the employees as a group. This was followed, in terms of rated preference, by the representative systems of works councils and Health and Safety Committees. These preferences seem to reflect a wish for a large degree of direct participation with one's work colleagues as a group. As regards the interplay between working time and social time for the three team groups, our analyses showed that shift workers in systems with four and five teams reported taking slightly more initiatives to ensure the quality of their social activities than those working in systems with six teams. There were no substantial differences in influence on sleep and well-being.

Finally, the results showed that fewer shift workers in systems with six teams wished to change to daytime work, especially without (but even with) unchanged salary and working conditions. If these results are compared to respondents' satisfaction with working hours, some apparent contradictions become apparent. Shift workers in four-team systems have the smallest influence by far on working-hour arrangements, while a higher proportion of five-team shift workers than six-team shift workers reported wishing to change to daytime work only. At the same time, however, shift workers in four-team systems were also the most satisfied with working hours. These results may indicate that the two different expressions of satisfaction (satisfaction with working hours, and wishes to change to daytime work only, respectively) measure two different aspects of respondents' attitudes towards working hours. Based on the distribution of the results reviewed above, on interpretations of meaningful associations, and on comparisons with findings in other studies (see section 2), shift workers' wishes to change may reflect their attitudes to shift work and the shift system itself. Meanwhile, expressions of satisfaction with working hours may, to a great extent, express respondents' attitudes to the way working hours are managed. Continuing along these lines of interpretation, the results, taken in total, could imply that fewer shifts outside daytime hours and less weekend work, as experienced in systems with six teams, are needed to ensure the quality of employees' activities and social lives. These findings may reflect the fact that a schedule with fewer shifts outside daytime hours and less weekend work, as in six-team systems, does not necessarily in itself lead to greater satisfaction with working hours, but that this satisfaction will interact with and depend upon the level of changes to the planned schedules. It can reasonably be assumed that shift systems with six teams, compared to those with four or five teams, have the potential to offer better quality in social life, but that the materialization of these depends on the organizational shape and the use of flexibility in the working-time schedules applied.

8. CONCLUSIONS AND PERSPECTIVES

The general aim of this project was to investigate how shift work was organized at company level, and to shed light on the interaction of this process with participation in its diverse forms as well as the internal dynamics within a number of Norsk Hydro companies. It should be noted that the present study did not aim to investigate organizational participation in general with its prerequisites and operational frameworks in a cross-national approach. Targeting a specific focus area to investigate the practice of participation offered us opportunities to estimate the importance and potential of participation relative to the development within this focus area – in an interplay with the area's organizational conditions for productivity. Against this background we were able to set up perspectives for an innovative organizational participation process within the area of shift work. This enabled us to explore and propose general perspectives on the developmental dynamics of organizational participation; perspective that go beyond identifying opportunities to work with control distribution and flexibility from a participatory point of view.

Conclusions

The results from the project's questionnaire phase documented the already established knowledge about the social effects of shift work and its influence on attitudes to work, including reduced work satisfaction (see section 2). The questionnaire phase also pointed to the fact that schedule design influenced the social costs experienced by shift workers. As a new dimension, the study further suggested that the effects of shift work were not only a result of the way the schedule was designed, but also a consequence of the way the planned schedule and the working hours were managed. This will have increased relevance as the importance and development of operational flexibility increases, for instance through the use of more teams to fulfil operational demands. These issues have been specified and clarified further elsewhere (in Jeppesen, Kleiven & Bøggild 2004). The substantiation of our present findings concerning the social effects of shift work (note that health effects were not investigated here) emphasized the need for developing employee participation in the organization of shift work. This need was especially notable because of the value such participation might have in designing shift schedules that offer greater congruence between the working lives and social lives of shift workers (Jeppesen 2003). From this angle the questionnaire phase of the present study produced strong arguments for supporting participatory processes, not only in the design of shift schedules, but also in the day-to-day management of shift workers' hours.

The interviews showed that management tended to have decision-making authority within the regulatory frameworks for applying employees' working hours to fulfil productivity demands, and hence had decision-making authority when it came to organizing shift work. This included the conditions determining the shift system used, such as tasks, the number of teams and employees, and the type of shift system itself. Management authority also included (with some variation) the distribution of employees according to task types and functional demands, as well as the placing of employees in the different teams and schedules.

While the choice of shift system (involving such issues as production hours and number of applied teams) was management's prerogative, the employees, within the given frameworks, has extensive decision-making authority in the designing of schedules. In other words, there were rights and responsibilities that management assigned to the employees, typically by means of, or in collaboration with, various forums for employee representation. Employee authority was limited on issues like whether a new schedule would trigger hiring of extra people, would affect compensation, or would meet fluctuations in productivity. Often the granting of employee authority was accompanied by a few selected operational demands, such as the same schedule for all production employees, or no 12-hour shifts outside weekends. At the same time, the shift system type and schedule design could imply that employees' working hours might be based on conditions entailing more frequent changes to the shift plan or more overtime. This "space" for displaying needs, demands, and preferences was identified as an area in which organizational tensions manifested themselves around how shift work was organized. It was within this space that employee participation was displayed in its various forms with different intensities and internal dynamics. In addition, it was here, too, that we found manifestations of the parties' attention to interests and desire for control, as well as its utilization. Below we consider themes identified in the interaction between informal and formal, and between direct and representative participation, and in the mutual interaction between these factors.

In the companies with works-council-like bodies (WCBs) composed of elected employee representatives, the extension of employee participation raised special demands in relation to shift work. These demands had to do with managing the responsibility for shift design (which, including health conditions, had been left to the WCB), and interacting with direct participation in such a way as to stimulate participatory practices. The cases also highlighted that as a part of direct participation, employees should not be left with the (regulatory) responsibility for health and safety without a regulatory framework. In particular, this practice should not exist in companies where there are internal conflicts in balancing financial considerations with health and social conditions.

In spite of differences, both Sweden and Italy represented an ongoing dialogue between representatives and employees, including feedback about possibilities and points of view. This gave the process an innovative quality. We found that this interactive practice in developing the schedule design contributed to reducing tensions and potential conflicts between employees, and also to creating forms of participation that meant greater involvement of employees' views in the design process.

In Denmark and Norway, the companies' formal joint bodies were, in fact, made redundant when it came to considering shift work, even while employees were ensured an influence not found in the regulations, which was handed to them by management (though it now rested on an informal basis). In addition, there was an existing tradition of employee influence on the schedule, exerted through employees voting within the framework set up by the shift system itself and by management. This framework established the conditions and options for shift-system design. The informal system also indicated greater management ability to set the agenda for issues to be discussed. The company in France, which also had a joint committee, exemplified a situation where, in reality, the employees' influence on shift-work design rested on informal conditions, with the accompanying uncertainty potentially linked to the informal nature of the arrangement. These aspects accentuated not only the ambivalence of informal participation, but also its vulnerability, as a means of regulation, to different attitudes and divergent interests.

This could, in turn, generate unintended organizational effects, such as a weaker foundation for developing employee participation in the field of shift work – a field where employee participation increases the possibilities for developing schedules that are in concordance with employees' needs and wishes (Jeppesen 2003). Informal conditions might also erode the function of the formal participatory bodies or joint committees, interfering with the interaction between representative and direct participation and thereby disrupting the potential stimulation of an innovative employee participatory process. On the other hand, the employees did receive an ongoing influence that they had no possibility of obtaining based on the existing formal regulations.

Analysing statements from the interview participants, we found that management representatives generally estimated that employees had more influence on shift-work issues than was perceived by employee representatives themselves. The smallest differences were found in the three companies with a WCB composed of employee representatives elected by and among the employees, and in Norway. In most of these companies, employee influence rested on a formal foundation. It was also in these four companies, and in Sweden, that employee influence was rated highest by the interviewees, across the companies. One could reasonably infer from the results that beyond the actual level of influence in the workplace, employees' experience of influence were mainly linked to the influence's foundation and structural form, while management's experience was far more independent of these factors. It must be emphasized, however, that the influence ratings were probably also linked to how topical the issues were, further implying that a time dimension was involved in rating the interplay between shift-schedule design and influence. In short, interviewees might have thought: How long ago did influence last have to be applied? And how great an effect did the influence actually have?

A marked tendency concerning flexibility was that all companies, with some variation, experienced an ongoing demand for developing operational flexibility. Much effort was expended, and many ideas proposed, to satisfy company demands for operational flexibility, and to develop this in an interaction with functional flexibility. When it came to individual or group-based flexibility, however, there were fewer ideas, and less creativity and innovative thinking on the agenda.

This study also clarified the importance of looking at the way sched-uled plans are actually managed, and at the impact of employees' actual working hours on their assessment of the effects of shift work, in addition to employee assessments based on the shift schedule alone. Depending on the nature of the applied shift system, the management of working hours influences the level of unpredictability and irregularity – which can be indicators of stress, strain, and dissatisfaction with working hours (see section 2). We found it likely that with an increased development of shift-work organization based on a demand for operational flexibility, with a growing number of teams and standby or on-call duties, and with an absence of substitutes in the individual teams, the number of deviations from the scheduled plans would increase. Such a scenario was illustrated in section 7 by the results in the questionnaire phase, where our findings pointed to a link between an increase in the application of teams and the degree of deviations in the planned schedules. Continuous production imposes special demands on the design, planning, and management of schedules when the goal is integrating individual and operational demands. This is an interesting area for future field research on shift work and working time. Regardless of the conditions and frameworks under which the above-mentioned initiatives would be implemented (and these would be decided in local discussions and/or negotiations), the process could create new opportunities for the employees and the organization.

Regarding the attention paid to health and safety when organizing shift work, the companies' Health & Safety Committees (HSCs) had not been involved in organizing shift work or designing schedules, no matter what other types of representative participation the company had. The health aspects the HSCs had considered included well-being, sleepiness, fatigue, and social conditions, but did not include the risk of illness or long-term effects. These two aspects were typically handled by the employees or sometimes by their unions. A lack of information on health aspects in shift work was evident in relation to illness risks and long-term effects, and to preventive strategies, including ergonomic recommendations. At the same time it should be emphasized that there was a general demand to promote ergonomic framework conditions for designing shift schedules that could more effectively reduce the risk of long-term effects. The interaction between preventive and compensatory measures for shift workers have been summarized by Knauth and Hornberger (2003), and ergonomic recommendations for the designing of schedules are attached as an appendix to this report.

At the companies, health examinations were not found to include a preventive strategy associated with the design and discussion of shift schedules. Rather, results were discussed at an individual level with regard to possibilities for reassignment. In this way, shift-related health problems were found to be individualized and largely linked to the individual employee rather than to the shared work environment.

As concerns the potential limitations of this study, it should be noted that neither the companies nor the cases were necessarily representative other than being subject to different kinds of national regulations and traditions. On the other hand, the similarities in terms of production, science, sector, technology, and work organization, as well as their belonging to the same multinational company, offered special opportunities to examine differences in the dynamics of organizational participation. The study sought to optimize similarities in the fields of production and organization in an attempt to reduce differences in contextual dependency, even though this would vary naturally according to national regulations on participation, attitudes to cooperation, specific organizational traditions, and management strategies. The dynamic interplay between shift work, regulatory frameworks, and implementation of participation was also a major focus issue for this investigation.

Despite the use of simultaneous interpreting and back translation, we cannot rule out the possibility of linguistic uncertainties and inaccuracies reflecting on the results. In addition, a member of the researcher group was employed in the Norwegian company as chief medical doctor in the health department, which might have influenced the responses obtained, particularly in Norway. Furthermore, we must emphasize that the ongoing personnel reductions taking place to varying degrees at all the participating companies during the period of this study could very well have influenced attitudes to cooperating. However, during the interviews most participants mentioned that they were able to distinguish between the two different situations, and between local and central decisions. The interviewees also reported that they were interested in problems related to shift work. Irrespective of any effect on the interview participants, the redundancies clearly affected the number of employees participating in the questionnaire research, in that potential respondents did not wish to contribute to this aspect of the research. Finally, although a higher response rate in the questionnaire phase would have been desirable, we found no indication of systematic drop-out at any one company compared to the others.

Perspectives

In spite of, or perhaps precisely because of, its complexity, the field of shift work eminently exemplifies the possibilities for developing participatory practices by sharing control and utilizing opportunities for giving attention to mutual interests.

A key finding of the analyses in this report was deducing the concept of collective direct participation, which was seen in the ongoing interaction between the representatives and employees in Sweden and in Italy to help develop and implement schedule designs. We assume that by virtue of its very nature, direct collective participation will contribute to reducing 'power distance', which is an important dimension in the practice of participation (Sagie & Aycan 2003).

In the field of shift work, we believe it is possible to optimize organizational participation within the established frameworks. Our findings suggest this might be achieved by integrating the formal basis of representative participation (as displayed in Germany and the Netherlands) with some sort of formal collective participation to ensure ongoing interaction and dialogue about the company's schedule design. At the same time, the shift plans could be managed by a team-based participatory practice that could act autonomously within the frameworks of the production demands existing at any given time. This would not only reduce power distance, but also be an essential step in involving and utilizing the employees' knowledge and experience as part of their own decision-making processes. It could also facilitate the integration of individual and group-based flexibility with operational demands. In all events, it is not unreasonable to assume that the innovative developmental participatory dynamic arising from such steps would hold a practical value that could be conveyed to, and benefit, other areas within the organization.

9. REFERENCES

Alfredsson L, Åkerstedt T, Matsson M & Wilborg B, 1991. Self-reported health and well-being amongst night security guards with a comparison of the working population. *Ergonomics*, vol. 34, no. 5, 525-30.

Angersbach D, Knauth P, Loskant H, Karvonen MJ, Undeutsch K & Rutenfranz J, 1980. A retrospective cohort study comparing complaints and diseases in day and shift workers. *International Archives Occupational Environmental Health*, 456, 127-40.

Anxo D & Lundström S, 1998. Working time policy – a European Perspective. *The Committee for Working Life Research*, Stockholm (in Swedish).

Barton J, 1994. Choosing to work at night: a moderating influence on individual tolerance to shift work. *Journal of Applied Psychology*, 64, 449-54.

Barton J & Folkard, S, 1991. The response of day and night nurses to their work schedules. *Journal of Occupational Psychology*, 64, 207-18.

Barton J, Folkard S, Smith L & Poole C, 1994. Effects on health of a change from a delaying to an advancing shift system. *Occupational Environmental Medicine*, 51, 749-55.

Barton J, Spelten E, Totterdell P, Smith L, Folkard S & Costa G, 1995. The Standard Shift Work Index: a battery of questionnaires for assessing shift work related problems. *Work & Stress*, 9, 4-30.

Bisanti L, Olsen J, Basso O, Thonneau P & Karmaus W, 1996. Shift work and subfecundity: A European multicenter study. *Journal of Occupational and Environmental Medicine*, 38, 352-58.

Bjørner JB, Damsgård MT, Watt T, Bech P, Rasmussen NK, Kristensen TS, Modvig J & Thunedborg K, 1997. Danish manual to SF-36: a questionnaire about health status. *Lif*, Copenhagen (in Danish).

Bodin L, Axelsson G & Ahlborg G, 1999. The association of shift work and nitrous oxide exposure in pregnancy with birth weight and gestational age. *Epidemiology*, 10, 429-36.

Bohle P & Tilley AJ, 1989. The impact of night work on psychological well-being. *Ergonomics*, vol. 32, no. 9, 1089-99.

Bohle P & Tilley AJ, 1998. Early experiences of shiftwork: Influences on attitudes. *Journal of Occupational and Organizational Psychology*, 71, 61-79.

Büssing A, 1996. Social tolerance of working time scheduling in nursing. *Work & Stress*, vol. 10, no. 3, 238-50.

Bøggild H & Knutsson A, 1999. Shift work, risk factors and cardiovascular disease. *Scandinavian Journal of Work, Environment and Health*, 25(2), 85-99.

Bøggild H, Burr H, Tüchsen F & Jeppesen HJ, 2001. Work environment of Danish shift and day workers. *Scandinavian Journal of Work, Environment and Health*, 27(2), 97-105.

Bøggild H & Jeppesen HJ, 2001. Intervention in shift scheduling and changes in biomarkers of heart disease in hospital wards. *Scandinavian Journal of Work, Environment and Health*, 27(2), 87-96.

Comperatore CA & Krueger GP, 1990. Circadian Rhythm, desynchronosis, jet lag, shift lag and coping strategies. *Occupational Medicine: State of the Art Reviews*, vol. 5, no. 2, 323-41.

Cook JD, Hepworth SJ, Wall TD & Warr PB, 1981. The experience of work: a compendium and review of 249 measures and their use. *Academic Press Inc.*, London.

Corlett EN, Queinnec Y & Paoli P, 1988. Adapting shift work arrangements. *European Foundation for the Improvement of Living and Working Conditions*, Dublin, Ireland.

Costa G, 1996. The impact of shift and night work on health. *Applied Ergonomics*, vol. 27, no. 1, 9-16.

Costa, G, 1997. The problem: shiftwork. *Chronobiology International*, 14 (2), 89-98.

Dachler HP & Wilpert B, 1978. Conceptual dimensions and boundaries of participation in organizations: A critical evaluation. *Administrative Science Quarterly*, 23, 1-39.

Davis S, Mirich DK & Stevens RG, 2001. Night shift work, light at night, and risk of breast cancer. *Journal of the National Cancer Institute*, 93, 1557-62.

Danish Parliament, 2004. The Working Environmental Act. *Legislation no. 442, 09/06/2004*. Copenhagen.

EIROnline (2000): Working time developments – 2000, *European Industrial Relations Observatory On-line*, European Foundation, Dublin.

European Commission, 1989. On the introduction of measures to encourage improvements in the safety and health of workers at work. *Council directive of 12 June 1989; 89/391/EEC*, Brussels.

European Commission, 1990. Community Charter of the Fundamental Social Rights of Workers. *Office for Official Publications of the European Communities*, Luxembourg.

European Commission, 1993. Concerning certain aspects of the organization of working time. *Council directive of 23 November 1993; 93/104/EC*, Brussels.

European Commission, Employment and Social Affairs, 1998. Working time: Research and development 1995-1997. *Office for Official Publications of the European Communities*, Luxembourg.

European Parliament and the Council, 2003. Concerning certain aspects of the organization of working time. *Directive of 4 November 2003, 2003/88/EC*, Brussels.

Escribà-Agüir V, 1992. Nurses' attitudes towards shiftwork and quality of life. *Scandinavian Journal of Social Medicine*, vol. 20, no. 2, 115-18.

Fortier I, Marcoux S & Brisson J, 1995. Maternal work during pregnancy and the risk of delivering a small-for-gestational-age or preterm infant. *Scandinavian Journal of Work, Environment and Health*, 21, 412-18.

Folkard S, 1992. Is there a "best compromise" shift system? *Ergonomics*, vol. 35, no. 12, 1453-63.

Folkard S, 1996. Biological disruptions in shiftworkers. In: Colquhoun WP, Costa G, Folkard S & Knauth P. *Shiftwork – Problems and solutions*. Peter Lang Verlag, Frankfurt am Main, 29-61.

Freese M & Semmer N, 1986. Shift work, stress and psychosomatic complaints: a comparison between workers in different shift work schedules, non-shift workers and former shift workers. *Ergonomics*, 29, 99-114.

Gill C, 1993. Participation in health and safety within the European Community. *European Foundation for the Improvement of Living and Working Conditions*, Dublin, Ireland.

Gold DR, Rogacz S, Bock N, Tosteson TD, Baum TM, Speizer RE & Czeisler CA, 1992. Rotating shift work, sleep, and accidents related to sleepiness in hospital nurses. *American Journal of Public Health*, 82, 1011-14.

Gordon N, Cleary P, Parker C & Czeisler C, 1986. The prevalence and health impact of shift work. *American Journal of Public Health*, 76, 1225-28.

Grzech-Sukalo H & Nachreiner F, 1998. Structural properties of shift schedules, employment of partners, and their effects on workers' family and leisure activities. *International Journal of Occupational and Environmental Health*, vol. 3, no. 3, 67-70.

Hansen J, 2001. Increased breast cancer risk among women who work predominantly at night. *Epidemiology*, 12, 74-77.

Haider M, Kundi M & Koller M, 1981. Methodological issues and problems in shift work research. In: Johnson LC, Tepas DI, Colquhoun WP & Colligan MJ (eds). *The twenty-four hour workday: proceedings of a symposium on variations in work sleep schedules*. NIOSH, Ohio, 197-220.

Harrington JM, 1978. Shiftwork and health. A critical review of the literature. *University of London*, London.

Hornberger S & Knauth P, 1993. Inter individual differences in the subjective valuation of leisure time utility. *Ergonomics*, vol. 36, nos 1-3, 255-64.

Hornberger S & Knauth P, 1998. Follow-up study on effects of a change in shift schedule on shift workers in the chemical industry. *International Journal of Industrial Ergonomics*, 21, 249-57.

Härmä M, 1996. Ageing, physical fitness and shift work tolerance. *Journal of Applied Ergonomics*, 27, 25-29.

Härmä MI, Hakola T, Åkerstedt T & Laitinen JT, 1994. Age and adjustment to night work. *Occupational and environmental medicine*, 51, 568-73.

International Labour Office (ILO) 1990. The hours we work: New work schedules in policy and practice. *Conditions of work digest*, vol. 9, no. 2. International Labour Office, Geneva.

Infante-Rivard C, David M, Gauthier R & Rivard GE, 1993. Pregnancy loss and work schedule during pregnancy. *Epidemiology*, 4, 73-75.

Jeppesen HJ, 2003. Participatory approaches to strategy and research in shift work intervention. *Theoretical Issues in Ergonomic Science*, vol. 4, nos 3-4, 289-301.

Jeppesen HJ, Bøggild H & Larsen K, 1997. Regulations as Prevention Strategies for Shiftwork Problems. *International Journal of Occupational and Environmental Health*, vol. 3, no. 3, 82-87.

Jeppesen HJ & Bøggild H, 1998. The Management of Health and Safety in the Organization of Working Time at Local Level. *Scandinavian Journal of Work, Environment & Health*, vol. 24, suppl. 3, 81-87.

Jeppesen HJ, Kleiven M & Bøggild H, 2004. Can varying the number of teams in a shift schedule constitute a preventive strategy? *Journal of Public Health / Revista de Saú de Pública*, vol. 38, suppl. 47-55.

Jeffreys S, 2000. A Copernican Revolution in French Industrial Relations: Are the Times a' Changing, *British Journal of Industrial Relations*, 38:2, 241-60.

Kandolin I & Huida O, 1996. Individual flexibility: an essential prerequisite in arranging shift schedules for midwives, *Journal of Nursing Management*, no. 4, 213-17.

Karlsson B, Knutsson A & Lindahl B, 2001. Is there an association between shift work and having a metabolic syndrome? Results from a population based study of 27,485 people. *Occupational and Environmental Medicine* 58 (11), 747-52.

Kawachi I, Colditz GA, Stampfer MJ, Willett WC, Manson JE, Speizer FE & Hennekens CH, 1995. Prospective study of shift work and risk of coronary heart disease in women, *Circulation*, 92, 3178-82.

Kleiven M, Bøggild H & Jeppesen HJ, 1998. Shiftwork and Sickleave. A Case-Referent Study. *Scandinavian Journal of Work, Environment and Health*, vol. 24, suppl. 3, 128-33.

Koller M, 1983. Health risks related to shift work. *International Archives Occupational Environmental Health*, 53, 59-75.

Knauth P, Eichhorn B, Löwenthal I, Gärtner KH & Rutenfranz, 1983. Reduction of nightwork by re-designing of shift-rotas. *International Archives Occupational Environmental Health*, 51, 371-79.

Knauth P, 1993. The design of shift systems, *Ergonomics*, 36, 15-28.

Knauth P, 1996. Designing better shift systems, *Applied Ergonomics*, 27, no. 1, 39-44.

Knauth P & Rutenfranz J, 1976. Circadian rhythm of body temperature and re-entrainment at shift change, *International Archives of Occupational and Environmental Health*, 37, 125-37.

Knauth P & Kiesewetter E, 1987. A change from weekly to quicker shift rotations: a field study of discontinuous three shift workers, *Ergonomics*, 30, 1311-21.

Knauth P & Rutenfranz J, 1987. Shiftwork. In: Harrington JM. *Recent advances in occupational health*, Churchill Livingstone, London, 263-81.

Knauth P & Costa, G, 1996. Psychosocial effects. In: Colquhoun WP, Costa G, Folkard S & Knauth P. *Shiftwork – Problems and solutions*, Peter Lang Verlag, Frankfurt am Main, 89- 112.

Knauth P & Hornberger S, 1998. Changes from weekly backwards to quicker forward rotating shift systems in the steel industry, *International Journal of Industrial Ergonomics*, 21, 267-73.

Knauth P & Hornberger S, 2003. Preventive and compensatory measures for shift workers, *Occupational Medicine*, 53, 109-16.

Knutsson A, 1989. Shift work and coronary heart disease. *Scandinavian Journal of Social Medicine*, 44 suppl. 1-36.

Knutsson A & Bøggild H, 2000. Shift work and cardiovascular disease: review of disease mechanisms, *Review Environ Health*, 15, 359-72.

Kogi K, 1995. Increasing flexibility in shift work arrangements, *Work & Stress*, vol. 9, no. 2/3, 211-18.

Koller M, Kundi M & Cervinka R, 1978. Field studies at an Austrian oil refinery I: Health and psychosocial wellbeing of workers who drop out of shiftwork, *Ergonomics*, vol. 21, no. 10, 835-47.

Kundi M, Koller M & Stefan H *et al.*, 1995. Attitudes of nurses towards 8-h and 12-h shift systems, *Work & Stress*, vol. 9, no. 2/3, 134-39.

Kundi M & Wöckinger G, 2000. Psychosocial effects and flexible shift work arrangements in hospital nurses. In: Hornberger S, Knauth P, Costa G & Folkard S (eds). Shiftwork in the 21st century, *Arbeitswissenschaft in der betrieblichen Praxis*, Band 17, Peter Lang Verlag, Frankfurt, 393-98.

Loudoun RJ & Bohle PL, 1998. Work/non-work conflict and health in shiftwork: Relationships with family status and social support. *International Journal of Occupational and Environmental Health*, suppl. vol. 3, no. 3, 71-77.

Lowden A, Kecklund G, Axelsson J & Åkerstedt T, 1998. Change from an 8-hour to a 12-hour shift, attitudes, sleep, sleepiness and performance. *Scandinavian Journal of Work, Environmental Health*, 24, suppl. 3, 69-75.

Monk TH, 1988. Coping with stress of shift work, *Work & Stress*, 2, 169-72.

Monk TH & Folkard S, 1992. *Making shiftwork tolerable*, Taylor & Francis, London.

Mozurkewich EL, Luke B, Avni M & Wolf FM, 2000. Working conditions and adverse pregnancy outcome: a meta-analysis, *Obstet Gynecol*, 95, 623-35.

Nilsson C, 1981. Social consequences of the scheduling of working hours. In: Reinberg A, Vieux N & Andlauer P. *Night and shiftwork. Biological and social aspects*, Pergamon Press, Oxford, 489-94.

Orth-Gomér K, 1983. Intervention on coronary risk factors by adapting a shift work schedule to biologic rhythmicity, *Psychosomatic Medicine*, vol. 45, no. 5, 847-54.

Paley MJ, Price JM & Thierry H, 1998. The impact of a change in rotating shift schedules: a comparison of the effects of 8, 10, 14 h work shifts, *International Journal of Industrial Ergonomics*, 21, 293-305.

Pellegrini C, 1998. Employment relations in Italy. In: Bamber GJ & Lansbury RD. *International and Comparative Employment Relations*, SAGE, London, 145-68.

Ponzellini AM, 2003. Worker Participation in Negotiating Working Time in Italy. In: Gold M (ed.). *New Frontiers of Democratic Participation at Work*, Ashgate Publishing Limited, Aldershot, 249-72.

Rantanen J, 1995. Strategies for regulations and services in occupational health and safety. In: Rantanen J, Lehtinen S, Hernberg S, Lindström K, Sorsa M, Starck J & Viikari-Juntura E (eds). *Proceedings of the International Symposium 'From Research to Prevention'*, March 1995, Helsinki. Finnish Institute of Occupational Health, Helsinki, 158-66.

Regalia I & Regini M, 1998. Italy: The dual character of industrial relations. In: Ferner A & Hyman R. *Changing industrial relations in Europe*, Blackwell Publishers Ltd. Oxford, 459-503.

Rutenfranz J & Knauth P, 1986. Combined effects – Introductory remarks. In: Haider M, Koller M & Cervinka R (eds). *Night and shift work. Long-term effects and their prevention*, Verlag Peter Lang, Frankfurt, 67-74.

Sagie A & Aycan Z, 2003. A cross-cultural analysis of participative decision-making in organizations, *Human Relations*, 56, 4, 453-73.

Salamon M, 1987. *Industrial Relations*, Prentice Hall, London.

Schernhammer ES, Laden F, Speizer FE, Wilett WC, Hunter DJ, Kawachi I, *et al.*, 2001. Rotating night shifts and risk of breast cancer in women participating in the Nurses' Health Study, *Journal of the National Cancer Institute*, 93, 1563-68.

Scott AJ, 2000. Shift work and health, *Primary Care*, 27(4),1057-78.

Scott, AJ & Ladou J, 1990. Shift work: effects on sleep and health with recommendations for medical surveillance and screening. In: Scott AJ & Ladou J (eds). *Occupational Medicine: State of the art reviews*, Hanley & Belfus Inc., Philadelphia.

Smith L, Folkard S & Poole C, 1994. Increased injuries on night shift, *Lancet*, 344, 1137-39.

Steenland K, 2000. Shift work, long hours, and cardiovascular disease: review. In: Schnall P, Belkic K, Landsbergis P & Baker D (eds). *The work place and cardiovascular disease*, Hanley & Belfus Inc., Philadelphia, 7-17.

Taylor PJ & Poccock SJ, 1972. Mortality of shift and day workers 1956-68, *British Journal of Industrial Medicine*, 29, 201-7.

Tucher P, Smith L, Macdonald I & Folkard S, 1998. The impact of early and late shift change-overs on sleep, health and well-being in 8 and 12 hour shift systems, *Journal of Occupational Health Psychology*, 3, 265-75.

Tüchsen F, Jeppesen HJ & Bach E, 1994. Employment Status, Non Daytime Work and Gastric Ulcer in Men, *International Journal of Epidemiology*, vol. 23, 365-70.

Zhu JL, Hjøllund NH, Bøggild H & Olsen J, 2003. Shift work and subfecundity: a causal link or an artefact, *Journal of Occupational Environmental Medicine*, 60, E, 12.

Walker J, 1985. Social problems of shiftwork. In: Folkard S & Monk TH (eds). *Hours of work*, John Wiley and Sons Ltd., Chichester, 211-25.

Waterhouse JM, Folkard S & Minors DS, 1993. Shiftwork, health and safety: an overview of the scientific literature 1978-1990, *Her Majesty's Stationary Office*, London, 1-31.

Wedderburn A (ed.), 1993. Social and family factors in shift design, *Bulletin for European Studies of Time* (BEST), no. 5, European Foundation for the Improvement of Living and Working Conditions, Loughlinstown House, Dublin.

Wedderburn A (ed.), 1994. Instruments for designing, implementing and assessing working time arrangements, *Bulletin for European Studies of Time* (BEST), no. 7, European Foundation for the Improvement of Living and Working Conditions, Loughlinstown House, Dublin.

Wedderburn A (ed.), 2000. Shift work and health, *Bulletin for European Studies of Time* (BEST), no. 9, European Foundation for the Improvement of Living and Working Conditions, Loughlinstown House, Dublin.

Williamson AM & Sanderson JW, 1986. Changing the speed of shift rotation: a field study, *Ergonomics*, 29, 1085-96.

Wilpert B, 1998. A view from Psychology. In: Heller F, Pusic E, Strauss G & Wilpert B (eds). *Organizational Participation*, Oxford University Press, New York, 40-64.

Åkerstedt T, 1985. Adjustment of physiological circadian rhythms and sleep-wake cycle to shift work. In: Folkard S & Monk TH (eds). *Hours of work*. John Wiley and Sons Ltd., Chichester, 185-97.

Åkerstedt T, 1990. Psychological and physiological effects of shiftwork. Scandinavian Journal of *Work, Environment and Health*, 16, suppl. 1, 67-73.

Åkerstedt T & Knutsson A, 1994. Shiftwork. In: Levi BS & Wegman DH (eds). *Occupational health, recognizing and preventing work related disease*, Little, Brown & Co., Boston, 407-17.

10. APPENDICES

APPENDIX 1

FOURTEEN RULES FOR DESIGNING
A GOOD SHIFT SYSTEM

1. Minimize permanent nights.
2. Minimize night-shift sequences: schedule only 2-4 night shifts in succession.
3. Avoid fast double-backs (short intervals of time off – 7, 8, or 10 hours – between two shifts).
4. Plan rotas with some weekends off.
5. Avoid overlong work sequences.
6. Arrange shift length to reflect task loads (the length of the shift should depend on the physical and mental load involved in performing the tasks).
7. Consider shorter night shifts.
8. Rotate forwards.
9. Delay morning start time (the morning shift should not begin too early).
10. Make shift-change times flexible if possible.
11. Keep rotas regular.
12. Allow some individual flexibility.
13. Limit short-term rota changes.
14. Give timely notice of rotas.

These rules are based on ergonomic and biological health criteria, and some companies may experience them as being in opposition to social wishes. Although adherence to all of the rules is not a must, they do represent various recommendations for using shift-work design to prevent adverse affects. (Based on *Guidelines for shift workers, 1991*. Bulletin of European Studies on Time (BEST), no. 3, European Foundation for the Improvement of Living and Working Conditions, Dublin).

APPENDIX 2

PROCESS RECOMMENDATIONS FOR IMPLEMENTING OR ALTERING EXISTING SHIFT SCHEDULES

1. Clarify whether it is practicable to design new schedules based on prevailing legislation and agreements, and on existing resources and tasks, or whether a new design will require changes.
2. Clarify whether external assistance is necessary to commence the process.
3. Ensure support from management, and stipulate the determination frameworks that apply for the employee participants.
4. Have the decision-making authority on schedule design lie with the employee participants.
5. Allow the time-frames for accomplishing the process to be sufficiently long.
6. Have the employee participants work out the framework for how the process will unfold.
7. Make sure some of the participants are prepared to undertake responsibility for the process as it progresses, and to be part of a working group.
8. Establish a structure for the activities of the working group.
9. Ensure employee motivation for participating in the process of altering the schedules.
10. Allocate specific time and resources to the process.
11. Ensure ongoing participative discussions and activities.
12. Secure a continuously high level of information to all.
13. Have the participants discuss, and stipulate in advance, the decision-making principles that apply when introducing schedule changes.
14. Test a new schedule for a period of 6-12 months and evaluate before making a final decision on the future schedule.
15. Establish, in advance, the principles for how to proceed and reach a final decision after the test period.
16. Avoid too many other parallel activities during the process.

These recommendations are derived from experiences obtained during intervention studies of shift-schedule design in hospitals based on participatory processes. They are intended for others contemplating a process aimed at altering applied shift schedules. (Jeppesen HJ & Bøggild H, 2000, *Prevention in shift work in hospitals – a participatory intervention study* (in Danish). The Danish Work and Environmental Foundation, Copenhagen, Denmark).

APPENDIX 3

PARTICIPATION AND PREVENTION WHEN ORGANIZING SHIFT WORK AT COMPANY LEVEL IN VARIOUS EUROPEAN COUNTRIES

Individual company reports

Supplementary individual company reports based on the questionnaire research in

3.1 Italy
3.2 Sweden
3.3 Norway
3.4 East Germany
3.5 The Netherlands
3.6 Denmark

Supplementary report – Italy
Norsk Hydro

Introduction and background

The research group's reporting on the HAPCA project consists of a main report and a set of appendices that includes company-specific supplements for the companies that participated in the questionnaire research. The study was supported by Norsk Hydro's Research Foundation and NHO's Work Environment Research Foundation, Norway.

In the main, or joint, report we first describe the overarching framework of the project in terms of its purpose and background, design, and methods of data collection, as well as the strategies used in preparing and organizing the project. We then give an account of the investigations, data collection, analyses, and description, followed by our interpretation of the results within the areas investigated.

Originally, the participating companies in the study were Norsk Hydro's factories in Italy, France, the United Kingdom, the Netherlands, former East Germany, former West Germany, Sweden, and Norway. All of these sites were Hydro Agri Europe companies. In addition, we chose to include a site in Denmark, which was from Hydro Aluminium. Before data collection began, the factory in the UK was shut down and was therefore eliminated from the study.

The planned collection of data from different sources was carried out in a variety of ways. This process is described more fully in the main report. In these individual company reports we account for what happened within the individual areas. The interviews were all carried out as originally planned, with at least five interviewees from each company (representatives from management and employees, plus one person from the HR department). The collected data were analysed, and the results were communicated to outline the tasks and functions of the health and safety committee, the company's handling of work-environment issues when organizing shift work, the related opportunities and limitations, and employees involvement in the process. Furthermore, our analyses determine the nature of the company's existing shift system, and we look at the themes of shift-system responsibility, design background, employee involvement (and its significance), and issues of health and safety. Our intention with the interviews was that the data obtained would enable us to perform general analyses and cross-company comparisons of shift-work issues, and also enable us to analyse at company level to identify features of specific and shared importance. Note that our analyses of interview data is not reported on an individual company level, but only in the main report. This ensures the interviewees' anonymity, as it prevents identification of any single person's utterances and views.

The questionnaire survey was originally initiated on behalf of the employee representatives in the European Works Council, who wanted to give the employees an opportunity to express their views and assessments. The research team and the central project group supported this. Such a questionnaire investigation was then discussed and planned in collaboration with the participating companies. It later turned out that only the companies and employees in E Germany, Denmark, Italy, Norway, the Netherlands, and Sweden wished to participate. The questionnaires were translated from a common version into the different languages of the participating companies and then back-translated, but minor linguistically based differences between the country-specific versions cannot be ruled out. Questionnaires were handed out by the company and collected by the union representative (steward) in sealed envelopes. The reply rate relative to the questionnaires handed out varied considerably: from 25% to 64%. The rather low response rates diminish the strength of the interpretations and conclusions, and the potential for generalizing our findings. This consideration is especially pertinent here because we have no knowledge about potential respondents' reasons for not participating. These aspects are discussed more fully later, in the section on analyses and descriptions of the questionnaire data, but it is important to view our interpretations and discussions in this light.

In the individual companies, the number of participants is generally too small to further divide the participants in the analyses, for instance into day and shift workers. Comparative analyses of different groups in accordance with their working hours and other conditions have thus been carried out across all participants. Analyses of these aspects at company level will be prone to statistical uncertainty because of the scattered data. Because this has affected the possibilities for analysis, and the certainty of conclusions on possible differences, these comparative group analyses are only described in the main report.

However, for a number of selected questions, comparative analyses have been made between employees in individual companies versus the rest of the companies. These analyses form the background of the specific supplements for each of the participating companies, since the findings may be used to determine what initiatives the company might take.

Unfortunately, it turned out that the factual data on accidents were too scattered, too sparse, and too variable. The data also reflected insufficient accident reporting in several companies, especially for the collection period in 2000. Consequently, trustworthy analyses could not be undertaken. The quality of these data presumably relates to differences in the evaluation and incidence of events registered as accidents of different severity within different companies. This is reflected in the considerable heterogeneity in the accident data the companies have reported to the project. Thus, accident data were left out, both in the main report and in the supplements.

Similarly, it turned out to be impossible to obtain the necessary data on illness reports, typically because in a number of cases such reports did not exist as digital data or usable files within the project time-frame. Hence, data for illness/absence reports are not a part of this final report or analyses.

We assumed that factual data concerning shift systems (the distribution of staff and the system design) would be known to the participating companies. We therefore considered it unnecessary to report back these data, mentioning them instead in the comparisons and evaluations of the participating companies' organization of shift work, and the design of the applied shift systems.

On this background the supplementary reports have been organized to review the results of the questionnaires with ongoing discussions and a concluding summary. Furthermore, specific appendices with ergonomic rules for designing a good shift system (Appendix 1) and recommendations for implementing or altering shift systems (Appendix 2) have been added, both to the supplements and to the main report. Hopefully, in line with our intentions, these can be a point of focus for discussions and initiatives about how to organize working hours.

ANALYSES AND DESCRIPTION OF QUESTIONNAIRE DATA

While reviewing the results in the sections below, we sometimes use the expression "significance" or "statistical significance" when referring to differences between groups. "Significant" differences are differences that occur with a certain minimal probability (p). A p-value of, for example, 0.05 indicates that the probability that the differences found are a result of chance is less than 5%. Put simply, the concept of significance helps express one's confidence as to whether there are differences between the analysed groups or not. As noted, a significance level of 0.05 reflects a probability of less than 5% that any differences observed are coincidental. If the significance were 0.01, then the probability of chance would be less than 1%. When referring to the degree of significance in the results sections, a significance of 5% or less is marked by *, 1% or less by **, and 0.1 % or less by ***.

Similar to the presentation of our analyses in the main report and the supplementary reports for the other individual companies, here, in reviewing the results, we focus primarily on the significant findings. Exceptions are made when the results themselves, independently of comparisons with results from other companies, give us important information about issues such as age or attitudes to shift-system alterations. The analyses themselves have been carried out by comparing the employees at Hydro Italy with the participants from all other companies considered as a total group.

The analyses were carried out at group level, and accordingly the description of results will only be related to group data. The variables examined reflect those questions from the questionnaire that concern characteristics of the participants relating to social conditions such as age, household members, seniority, and working hours. In addition, information about attitudes and wishes for alterations to the current working-time systems in the company are considered. Finally, we present and discuss responses concerning satisfaction and dissatisfaction with different features of the work itself and its organization, and with cooperation and influence.

The response rate is very important in all questionnaire research, since a large drop-out rate means more uncertainty in the interpretations and generalizations of the results – that is, a high response rate means more robust interpretations are possible based on more representative data. This is linked to the lack of knowledge about how people who have not filled out the questionnaires would have responded. This might affect the results, although not necessarily. At the same time, drop-out can be "obliquely" distributed, so that it may be associated with one or more specific groups, such as day workers or shift workers without night shifts. In this case it would be the answers from these groups that primarily confounded the analyses. The degree of uncertainty likewise depends on the whether or not the drop-out is systematic, which could mean that it primarily occurs among people with specific attitudes such as satisfaction with working hours, or dissatisfaction with work conditions. In this way certain attitudes can be over- or underrepresented. We do have some information about the drop-out distribution in groups with different working hours, which we can draw on when interpreting the statistical results of the analyses. Even so, this type of problem, which exists in all investigations, cannot be resolved in this project, because we do not have sufficient information. In addition to this, national differences between labour market, and cultures and traditions, are likely to have influenced some of the responses, which is important to bear in mind when interpreting the differences in the analysis results between the participating companies. At the same time, the strength of these comparative analyses lies in the fact that they have been carried out between companies in the same sector of the chemical industry, which therefore generally have the same kind of production and technology (with the exception of Denmark, as already mentioned). Furthermore, in all the companies most of the employees in production units worked in continuous production, 24 hours a day, which hence applied to the participants in this investigation. In relation to this, the dominating shift systems (again with the exception of Denmark, which operates fixed shifts) are designed as continuous three-shift systems worked by four, five, or six shift teams in the individual companies.

There are differences in the shape of the actual shift systems' design in terms of, for example, their speed of rotation and start and end times, but all share conditions like changing working hours through day, evening and night shifts, and working on weekdays and weekends. (Further accounts of the actual shift systems can be found in the main report.) These shared conditions form the basis for comparing results between and across the companies in order to throw light on the possible influence of national traditions and culture in individual companies, as well as variations in working hours and work-organizational conditions. However, these comparative analyses and interpretations are only partly related to analyses of the questionnaire data and to a large extent rest on our analyses of the interview data.

THE QUESTIONNAIRE PHASE IN ITALY

In the following the results are divided into a number of sections that cover characteristics of the participants or "respondents", factors related to working hours, and work satisfaction. In the analyses, Italy was compared with the group of other companies as a whole.

The questionnaire process
The questionnaires were distributed and collected in the period from May to June 2000. At the company in Italy, 86 questionnaires were handed out and 54 returned. Three of these questionnaires had to be rejected, however, on account of insufficient or lacking information, which left 51 for the analyses. This corresponds to a response rate of 59%. Employee representatives were responsible for taking care of the returned questionnaires and passing them on to the research group with assistance from the HR department. The analyses presented below are thus based on 623 respondents (572 from the other companies and 51 from Italy). These numbers vary in relation to the analyses, because not everyone responded to all the questions.

Respondents
The 51 completed questionnaires came from 9 day workers and 42 shift workers, corresponding fairly well to the original distribution, but with a slightly higher response rate among day workers. Nearly all of the participating shift workers had shift work with night work.

At Hydro Italy, a similar gender distribution applied as in the other companies producing fertilizers (96% male vs 4% female), with very few women working in the production areas. In Italy, however, no women participated in the survey. In Norway 92% of the respondent sample were men. This is certainly related to the nature of production, but cultural traditions may also be of importance. Only Norsk Hydro Denmark, involved in aluminium production, has a different distribution, with as many women as men, but again, social conditions may be of importance here.

The age distribution in Italy was significantly different (***) from the group of other companies, especially for the two lowest age groups (up to 29 years and from 30 to 39 years), where, the largest differences were found. Italy had a fairly equal distribution, with 29% of the employees in the age group up to 29, and 23% in the 30-39 age group, whereas the other companies only had 7% of the employees in the group up to 29, but 35% in the 30-39 age group. The other age groups have an even distribution with around ⅓ in the 40-49 group and 17% in the 50-59 group. Italy, therefore, had a more equal allocation of employees across the age groups and a younger employee group than the other companies. Obviously related to the age distribution, fewer (***) of the employees in Italy (63%) were married or cohabitating than employees at the rest of the companies (82%), but there were no differences between the groups in the number of children living at home.

Despite the differences in age between Italy and the other companies, no differences were found in the distribution of seniority. Both in Italy and in the group of other companies the largest groups of employees, 45% and 52% respectively, have 11-25 years of seniority. In Italy, 51% reported involvement in management tasks compared to 31% in the other companies, so here the difference was significant (**).

This level of managerial activity was relatively high in Italy, and this suggested that certain tasks connected to the performance of work with specific responsibility to, but not necessarily authority over other employees, may be included in the responses. Only a small group in Italy (8%) against 23% at the other companies stated that they were involved in representative tasks. Regarding the distribution of roles at work, 35% reported being operators outside the control room, 25% operators both in and outside the control room, 24% operators in the control room, and 10% in the laboratory. Substantial differences (***) can be seen compared to the other companies, where only 9% reported being operators outside, 35% both in and outside control room, and 2% inside. At the other companies only 2% noted laboratory roles, while 15% reported maintenance roles compared to none in Italy.

Working time

The distribution of the employees in Italy according to their working-time system is shown in Table 1. The majorities, both at the other companies and in Italy, had shift work with night shifts, but in Italy it was 75% of respondents compared to 58% in the other companies. The other group of importance in Italy is day workers, making up 18%, which corresponds to the proportion of day workers at the other companies.

Changes in the scheduled working time: There was no difference between Italy and the other companies. In Italy, 44% had worked more than 5 extra hours outside normal working hours during the last four weeks. Regarding changes beyond one hour in the working-time schedule itself within the last four weeks, some differences were identified between Italy and the rest (**), where 44% in Italy, against 33% in the rest, had their schedules changed two times or more. These two questions can be said to reflect flexibility for the companies with regard to organizing and changing the working-time schedules, and the employees in Italy appear to have a higher risk in this regard compared to the employees in the other companies.

Employees' current working hours (in %)	Other companies	Italy
Day work only	18	18
Shift work without night shifts	8	6
Shift work with night shifts	58	75
Evening work only	1	-
Night work only	5	-
Day work with on-call work	9	–
Weekend work only	2	-
Other	-	1

TABLE 1 *Current working hours.*

As for own influence on the organization of working time, the figure below illustrates the distribution in percentages of the replies to the question "To what degree do you experience that you have influence on your current working-hour arrangements?"

Influence for oneself on working-hour arrangements (distribution in %)	None	Not much	Some	A good deal	Complete
The other companies	38	29	18	12	3
Italy	46	30	18	6	–

TABLE 2 *Personal influence on working hours.*

Table 2 shows no major or significant differences between Italy and the other companies. In Italy, 76% reported that they experienced little or no influence compared with 64% at the other companies. The next table illustrates the distribution of the replies to the question "To what degree do you experience that the employees as a group have influence on their current working-hour arrangements?"

Influence for the employees as a group on working-hour arrangements (distribution in %)	None	Not much	Some	A good deal	Complete
The other companies	25	31	28	14	2
Italy	26	42	18	12	2

TABLE 3 *Group influence on working hours.*

Table 3 again shows no significant differences between Italy and the other countries, but still a majority of 68% stated that they experienced little or no influence. Thus, it is not only as individuals but also as a collective that the employees in Italy reported an absence of influence on working-hour arrangements. It is notable that there is a difference of only 8% in the number of employees that reported 'none' or 'not much' influence in their perceptions as individuals and as a group.

The next table illustrates the distribution of replies, between Italy and the other companies, to the question "Who do you think should have the most influence on the design of shift work in order to ensure that the employees' health and safety is taken care of?" (Only one answer could be given.)

Attitude to who should have most influence on shift work to ensure health and safety	Other companies	Italy
You yourself	8	10
The employees as a group	55	26
Representatives / unions	7	16
Health and Safety Committees	9	28
Works councils	19	14
Management / supervisors	3	6

TABLE 4 *Preference as to who should have influence on working hours.*

The total distribution of the results between Italy and the other companies was significantly (***) distinct. The differences are particularly linked with categories 'employees as a group', 'Health and Safety Committees', and 'representatives/unions'. In Italy it is characteristic that a majority indicated a preference for influence to be allocated to formal agents in the organizational system, whereas the majority at the other companies tended to prefer the employees as a group as a means of influence. Italy was the only company where the largest group of employee responses indicated the Health and Safety Committee as a preferred source of influence, and where less than half responded the employees as a group. The differences in the distribution of answers between Italy and the other companies, both as a group and as individual companies, were so pronounced that besides variations in attitudes and the number of employees holding management tasks, we suspect that variations in traditions and structures for regulating the labour market may also be of importance. Experiences and expectations concerning employee control or cooperation in the organization may play a role, too. In addition, the results could indicate differences in organizational practices for managing working time and handling health and safety issues.

Conditions of importance (reasons) for working the actual working-time system: Significant differences (*) were found for three areas. In Italy 63%, against 43% at the other companies, (*) stated that the reason "fits better with my family life" was not important. Regarding the reason "pays better", variations could be seen distributed across the response categories, where only 10% in Italy compared to 24% elsewhere said it held no importance. On the other hand, 30% elsewhere, against 22% in Italy, reported it to be a very important reason. However, in general it can be stated that the employees in Italy were more prone to report pay as more important. The reason "gives greater personal freedom" was reported to be important or very important by 36% of the employees at the other companies, compared to 19% in Italy. It should also be emphasized that, even when no significant differences were found, 55% and 54% of the employees in Italy, against 40% and 42% at the other companies, reported that the following reasons, respectively, for working on the existing work schedule were important or very important: "the only possibility of obtaining work at this workplace", and "the only possibility to continue at this workplace". Furthermore, 43% in Italy, compared to 29% elsewhere, reported that "the only possibility if I wanted a job" was important or very important as a reason. In summary it can be suggested that for employees in Italy, reasons related to having a job and having it at this particular workplace appeared to play a more important role for working the actual working hours than reasons related to family life, pay, and personal freedom.

The questionnaire also had a measure that evaluated the current shift system with several sub-questions. The table below shows the distribution of answers in percentages for all the different sub-questions. Examination of these responses at the Italy site could give cause to consider potential changes and initiatives. Comparisons with the other companies are not illustrated, as this would not be so informative because the other companies operated different work schedules.

The majority of answers to the different sub-questions for the other companies as a group was in the category 'Appropriate number', whereas the distribution of the answers from the employees in Italy was much more scattered. This could be interpreted as expressing a desire to re-design the working-time schedules operated at the Italy site. The desire for changes appeared to be primarily concentrated around night work, length of night shifts, number of weekends off, and also the length of weekend shifts.

	Far too few		Appropriate number		Far too many	Not relevant
a) Number of day shifts per month	16	3	43	11	5	22
b) Number of evening shifts per month	–	–	37	13	37	13
						Cont. next page

c) Number of night shifts per month	3	3	21	29	34	11
d) Number of day shifts in a row	3	17	49	3	14	14
e) Number of evening shifts in a row	3	11	46	11	16	14
f) Number of night shifts in a row	3	11	41	16	19	11
g) Number of week-ends off	38	14	3	5	27	14
h) Number of hours on day shift	–	16	41	19	13	13
i) Number of hours on evening shift	3	5	49	–	30	14
j) Number of hours on night shift	3	3	22	14	49	11
k) Number of hours on weekend shift	8	8	11	14	42	17
	Too early		Appropriate		Too late	Not relevant
j) Start time for day shifts	50	13	21	–	–	16
k) Start time for evening shifts	11	5	50	5	5	24
l) Start time for night shifts	13	3	47	5	11	21

TABLE 5 *Perceptions of shift-system features.*

A majority reported the start time of the day shift as being too early or much too early. Some of the dimensions hold a potential for change within the existing conditions, whereas others, such as the number of night shifts and weekend shifts, would require discussions on the number of crews or teams and number of employees involved, as well as the distribution of tasks among the employees.

Considering the question "Satisfaction with your working hours", the distribution, in percentages, is illustrated in the table below for Italy compared with the other companies.

Distribution in % of answers to "satisfied with working hours"	Very satisfied	Generally satisfied	Neither satisfied nor dissatisfied	Generally dissatisfied	Very dissatisfied
The other companies	15	34	37	10	4
Italy	12	36	42	8	2

TABLE 6 *Satisfaction with working hours.*

No significant differences were observed between the two groups. Around half of the employees, both in Italy and the other companies, stated that they were satisfied, and only 10% in Italy stated that they were dissatisfied. To some extent these results may appear to run counter to those for the reasons for working shift work, the experience of low influence on the design, and apparent desires for altering the schedules in operation. However, other research in the area has indicated that this might, at least in part, be a consequence of no vision or knowledge of suitable alternatives, or a result of difficulties experienced in changing the actual shift systems that are operating. The responses do not necessarily imply that alterations would not be appropriate, because they may also be related to the individual amount of knowledge about possibilities for change, and to how to approach and combine health and social considerations.

In order to obtain additional information on the levels of satisfaction with the actual applied working-time systems, the participants were asked if they would change to daytime work if they had the opportunity. A second question asked if they would change to daytime work without it affecting pay or other working-time conditions. The distribution of responses is shown below. Note that only shift workers completed these questions.

If given opportunity to change to daytime work only (in %)	Yes	No	Don't know
Other companies	32	42	26
Italy	71	10	20

TABLE 7 *Responses about changing to day work.*

If given opportunity to change to daytime work without affecting pay or work conditions (in %)	Yes	No	Don't know
Other companies	62	24	15
Italy	87	3	11

TABLE 8 *Responses about changing to day work with pay and conditions unchanged.*

Significant differences (*** and **) were found in the responses between Italy and the rest of the companies for both questions. The results from the first question, about changing to day work without any compensation, show a very high percentage of shift workers in Italy (71%) against 32% elsewhere who would change if the opportunity was given, while only 10% would remain. If compensation is included, the differences between Italy and the other companies were smaller (**), but the actual numbers of employees who wanted to change were higher still, with 87% in Italy and 62% elsewhere who would change, and only one employee in Italy who would not. Therefore, even if no compensations were included, close to three quarters of the employees in Italy would change shift work to day work if given the opportunity. This underlines our suggestion that the question about general satisfaction with working hours has several dimensions built into it, and that the results should be interpreted cautiously.

Work satisfaction

The question about the degree of employees' satisfaction with their present work situation consists of a number of sub-questions that covered most aspects of a job situation. We present the distribution of answers on all the sub-questions (see Table 9 below) in the belief that it could facilitate the discussions at the company about introducing change initiatives if certain issues appeared to be problematic.

A seven-point (Likert-type) response scale, ranging from 'very dissatisfied' to 'very satisfied', was applied to each sub-question. In Table 9 the three response categories concerning 'dissatisfied' have been combined into one category, and the same applies to 'satisfied', while the neutral category for 'neither satisfied nor dissatisfied' has been maintained. In the analyses the responses from the employees in Italy (denoted by I) are compared with the employees at the rest of the companies (denoted by R), and significant differences are indicated with a number of stars (* ≤ 0.05, ** ≤ 0.01 and *** ≤ 0.001) depending on the degree of confidence

PARTICIPATION AND PREVENTION

with which the results indicate differences between Italy and the other companies. Arrows have also been inserted for the sub-questions where reliable differences were found. The direction of the arrows shows the direction of the differences in satisfaction levels. If the direction of the arrow points towards the company in question, which here is Italy (I), the level of employee satisfaction concerning that dimension is higher in Italy than in the rest of the companies, and vice versa if the arrow points towards R.

When interpreting the results it is important to look not only at the differences between the companies, but also at how the responses are dispersed on the different categories for the single sub-question at the given company. In this way, we sometimes found that even a considerable difference in the distribution of responses between satisfied and dissatisfied had no apparent significance, because the same differences occurred in the other companies. Additionally it should be emphasized that, beyond existing differences in conditions for the individual dimensions, variations in culture and traditions are likely to have influenced responses to the questions.

Italy (I) compared with the rest of the companies (R) on the dimensions of satisfaction		Very dissatisfied. Dissatisfied. Slightly dissatisfied		Indifferent	Slightly satisfied. Satisfied. Very satisfied	
a. Your physical working conditions	I	48	⇑	12	40	*
	R	30		11	59	
b. Freedom to carry out your work	I	30	⇑	26	44	***
	R	18		10	73	
c. Your colleagues at work	I	18	⇑	22	60	***
	R	13		5	81	
d. The recognition you get for your work	I	59	⇑	16	24	***
	R	37		12	52	
e. Your immediate supervisor	I	37	⇑	24	39	*
	R	30		14	56	
f. The amount of responsibility you get	I	55	⇑	14	31	***
	R	14		11	70	
g. Your pay conditions	I	54		6	40	
	R	39		11	49	
					Cont. next page	

h. Opportunities to use your abilities	I	55	⇑	21	23	***
	R	29		12	59	
i. Cooperation between management and employees	I	63		10	27	
	R	47		10	43	
j. Your opportunities for promotion	I	55		18	27	
	R	40		24	36	
k. The manner in which the workplace is run	I	67	⇑	10	22	*
	R	46		16	39	
l. The attention your suggestions receive	I	58	⇑	23	19	***
	R	35		20	45	
m. Your working time	I	69	⇑	2	29	***
	R	30		11	59	
n. Variety in your work	I	65	⇑	10	24	***
	R	23		13	64	
o. Security in your employment	I	76	⇑	8	16	***
	R	32		12	57	
p. Your influence on the arrangement of your work	I	46	⇑	31	23	***
	R	27		22	51	
q. The extent of work tasks	I	49	⇑	31	20	***
	R	21		16	63	
r. The pace of work	I	62	⇑	14	24	***
	R	20		18	62	
s. Clarity of your tasks at work	I	64	⇑	4	32	***
	R	22		12	66	
t. Your possibilities for personal development	I	57	⇑	16	27	**
	R	35		14	51	

TABLE 9 *Work satisfaction.*

Table 9 presents the results quite clearly. Consequently, only limited additional comments are made here. Significant differences were obtained for all sub-questions, except three, with a higher dissatisfaction reported in Italy than in the rest in all cases. In 13 areas of work satisfaction the results were highly significant (***). In 14 of the dimensions a majority of the answers from the employees in Italy indicated different degrees of dissatisfaction. These dimensions were primarily centred on some aspects of management, the organization of work, and personnel policies. Furthermore, the employees' responses regarding working time again suggested that generally the employees in Italy (69%) were dissatisfied with their working hours compared to 29% expressing satisfaction.

CONCLUDING REMARKS

This supplementary report on the Norsk Hydro site in Italy has presented an overview of the research carried out. The nature of the shift systems, the background for the design, the employees' involvement and influence, and also the issues of system and work satisfaction were considered.

The participating employees in Italy reported low influence on the arrangement of their working-time hours at both individual and group level. In relation to some variations in the results it is fair to suggest that, in general, the employees tended to be dissatisfied with their working time and the actual schedules. The dissatisfaction was indicated by the employees' assessment of the shift schedules being worked, and their responses indicate specific problematic features of the schedules that could feed in to initiatives to design more appropriate schedules. The desire to alter the working-time system was further illustrated by the employees' indications that they would change to day work if they had the opportunity, with or without any kind of compensation. This group was, proportionately, significantly larger than at the other companies.

It is reasonable to suggest that one of the barriers to the implementation of new schedules may be a lack of knowledge about applicable methods and principles for the design of work schedules that integrate health and social considerations. The employees' expressions of satisfaction with their working hours could be taken to illustrate the above themes whereby, given the circumstances, knowledge about better solutions for designing and changing shift systems might not be available to the shift workers themselves, and therefore, in the face of no alternatives, one has to be satisfied. At another level the employees also expressed considerable dissatisfaction with their working hours. Hence, it is likely that the evaluation of a given shift schedule will be undertaken based on one's knowledge of applicable alternatives.

The dissatisfaction in Italy did not only relate to working hours, but could be found for most of the dimensions of work satisfaction. On the basis of the available research data it was not possible to estimate to what degree this reflects the experience of the actual conditions, or whether it can be partly attributed to a destabilization effect originating in working-time issues.

The composition of the employee respondent group in Italy differed from the employee groups participating at the other companies. This may also have influenced the results. In Italy around half of the respondents reported that they were involved in management tasks to some degree, and nearly no one reported having representative tasks. They also had different working roles compared to elsewhere with a higher proportion being operators in the control the room, and none reporting maintenance roles. Simultaneously, they expressed a belief in the formally established systems for employee influence and cooperation as the best approaches to managing employee health and safety in relation to shift work.

In summary, the results of the analyses and interpretations suggest a number of issues to consider in terms of possibly altering the shift schedules. These issues raise challenges for both the company and the employees to initiate discussions about practicable new activities and strategies regarding aspects of the employees' work situation.

Supplementary report – Sweden
Norsk Hydro

Introduction and background

The research group's reporting on the HAPCA project consists of a main report and a set of appendices that includes company-specific supplements for the companies that participated in the questionnaire research. The study was supported by Norsk Hydro's Research Foundation and NHO's Work Environment Research Foundation, Norway.

In the main, or joint, report we first describe the overarching framework of the project in terms of its purpose and background, design, and methods of data collection, as well as the strategies used in preparing and organizing the project. We then give an account of the investigations, data collection, analyses, and description, followed by our interpretation of the results within the areas investigated.

Originally, the participating companies in the study were Norsk Hydro's factories in Italy, France, the United Kingdom, the Netherlands, former East Germany, former West Germany, Sweden, and Norway. All of these sites were Hydro Agri Europe companies. In addition, we chose to include a site in Denmark, which was from Hydro Aluminium. Before data collection began, the factory in the UK was shut down and was therefore eliminated from the study.

The planned collection of data from different sources was carried out in a variety of ways. This process is described more fully in the main report. In these individual company reports we account for what happened within the individual areas. The interviews were all carried out as originally planned, with at least five interviewees from each company (representatives from management and employees, plus one person from the HR department). The collected data were analysed,

and the results were communicated to outline the tasks and functions of the health and safety committee, the company's handling of work-environment issues when organizing shift work, the related opportunities and limitations, and employees involvement in the process. Furthermore, our analyses determine the nature of the company's existing shift system, and we look at the themes of shift-system responsibility, design background, employee involvement (and its significance), and issues of health and safety. Our intention with the interviews was that the data obtained would enable us to perform general analyses and cross-company comparisons of shift-work issues, and also enable us to analyse at company level to identify features of specific and shared importance. Note that our analyses of interview data is not reported on an individual company level, but only in the main report. This ensures the interviewees' anonymity, as it prevents identification of any single person's utterances and views.

The questionnaire survey was originally initiated on behalf of the employee representatives in the European Works Council, who wanted to give the employees an opportunity to express their views and assessments. The research team and the central project group supported this. Such a questionnaire investigation was then discussed and planned in collaboration with the participating companies. It later turned out that only the companies and employees in E Germany, Denmark, Italy, Norway, the Netherlands, and Sweden wished to participate. The questionnaires were translated from a common version into the different languages of the participating companies and then back-translated, but minor linguistically-based differences between the country-specific versions cannot be ruled out. Questionnaires were handed out by the company and collected by the union representative (steward) in sealed envelopes. The reply rate relative to the questionnaires handed out varied considerably: from 25% to 64%. The rather low response rates diminish the strength of the interpretations and conclusions, and the potential for generalizing our findings. This consideration is especially pertinent here because we have no knowledge about potential respondents' reasons for not participating. These aspects are discussed more fully later, in the section on analyses and descriptions of the questionnaire data, but it is important to view our interpretations and discussions in this light.

In the individual companies, the number of participants is generally too small to further divide the participants in the analyses, for instance

into day and shift workers. Comparative analyses of different groups in accordance with their working hours and other conditions have thus been carried out across all participants. Analyses of these aspects at company level will be prone to statistical uncertainty because of the scattered data. Because this has affected the possibilities for analysis, and the certainty of conclusions on possible differences, these comparative group analyses are only described in the main report.

However, for a number of selected questions, comparative analyses have been made between employees in individual companies versus the rest of the companies. These analyses form the background of the specific supplements for each of the participating companies, since the findings may be used to determine what initiatives the company might take.

Unfortunately, it turned out that the factual data on accidents were too scattered, too sparse, and too variable. The data also reflected insufficient accident reporting in several companies, especially for the collection period in 2000. Consequently, trustworthy analyses could not be undertaken. The quality of these data presumably relates to differences in the evaluation and incidence of events registered as accidents of different severity within different companies. This is reflected in the considerable heterogeneity in the accident data the companies have reported to the project. Thus, accident data were left out, both in the main report and in the supplements.

Similarly, it turned out to be impossible to obtain the necessary data on illness reports, typically because in a number of cases such reports did not exist as digital data or usable files within the project time-frame. Hence, data for illness/absence reports are not a part of this final report or analyses.

We assumed that factual data concerning shift systems (the distribution of staff and the system design) would be known to the participating companies. We therefore considered it unnecessary to report back these data, mentioning them instead in the comparisons and evaluations of the participating companies' organization of shift work, and the design of the applied shift systems.

On this background the supplementary reports have been organized to review the results of the questionnaires with ongoing discussions and a concluding summary. Furthermore, specific appendices with ergonomic rules for designing a good shift system (Appendix 1) and recommendations for implementing or altering shift systems (Appendix

2) have been added, both to the supplements and to the main report. Hopefully, in line with our intentions, these can be a point of focus for discussions and initiatives about how to organize working hours.

ANALYSES AND DESCRIPTION OF QUESTIONNAIRE DATA

While reviewing the results in the sections below, we sometimes use the expression "significance" or "statistical significance" when referring to differences between groups. "Significant" differences are differences that occur with a certain minimal probability (p). A p-value of, for example, 0.05 indicates that the probability that the differences found are a result of chance is less than 5%. Put simply, the concept of significance helps express one's confidence as to whether there are differences between the analysed groups or not. As noted, a significance level of 0.05 reflects a probability of less than 5% that any differences observed are coincidental. If the significance were 0.01, then the probability of chance would be less than 1%. When referring to the degree of significance in the results sections, a significance of 5% or less is marked by *, 1% or less by **, and 0.1 % or less by ***.

Similar to the presentation of our analyses in the main report and the supplementary reports for the other individual companies, here, in reviewing the results, we focus primarily on the significant findings. Exceptions are made when the results themselves, independently of comparisons with results from other companies, give us important information about issues such as age or attitudes to shift-system alterations. The analyses themselves have been carried out by comparing the employees at Hydro Sweden with the participants from all other companies considered as a total group.

The analyses were carried out at group level, and accordingly the description of results will only be related to group data. The variables examined reflect those questions from the questionnaire that concern characteristics of the participants relating to social conditions such as age, household members, seniority, and working hours. In addition, information about attitudes and wishes for alterations to the current working-time systems in the company are considered. Finally, we present and discuss responses concerning satisfaction and dissatisfaction with different features of the work itself and its organization, and with cooperation and influence.

The response rate is very important in all questionnaire research, since a large drop-out rate means more uncertainty in the interpretations and generalizations of the results – that is, a high response rate means more robust interpretations are possible based on more representative data. This is linked to the lack of knowledge about how people who have not filled out the questionnaires would have responded. This might affect the results, although not necessarily. At the same time, drop-out can be "obliquely" distributed, so that it may be associated with one or more specific groups, such as day workers or shift workers without night shifts. In this case it would be the answers from these groups that primarily confounded the analyses. The degree of uncertainty likewise depends on the whether or not the drop-out is systematic, which could mean that it primarily occurs among people with specific attitudes such as satisfaction with working hours, or dissatisfaction with work conditions. In this way certain attitudes can be over- or underrepresented. We do have some information about the drop-out distribution in groups with different working hours, which we can draw on when interpreting the statistical results of the analyses. Even so, this type of problem, which exists in all investigations, cannot be resolved in this project, because we do not have sufficient information. In addition to this, national differences between labour market, and cultures and traditions, are likely to have influenced some of the responses, which is important to bear in mind when interpreting the differences in the analysis results between the participating companies. At the same time, the strength of these comparative analyses lies in the fact that they have been carried out between companies in the same sector of the chemical industry, which therefore generally have the same kind of production and technology (with the exception of Denmark, as already mentioned). Furthermore, in all the companies most of the employees in production units worked in continuous production, 24 hours a day, which hence applied to the participants in this investigation. In relation to this, the dominating shift systems (again with the exception of Denmark, which operates fixed shifts) are designed as continuous three-shift systems worked by four, five, or six shift teams in the individual companies.

There are differences in the shape of the actual shift systems' design in terms of, for example, their speed of rotation and start and end times, but all share conditions like changing working hours through day, evening and night shifts, and working on weekdays and weekends. (Further accounts of the actual shift systems can be found in the main report.) These shared conditions form the basis for comparing results between and across the companies in order to throw light on the possible influence of national traditions and culture in individual companies, as well as variations in working hours and work-organizational conditions. However, these comparative analyses and interpretations are only partly related to analyses of the questionnaire data and to a large extent rest on our analyses of the interview data.

THE QUESTIONNAIRE PHASE IN SWEDEN

In the following account the results are divided into a number of sections that cover characteristics of the participants or "respondents", factors related to working hours,, and work satisfaction. In the analyses, Sweden was compared with the group of other companies as a whole.

The questionnaire process
The questionnaires were distributed and collected in the period from May to June 2000. At the company in Sweden, 171 questionnaires were handed out and 108 returned, which corresponds to a response rate of 59%. Shop stewards were responsible for taking care of the returned questionnaires and passing them on to the research group. The analyses presented below are thus based on 623 respondents (515 from the other companies and 108 from Sweden). These numbers vary in relation to the analyses, because not everyone responded to all the questions.

Respondents
The proportions of returned questionnaires from day workers and shift workers with night work were very similar. The next-largest return came from day workers with on-call shifts, followed by shift work without night work.

At Hydro Sweden, the same gender distribution applies as in the other companies producing fertilizers (96% male vs 4% female), with very few women working in the production areas, and thus also few being potential employee participants in the project. In Sweden, 90% of the participants in the survey were men and 10% were women. This is certainly related to the nature of production, but cultural traditions may also be of importance. Only Norsk Hydro Denmark, involved in aluminium production, has a different distribution, with as many women as men, but again, social conditions may be of importance here.

PARTICIPATION AND PREVENTION

The age distribution in Sweden differs from the other companies (***) with the greatest variances found from 40 years of age and over. For the employees aged 40-49 Sweden had 25% and the rest if the companies 38%, for the age group 50-59 Sweden had 24% against 17% in the rest, and from 60 years and over Sweden had 8% against 1%. Regarding marital status, Sweden had more unmarried respondents (27%) than the rest (18%). More employees in Sweden (58%) had one child or more living at home, compared to 46% in the other companies.

There were differences (**) in the distribution of seniority across the applied categories between Sweden and the other companies. More employees in Sweden than in the rest of the companies had a seniority of 2-10 years, and of more than 25 years. In the 11-24-year seniority group, however, the proportion was lower in Sweden (41%) than elsewhere (53%). Regarding involvement in management tasks and representative tasks, no differences were found. Regarding the distribution of roles at work in Sweden, 24% stated they had maintenance roles, 15% were operators outside the control room, 14% were operators both in and outside the control room, 18% reported 'other' roles, 11% shipment roles, and 10% laboratory roles. The proportions at the other companies for the maintenance, shipment, and laboratory categories were 11%, 1%, and 1%, respectively. These variations in roles may explain some of the differences found between Sweden and the other companies.

Working time
The distribution of the employees in Sweden, according to their working-time systems, is shown in the table below. There was a significant difference (***) between Sweden and the rest for three working-time groups. Shift work with night shifts had a clear majority at the other companies, whereas Sweden had two groups of equal size; day workers and shift workers with night shift. This also applies for the group with on-call work. These findings suggest differences in both size (proportion of the responses) and character that may contribute to explaining some of the differences between Sweden and the rest of the companies for some of the effects related to working time.

Employees' current working hours (in %)	Other companies	Sweden
Day work only	14	39
Shift work without night shifts	8	8
Shift work with night shifts	64	38
Evening work only	1	-
Night work only	6	-
Day work with on-call work	6	15
Weekend work only	2	-
Other	-	-

TABLE 1 *Current working hours.*

Changes in the scheduled working time: Compared to the rest of the companies, around half of the employees in Sweden reported having extra hours beyond the normal employment time within the last four weeks. However, the half having extra hours had significantly more (**) extra hours than the rest, and around one third stated that they had worked between 11 and 40 extra hours. Regarding changes of more than one hour in the working-time schedule itself within the last four weeks, no valid differences were identified, but around one third, both in Sweden and in the other companies, said that this had been the case. These two questions can be said to reflect a flexibility for the companies with regard to organizing and changing the working-time schedules.

Individual and group influence on the organization of working time: The table below illustrates the distribution in percentages of the replies to the question "To what degree do you experience that you have influence on your current working-hour arrangement?"

Influence for oneself on working-hour arrangements (distribution in %)	None	Not much	Some	A good deal	Complete
The other companies	41	30	16	11	2
Sweden	31	23	26	14	6

TABLE 2 *Personal influence on working hours.*

The table shows that the employees in Sweden reported that as individuals, they have influence on their working-hour arrangements to a significantly higher degree (**) than elsewhere. 46% responded that they experience 'some' to 'complete' influence, compared to 29% at the other companies. The differences in this distribution of employees between the working-time systems may be centrally important for interpretation. The next table illustrates the distribution of reported influence on working-time arrangements for the employees as a group.

Influence for the employees as a group on working-hour arrangements (distribution in %)	None	Not much	Some	A good deal	Complete
The other companies	27	33	26	12	2
Sweden	20	23	32	23	3

TABLE 3 *Group influence on working hours.*

Table 3 shows significant (**) differences between Sweden and the others, with considerably more influence as a group reported in Sweden: 43% in Sweden, compared to 60% at the other companies, reported that they experience employees as having 'none' or 'not much' influence on working hours as a group.

The next table illustrates the distribution of replies, between Sweden and the other companies, to the question "Who do you think should have the most influence on the design of shift work in order to ensure that the employees' health and safety is taken care of?" (Only one answer could be given.) There was no difference in the distribution of results between Sweden and the other companies. For both, the category 'employees as a group', has more than half of the replies, followed by 'works council', with nearly one quarter in Sweden indicating this preference.

The results suggest that the employees would like to have the most influence on design of working-time schedules as a group (and this closely parallels the reported group influence in Table 3 above, which is also 58%). The low standing of Health and Safety Committees in terms of taking care of health and safety is a somewhat surprising finding.

Attitude to who should have most influence on shift work to ensure health and safety	Other companies	Sweden
You yourself	9	4
The employees as a group	52	58
Representatives / unions	8	5
Health and Safety Committees	11	9
Work councils	17	23
Management / supervisors	3	1

TABLE 4 *Preference as to who should have influence on working hours.*

Conditions of importance (reasons) for working on the actual working-time system: Significant differences (*) were found for all the applied arguments. In Sweden fewer employees than at the rest of the companies reported "the only possibility if I wanted a job" to be an important reason, but with responses spread across the reply categories. The same pattern was seen for the reason "the only possibility of obtaining work at this workplace". For the question "the only possibility to continue at this workplace", the difference was particularly noticeable for the category of "very important", which was stated by 36% of the employees elsewhere, but by only 17% in Sweden. Conversely, regarding the reason "fits better with my family life", 37% in Sweden reported this to be of importance, compared to 23% at the other companies. The reason "gives greater personal freedom" shows the same pattern, where 73% in Sweden compared to 58% elsewhere reported "some importance" to "very important".

Thus the employees in Sweden were somewhat more likely to perceive their actual working hours as giving personal freedom and fitting better in with family life. The reason "pays better" was reported by 61% in Sweden, and 72% elsewhere, to be of "some importance" to "very important".

The questionnaire also had a measure that evaluated the current shift system with several sub-questions. Only shift workers were required to respond to these questions. The table below shows the distribution of answers in percentages for all the different sub-questions. Examination of these responses at the Swedish company could give rise to the consideration of potential changes. Comparisons with the other companies are not illustrated, as this would not be so informative because the other companies operated different work systems. However, it is

PARTICIPATION AND PREVENTION

worth pointing out that the distribution of answers is very much alike, with most responses in the 'not relevant' or 'appropriate' categories.

This suggests the majority were reasonably content with the features of their working-time system. There were sizable proportions of the respondents who reported too many day shifts (30%) and night shifts (21%) per month, too many consecutive night shifts (29%), and too many consecutive day shifts (30%). The number of weekends off was reported to be too few (44%), and 33% reported that the weekend shifts have too many hours. Start time for the day shifts was reported to be too early by 53%. This is the category where a majority of respondents wanted changes in the same direction.

	Far too few		Appropriate number		Far too many	Not relevant
a) Number of day shifts per month	2	9	45	15	15	15
b) Number of evening shifts per month	4	4	62	6	9	15
c) Number of night shifts per month	5	5	49	14	7	21
d) Number of day shifts in a row	–	5	59	16	14	7
e) Number of evening shifts in a row	2	7	68	7	7	7
f) Number of night shifts in a row	7	14	40	19	10	10
g) Number of weekends off	17	27	46	2	–	7
h) Number of hours on day shift	11	2	67	11	7	2
i) Number of hours on evening shift	7	–	73	9	7	4
j) Number of hours on night shift	12	2	54	20	5	7
k) Number of hours on weekend shift	–	–	60	19	14	7
	Too early		Appropriate		Too late	Not relevant
j) Start time for day shifts	40	13	48	–	–	–

Cont. next page

k) Start time for evening shifts	13	2	77	2	–	6
l) Start time for night shifts	9	5	63	7	9	7

TABLE 5 *Perceptions of shift-system features.*

Considering the question "Satisfaction with your working hours", the distribution of responses in percentages is illustrated in the table below for Sweden compared with the other companies.

Distribution in % of answers to "satisfied with working hours"	Very satisfied	Generally satisfied	Neither satisfied nor dissatisfied	Generally dissatisfied	Very dissatisfied
The other companies	15	33	39	10	5
Sweden	15	44	32	9	1

TABLE 6 *Satisfaction with working hours.*

No differences were found between the two groups regarding satisfaction with working hours. The majority in Sweden reported that they were "generally satisfied" or "extremely satisfied" with their working hours. It should be noted that the majority of the participating employees in Sweden were not shift workers, which makes the interpretation of the results of this question less certain in relation to shift work.

In order to obtain additional information about the levels of satisfaction with the actual working-time systems in operation, the participants were asked if they would change to daytime work if they had the opportunity. A second question asked if they would change to daytime work without it affecting pay or other working-time conditions. The distribution of responses is shown below. Note that only shift workers participated.

If opportunity to change to work only in daytime (answers in %)	Yes	No	Don't know
Other companies	38	38	24
Sweden	18	49	33

TABLE 7 *Responses about changing to day work.*

If given opportunity to change to daytime work without affecting pay or work conditions (in %)	Yes	No	Don't now
Other companies	66	21	14
Sweden	51	31	18

TABLE 8 *Responses about changing to day work with pay and conditions unchanged.*

For the question about change if the opportunity arose, a significantly (*) smaller proportion of the shift workers in Sweden (18%), compared to 38% elsewhere, wanted to change, but also a slightly larger proportion did not know. If a change would not affect pay or work conditions, no differences emerged between Sweden and the rest. This suggests that the extra pay as shift workers plays a role, but even so, a smaller part of the shift workers in Sweden (around a third of the group) would not want to change if given the chance. Around half the shift workers would change. This might also, as earlier questions showed, suggest the importance of family life and personal freedom as reasons for working shifts, at least for part of the group – but also that the ways of matching working-time schedules with social activities may vary among shift workers, depending on age, family structure, children, social activities, and so on.

Work satisfaction

The question about the degree of employees' satisfaction with their present work situation consists of a number of sub-questions that covered most aspects of a job situation. We present the distribution of answers on all the sub-questions (see Table 9 below) in the belief that it could facilitate the discussions at the company about introducing change initiatives if certain issues appeared to be problematic.

A seven-point (Likert-type) response scale, ranging from 'very dissatisfied' to 'very satisfied', was applied to each sub-question. In Table 9 the three response categories concerning 'dissatisfied' have been combined into one category and the same applies to 'satisfied', while the neutral category for 'neither satisfied nor dissatisfied' has been maintained. In the analyses the responses from the employees in Sweden (denoted by S) are compared with the employees at the rest of the companies (denoted by R), and significant differences are indicated with a number of stars ($* \leq 0.05$, $** \leq 0.01$ and $*** \leq 0.001$) depending on the degree of confidence with which the results indicate differences between Sweden and the other companies. Arrows have also been inserted for the sub-questions where reliable differences were found. The direction of the arrows shows the direction of the differences in satisfaction levels. If the direction of the arrow points towards the company in question, which here is Sweden (S), the level of employee satisfaction concerning that dimension is higher in Sweden than in the rest of the companies, and vice versa if the arrow points towards R.

When interpreting the results it is important to look not only at the differences between the companies, but also at how the responses are dispersed on the different categories for the single sub-question at the given company. In this way, we sometimes found that even a considerable difference in the distribution of responses between satisfied and dissatisfied had no apparent significance, because the same differences occurred in the other companies. Additionally it should be emphasized that, beyond existing differences in conditions for the individual dimensions, variations in culture and traditions are likely to have influenced responses to the questions.

Table 9 presents the results quite clearly. Consequently, only limited additional comments are made here. The factors with significant differences point in both directions. The employees in Sweden were more satisfied than elsewhere with the freedom to carry out the work and with their immediate supervisors. Besides freedom to carry out the work, the highest proportion of satisfaction was seen in relation to that with colleagues at work, which was also high for the rest of the companies.

Sweden (S) compared with the rest of the companies (R) on the dimensions of satisfaction		Very dissatisfied Dissatisfied Slightly dissatisfied		Indif-ferent	Slightly satisfied Satisfied Very satisfied	
a. Your physical working conditions	S	18	⇑	16	65	**
	R	34		10	56	
b. Freedom to carry out your work	S	4	⇑	9	88	***
	R	22		11	67	
c. Your colleagues at work	S	10		4	86	
	R	14		7	78	
d. The recognition you get for your work	S	30	⇑	21	50	**
	R	40		10	50	
					Cont. next page	

e. Your immediate supervisor.	S	14	⇑	19	67	***
	R	40		14	52	
f. The amount of responsibility you get	S	16		9	75	
	R	24		11	65	
g. Your pay conditions	S	54	⇑	22	25	***
	R	38		9	53	
h. Opportunities to use your abilities	S	27	⇑	16	57	
	R	32		12	56	
i. Cooperation between management and employees	S	41		14	45	
	R	50		9	41	
j. Your opportunities for promotion	S	50	⇑	26	25	*
	R	40		23	37	
k. The manner in which the workplace is run	S	45		22	33	
	R	48		14	38	
l. The attention your suggestions receive	S	34		27	39	
	R	37		19	44	
m. Your working time	S	29		11	60	
	R	34		10	56	
n. Variety in your work	S	18		12	70	
	R	28		12	59	
o. Security in your employment	S	47	⇑	17	36	***
	R	32		10	57	
p. Your influence on the arrangement of your work	S	24	⇑	33	43	*
	R	29		21	50	
q. The extent of work tasks	S	16		17	67	
	R	25		17	58	
r. The pace of work	S	18		23	59	
	R	25		16	59	
s. Clarity of your tasks at work	S	21		14	65	
	R	27		11	62	
t. Your possibilities for personal development	S	45	⇑	19	36	*
	R	36		13	51	

TABLE 9 *Work satisfaction.*

The employees in Sweden were considerably more dissatisfied with pay conditions and security in employment than the employees in the rest of the companies. Also, the Swedish employees were more dissatisfied with some of the dimensions of personnel policy. It should also be noted that for the items measuring cooperation, management, and influence (questions i, k, and l) the proportion of satisfied employees was below 50%. For the rest of the questions, more than half of the employees indicated that they were satisfied.

CONCLUDING REMARKS

This supplementary report on the Norsk Hydro site in Sweden has presented an overview of the research carried out. The nature of the shift systems, the background for the design, the employees' involvement and influence, and also the issues of system and work satisfaction were considered.

The employees in Sweden experienced more influence on working-time arrangements than elsewhere. A majority of the employees in Sweden would prefer the employees as a group to have most influence on the design of shift work to ensure health and safety. It was interesting that the employees in Sweden reported family and personal reasons for working shift work to a higher degree than at the other companies. Correspondingly, fewer employees in Sweden would want to change to day work if that were possible. However, it was also suggested that shift pay plays some role as a reason for working shifts – as around half would change to day work if pay were not affected.

In Sweden a majority of the shift workers suggested a certain feature of the shift schedule that they would want to change, namely, the starting time of day shifts. Regarding the design of shift work, the employees' responses suggest reasons for considering the possibility of initiating a participative process that could incorporate the wishes of the employees and integrate health and social perspectives. The responses also showed that different attitudes existed and suggest that difficulties may more easily be overcome by introducing more flexibility in autonomous working-time groups at different organizational levels in the company.

Furthermore, the distribution of the responses to the general satisfaction questionnaire with its sub-questions showed a general satisfaction with most work dimensions, but it also suggested some challenges for management and employees to consider in the future. This was particularly relevant to personnel policies and employee influence that relate to opportunities for advancement and personnel development, security in employment and how the workplace is managed in order to start discussions about practicable new initiatives.

Supplementary report – Norway
Norsk Hydro

Introduction and background

The research group's reporting on the HAPCA project consists of a main report and a set of appendices that includes company-specific supplements for the companies that participated in the questionnaire research. The study was supported by Norsk Hydro's Research Foundation and NHO's Work Environment Research Foundation, Norway.

In the main, or joint, report we first describe the overarching framework of the project in terms of its purpose and background, design, and methods of data collection, as well as the strategies used in preparing and organizing the project. We then give an account of the investigations, data collection, analyses, and description, followed by our interpretation of the results within the areas investigated.

Originally, the participating companies in the study were Norsk Hydro's factories in Italy, France, the United Kingdom, the Netherlands, former East Germany, former West Germany, Sweden, and Norway. All of these sites were Hydro Agri Europe companies. In addition, we chose to include a site in Denmark, which was from Hydro Aluminium. Before data collection began, the factory in the UK was shut down and was therefore eliminated from the study.

The planned collection of data from different sources was carried out in a variety of ways. This process is described more fully in the main report. In these individual company reports we account for what happened within the individual areas. The interviews were all carried out as originally planned, with at least five interviewees from each company (representatives from management and employees, plus one person from the HR department). The collected data were analysed,

and the results were communicated to outline the tasks and functions of the health and safety committee, the company's handling of work-environment issues when organizing shift work, the related opportunities and limitations, and employees involvement in the process. Furthermore, our analyses determine the nature of the company's existing shift system, and we look at the themes of shift-system responsibility, design background, employee involvement (and its significance), and issues of health and safety. Our intention with the interviews was that the data obtained would enable us to perform general analyses and cross-company comparisons of shift-work issues, and also enable us to analyse at company level to identify features of specific and shared importance. Note that our analyses of interview data is not reported on an individual company level, but only in the main report. This ensures the interviewees' anonymity, as it prevents identification of any single person's utterances and views.

The questionnaire survey was originally initiated on behalf of the employee representatives in the European Works Council, who wanted to give the employees an opportunity to express their views and assessments. The research team and the central project group supported this. Such a questionnaire investigation was then discussed and planned in collaboration with the participating companies. It later turned out that only the companies and employees in E Germany, Denmark, Italy, Norway, the Netherlands, and Sweden wished to participate. The questionnaires were translated from a common version into the different languages of the participating companies and then back-translated, but minor linguistically-based differences between the country-specific versions cannot be ruled out. Questionnaires were handed out by the company and collected by the union representative (steward) in sealed envelopes. The reply rate relative to the questionnaires handed out varied considerably: from 25% to 64%. The rather low response rates diminish the strength of the interpretations and conclusions, and the potential for generalizing our findings. This consideration is especially pertinent here because we have no knowledge about potential respondents' reasons for not participating. These aspects are discussed more fully later, in the section on analyses and descriptions of the questionnaire data, but it is important to view our interpretations and discussions in this light.

In the individual companies, the number of participants is generally too small to further divide the participants in the analyses, for instance

into day and shift workers. Comparative analyses of different groups in accordance with their working hours and other conditions have thus been carried out across all participants. Analyses of these aspects at company level will be prone to statistical uncertainty because of the scattered data. Because this has affected the possibilities for analysis, and the certainty of conclusions on possible differences, these comparative group analyses are only described in the main report.

However, for a number of selected questions, comparative analyses have been made between employees in individual companies versus the rest of the companies. These analyses form the background of the specific supplements for each of the participating companies, since the findings may be used to determine what initiatives the company might take.

Unfortunately, it turned out that the factual data on accidents were too scattered, too sparse, and too variable. The data also reflected insufficient accident reporting in several companies, especially for the collection period in 2000. Consequently, trustworthy analyses could not be undertaken. The quality of these data presumably relates to differences in the evaluation and incidence of events registered as accidents of different severity within different companies. This is reflected in the considerable heterogeneity in the accident data the companies have reported to the project. Thus, accident data were left out, both in the main report and in the supplements.

Similarly, it turned out to be impossible to obtain the necessary data on illness reports, typically because in a number of cases such reports did not exist as digital data or usable files within the project time-frame. Hence, data for illness/absence reports are not a part of this final report or analyses.

We assumed that factual data concerning shift systems (the distribution of staff and the system design) would be known to the participating companies. We therefore considered it unnecessary to report back these data, mentioning them instead in the comparisons and evaluations of the participating companies' organization of shift work, and the design of the applied shift systems.

On this background the supplementary reports have been organized to review the results of the questionnaires with ongoing discussions and a concluding summary. Furthermore, specific appendices with ergonomic rules for designing a good shift system (Appendix 1) and recommendations for implementing or altering shift systems (Appendix

2) have been added, both to the supplements and to the main report. Hopefully, in line with our intentions, these can be a point of focus for discussions and initiatives about how to organize working hours.

ANALYSES AND DESCRIPTION OF QUESTIONNAIRE DATA

While reviewing the results in the sections below, we sometimes use the expression "significance" or "statistical significance" when referring to differences between groups. "Significant" differences are differences that occur with a certain minimal probability (p). A p-value of, for example, 0.05 indicates that the probability that the differences found are a result of chance is less than 5%. Put simply, the concept of significance helps express one's confidence as to whether there are differences between the analysed groups or not. As noted, a significance level of 0.05 reflects a probability of less than 5% that any differences observed are coincidental. If the significance were 0.01, then the probability of chance would be less than 1%. When referring to the degree of significance in the results sections, a significance of 5% or less is marked by *, 1% or less by **, and 0.1 % or less by ***.

Similar to the presentation of our analyses in the main report and the supplementary reports for the other individual companies, here, in reviewing the results, we focus primarily on the significant findings. Exceptions are made when the results themselves, independently of comparisons with results from other companies, give us important information about issues such as age or attitudes to shift-system alterations. The analyses themselves have been carried out by comparing the employees at Hydro Norway with the participants from all other companies considered as a total group.

The analyses were carried out at group level, and accordingly the description of results will only be related to group data. The variables examined reflect those questions from the questionnaire that concern characteristics of the participants relating to social conditions such as age, household members, seniority, and working hours. In addition, information about attitudes and wishes for alterations to the current working-time systems in the company are considered. Finally, we present and discuss responses concerning satisfaction and dissatisfaction with different features of the work itself and its organization, and with cooperation and influence.

The response rate is very important in all questionnaire research, since a large drop-out rate means more uncertainty in the interpretations and generalizations of the results – that is, a high response rate means more robust interpretations are possible based on more representative data. This is linked to the lack of knowledge about how people who have not filled out the questionnaires would have responded. This might affect the results, although not necessarily. At the same time, drop-out can be "obliquely" distributed, so that it may be associated with one or more specific groups, such as day workers or shift workers without night shifts. In this case it would be the answers from these groups that primarily confounded the analyses. The degree of uncertainty likewise depends on the whether or not the drop-out is systematic, which could mean that it primarily occurs among people with specific attitudes such as satisfaction with working hours, or dissatisfaction with work conditions. In this way certain attitudes can be over- or underrepresented. We do have some information about the drop-out distribution in groups with different working hours, which we can draw on when interpreting the statistical results of the analyses. Even so, this type of problem, which exists in all investigations, cannot be resolved in this project, because we do not have sufficient information. In addition to this, national differences between labour market, and cultures and traditions, are likely to have influenced some of the responses, which is important to bear in mind when interpreting the differences in the analysis results between the participating companies. At the same time, the strength of these comparative analyses lies in the fact that they have been carried out between companies in the same sector of the chemical industry, which therefore generally have the same kind of production and technology (with the exception of Denmark, as already mentioned). Furthermore, in all the companies most of the employees in production units worked in continuous production, 24 hours a day, which hence applied to the participants in this investigation. In relation to this, the dominating shift systems (again with the exception of Denmark, which operates fixed shifts) are designed as continuous three-shift systems worked by four, five, or six shift teams in the individual companies.

There are differences in the shape of the actual shift systems' design in terms of, for example, their speed of rotation and start and end times, but all share conditions like changing working hours through day, evening and night shifts, and working on weekdays and weekends. (Further accounts of the actual shift systems can be found in the main report.) These shared conditions form the basis for comparing results between and across the companies in order to throw light on the possible influence of national traditions and culture in individual companies, as well as variations in working hours and work-organizational conditions. However, these comparative analyses and interpretations are only partly related to analyses of the questionnaire data and to a large extent rest on our analyses of the interview data.

THE QUESTIONNAIRE PHASE IN NORWAY

In the following, the results are divided into a number of sections that cover characteristics of the participants or "respondents", factors related to working, and work satisfaction. In the analyses, Norway was compared with the group of other companies as a whole.

The questionnaire process

The questionnaires were distributed and collected in the period from May to June 2000. At the company in Norway, the procedure with handing out the questionnaires was decentralized and no valid information existed about the number of questionnaires handed out to which groups of employees. Overall, 74 questionnaires were returned, which corresponds to a response rate of approximately 25% estimated from the factual information on number of employees in the production area. Shop stewards were responsible for taking care of the returned questionnaires and passing them on to the research group. The analyses presented below are thus based on 623 respondents, (549 from the other companies and 74 from Norway). These numbers vary in relation to the analyses, because not everyone responded to all the questions. On account of the very low response rate and with a skewed distribution across working schedules, the results have to be interpreted with caution.

Respondents

According to the factual information the questionnaires could, in principle, have been distributed to approximately 300 employees in production, of which about 180 were shift workers. The distribution of answers to the question about working-time system showed that of the 74 returned questionnaires, 72 respondents were shift workers with night work, 69 of whom worked continuous shift work (estimated from other replies) and only 2 of whom were day workers. This gave such a skewed reply distribution that it raises the question of whether, despite the agreed terms for the questionnaire research, the handing out of questionnaires and the requests to participate were very skewed (i.e. only a particular sub-sample of the workforce may have been approached in any numbers). However, these returns mean that the reply rate for shift workers is 40%, and of this group nearly all worked continuous shift work. This implies that the responses from the employees in Norway can virtually be seen as replies from employees with shift work, and that the interpretations have to consider this fact.

At Hydro Norway, a similar gender distribution applied as in the other companies producing fertilizers (96% male vs 4% female), with very few women working in the production areas, and thus also few being potential employee participants in the project. In Norway, 92% of the respondent sample were men. This is certainly related to the nature of production, but cultural traditions may also be of importance. Only Norsk Hydro Denmark, involved in aluminium production, has a different distribution, with as many women as men, but again, social conditions may be of importance here.

In Norway the employees were younger than in the rest of the companies. Norway had 56%, and the others 42%, in the age groups up to 40 years. The results were reversed for the older age groups. Norway had significantly more (*) single employees (28%) than the other companies (18%). No significant differences were observed in terms of the number of children living at home, which may be related to the differences in age distribution.

No significant differences were observed for seniority between the sample in Norway and the employees at the other companies as a whole. Compared to the other companies, fewer employees in Norway (**) reported involvement in management tasks. The numbers were 18% in Norway, compared to 35% elsewhere. It is suggested that minor job tasks with special possibilities for management-type activity may be included here. No differences were found for involvement in representative tasks (20% in Norway and 22% in the other companies). As a consequence of the skewed distribution of participating employees, a different distribution of roles at work (***) was observed. In Norway 74% reported being operators both in and outside the control room, compared with 29% in the other companies. None of the employees in Norway reported maintenance roles, compared to 15% elsewhere, and

12% (Norway) compared to 4% (the rest of companies) reported having more than one work role.

Working time

The distribution of the employees in Norway and the other companies according to their working-time system is shown in Table 1. Significant differences (***) were found here, but again the skewed distribution of the working-time groups in Norway played a decisive role. In Norway 97% worked shift work with night shifts, compared to 54% in the other companies as a group. An average of 20% of the other companies' employees reported working day work only, compared to 3% of the participating employees in Norway. None of the participants in Norway had other forms of working-time schedules. These differences may contribute to explaining some of the differences between Norway and elsewhere for some of the effect variables connected to working time.

Changes in the scheduled working time: No significant differences were seen between the employees in Norway and the employees in the other companies with regard to extra hours. Here, 40% in Norway and 53% elsewhere reported no extra hours during the last four weeks. Regarding changes beyond one hour in the working-time schedule within the last four weeks, no differences were found between the groups, but both in Norway and the other companies, around one third reported that they had experienced changes in that period. These two questions can be said to reflect flexibility for the companies with regard to organizing and changing the working-time schedules.

Employees' current working hours (in %)	Other companies	Norway
Day work only	20	3
Shift work without night shifts	9	–
Shift work with night shifts	54	97
Evening work only	1	-
Night work only	5	-
Day work with on-call work	9	–
Weekend work only	2	-
Other	-	-

TABLE 1 *Current working hours.*

Individual and group influence on the organization of working time:
The table below illustrates the distribution in percentages of the replies
to the question "To what degree do you experience that you have influence on your current working-hour arrangements?"

Influence for oneself on working-hour arrangements (distribution in %)	None	Not much	Some	A good deal	Complete
The other companies	38	28	20	12	3
Norway	45	36	9	8	1

TABLE 2 *Personal influence on working hours.*

Table 2 shows no major differences between the employees in Norway
and the rest of the companies concerning individual influence on own
working-time arrangements, but at the same time it is notable that 81%
in Norway and 66% in the other-countries group experience none or not
much influence. The next table illustrates the distribution of reported
influence on working-time arrangements for the employees as a group.

Influence for the employees as a group on working-hour arrangements (distribution in %)	None	Not much	Some	A good deal	Complete
The other companies	27	30	26	15	2
Norway	15	42	35	8	-

TABLE 3 *Group influence on working hours.*

There was a significant (*) difference between Norway and the other
companies. However, the picture was not clear because fewer employees
in Norway reported having no influence, whereas fewer employees in
Norway also reported having a good deal of influence. It was noticeable
that the changes in the level of reported influence between individual
and group level is much larger in Norway than elsewhere.

The next table illustrates the distribution of replies between Norway
and the other companies for the question "Who do you think should
have the most influence on the design of shift work in order to ensure
that the employees' health and safety is taken care of?" (Only one
answer could be given.)

Attitude to who should have most influence on shift work to ensure health and safety	Other companies	Norway
You yourself	8	8
The employees as a group	52	58
Representatives / unions	8	4
Health and Safety Committees	10	11
Works councils	18	18
Management / supervisors	3	-

TABLE 4 *Preference as to who should have influence on working hours.*

No significant differences were found in the distribution of results between Norway and the other companies. In both groups, more than 50% of the employees stated a preference for the employees as a group to have most influence. Similarly, in both groups around 29% wanted cooperative bodies to have the most influence in the form of works councils and Health and Safety Committees, to ensure health and safety. This is a somewhat surprising finding given that the issue in question is taking care of health and safety.

Conditions of importance (reasons) for working on the actual working-time system: Significant differences at various levels were found for all the applied arguments, but most of the categories appeared to be of greater importance for the employees in Norway than the other companies as a group. In Norway 39%, compared to 29% in the other companies (*), reported "the only possibility if I wanted a job" to be an important reason, and only 21% in Norway, compared to 40% elsewhere, attached no importance to this reason.

The same pattern (*) was observed for "the only possibility to continue at this workplace" as a reason. As for "obtaining work at this workplace" being the reason for working the current system, 60% in Norway reported this to be of importance, compared to 40% in the other companies (***). For the reason "fits better with my family life", the answers were distributed more in both ends of the answering continuum for the group of other companies (46% reported no importance, and 19% very important) as compared to Norway (33% reported no importance, and 12% very important), and differences were significant (**).

The reason "pays better" was less important to a higher proportion of employees in the other companies (*), as 25% stated this elsewhere, compared to only 11% in Norway. Nevertheless, 30% in both groups reported it to be a very important reason. Correspondingly, the reason "gives greater personal freedom" appeared to have considerably less importance to the employees in the other companies (***), as 33% elsewhere stated no influence, compared to only 14% in Norway. The relatively higher proportion of participating shift workers in Norway may have influenced the results here.

The questionnaire also had a measure that evaluated the current shift system with several sub-questions. The table below shows the distribution of answers in percentages for all the different sub-questions. Examination of these responses at the Norway site could give cause to consider potential changes. Comparisons with the other companies are not illustrated, as this would not be so informative because the other companies operated different work schedules. However, it is worth pointing out that the distribution of answers is very similar, with most responses in the 'appropriate' category.

Only shift workers were asked to answer these questions. For most of the sub-questions, with four exceptions, responses are similar, with a clear majority of answers being reported to be appropriate, especially in comparison to the distribution in the rest of the companies. Similar to the other companies, deviations from this relate, in particular, to the number of weekends off, which are estimated to be too few, while 41% compared to 51% find the weekend shifts (item 'k') too long. Particular to Norway is the fact that the numbers of day shifts. both in a row and per month, were reported as being too many by fairly large groups, 39% and 34%, respectively. As for start times for the different shifts, very clear majorities of 70% (day shifts), 84% (evening shifts), and 83% (night shifts) found them appropriate.

	Far too few		Appropriate number		Far too many	Not relevant
a) Number of day shifts per month	1	14	49	23	11	1
b) Number of evening shifts per month	–	3	77	13	6	1
c) Number of night-shifts per month	–	6	59	19	16	1
					Cont. next page	

PARTICIPATION AND PREVENTION

d) Number of day shifts in a row	3	7	49	17	22	1
e) Number of evening shifts in a row	–	3	75	12	9	1
f) Number of night shifts in a row	–	9	64	16	12	–
g) Number of weekends off	27	27	39	4	1	1
h) Number of hours on day shift	–	10	61	12	13	4
i) Number of hours on evening shift	–	1	74	12	7	6
j) Number of hours on night shift	–	6	61	13	14	6
k) Number of hours on weekend shift	1	3	51	19	22	4
	Too early		Appropriate		Too late	Not relevant
j) Start time for day shifts	8	14	70	4	1	1
k) Start time for evening shifts	3	4	84	3	4	1
l) Start time for night shifts	1	4	83	6	4	1

TABLE 5 *Perceptions of shift-system features.*

Considering the question "Satisfaction with your working hours", the distribution, in percentages, is illustrated in Table 6 below for Norway compared with the other companies.

Distribution in % of answers to "satisfied with working hours"	Very satisfied	Generally satisfied	Neither satisfied nor dissatisfied	Generally dissatisfied	Very dissatisfied
The other companies	16	37	33	10	4
Norway	1	19	68	8	4

TABLE 6 *Satisfaction with working hours.*

A significant difference (***) was found between the two groups, but the differences in the composition of the groups may have particular importance. That is to say, recall that the employees in Norway are nearly exclusively shift workers, and that the group of other companies consists of a mixture of employees with different working-time systems. Satisfaction is higher in the other companies, but a large proportion in Norway reported being neither satisfied nor dissatisfied. Only 14% and 12% in the two groups expressed being, in fact, dissatisfied, but similarly only 20% in Norway reported being, in fact, satisfied.

In order to obtain additional information on the levels of satisfaction with the existing working-time systems, the participants were asked if they would change to daytime work if they had the opportunity. A second question asked if they would change to daytime work without it affecting pay or other working-time conditions. These two questions were only for shift workers.

If given opportunity to change to daytime work only (in %)	Yes	No	Don't know
Other companies	39	39	22
Norway	19	42	39

TABLE 7 *Responses about changing to day work.*

If given opportunity to change to work in daytime work without affecting pay or work conditions (in %)	Yes	No	Don't know
Other companies	67	21	12
Norway	46	26	28

TABLE 8 *Responses about changing to day work with pay and conditions unchanged.*

There was a significant difference (**) between the groups for the question about changing to day work if the opportunity arose: A much higher proportion of the shift workers in the other companies would change to daytime work, while a higher proportion in Norway did not know. When the employees considered the issue of a change to day work that would not affect pay or work conditions, an even more robust difference (***) emerged: 67% in the other-companies group, compared to 46% in Norway, would change to daytime work. In addition, the proportion responding 'don't know' is also higher in Norway. These findings corresponded to the results, which showed pay and greater personal freedom as reasons for working the existing system, both of which were of higher importance in Norway than the other companies.

Work satisfaction

The question about the degree of employees' satisfaction with their present work situation consists of a number of sub-questions that covered most aspects of a job situation. We present the distribution of answers on all the sub-questions (see Table 9 below) in the belief that it could facilitate the discussions at the company about introducing change initiatives if certain issues appeared to be problematic.

A seven-point (Likert-type) response scale, ranging from 'very dissatisfied' to 'very satisfied', was applied to each sub-question. In Table 9 the three response categories concerning 'dissatisfied' have been combined into one category, and the same applies to 'satisfied', while the neutral category for 'neither satisfied nor dissatisfied' has been maintained. In the analyses the responses from the employees in Norway (denoted by N) are compared with the employees at the rest of the companies (denoted by R), and significant differences are indicated with a number of stars (* ≤ 0.05, ** ≤ 0.01 and *** ≤ 0.001) depending on the degree of confidence with which the results indicate differences between Norway and the other companies. Arrows have also been inserted for the sub-questions where reliable differences were found. The direction of the arrows shows the direction of the differences in satisfaction levels. If the direction of the arrow points towards the company in question, which here is Norway (N), the level of employee satisfaction concerning that dimension is higher in Norway than in the rest of the companies, and vice versa if the arrow points towards R.

When interpreting the results it is important to look not only at the differences between the companies, but also at how the responses are dispersed on the different categories for the single sub-question at the given company. In this way, we sometimes found that even a considerable difference in the distribution of responses between satisfied and dissatisfied had no apparent significance, because the same differences occurred in the other companies. Additionally it should be emphasized that, beyond existing differences in conditions for the individual dimensions, variations in culture and traditions are likely to have influenced responses to the questions.

Table 9 presents the results quite clearly. Consequently, only limited additional comments are made here. The factors with significant differences point in both directions. The actual participants in Norway only make up 25% of the potential employee participants, which may imply a skewed distribution between the actual responses and the potential responses if more employees had participated. Furthermore, nearly all of the participants from Norway are shift workers, in opposition to the mixture of working-time systems represented in the other group, and the analyses of differences between shift and day workers showed that shift workers were generally far more dissatisfied, also with the other dimensions of their working-life conditions, than day workers.

Norway (N) compared with the rest of the companies (R) on the dimensions of satisfaction		Very dissatisfied Dissatisfied Slightly dissatisfied		Indifferent	Slightly satisfied Satisfied Very satisfied	
a. Your physical working conditions	N	29		11	60	
	R	32		11	57	
b. Freedom to carry out your work	N	10		19	71	*
	R	20	⇑	10	70	
c. Your colleagues at work	N	6		10	85	
	R	15		6	79	
d. The recognition you get for your work	N	31		17	53	
	R	40		11	49	
e. Your immediate supervisor	N	32		22	46	
	R	30		14	56	
f. The amount of responsibility you get	N	15		24	61	***
	R	24	⇑	9	67	
g. Your pay conditions	N	38		22	40	**
	R	41	⇑	9	50	
h. Opportunities to use your abilities	N	27		18	55	
	R	32	⇑	12	56	
i. Cooperation between management and employees	N	44		24	32	***
	R	49	⇑	8	43	
j. Your opportunities for promotion	N	32		44	24	***
	R	43	⇑	21	36	
k. The manner in which the workplace is run	N	51		25	24	**
	R	47	⇑	14	39	
					Cont. next page	

l. The attention your suggestions receive	N	33		31	36	
	R	37		23	44	
m. Your working time	N	33	⇑	22	44	**
	R	33		9	58	
n. Variety in your work	N	25		19	56	
	R	27		11	62	
o. Security in your employment	N	25		14	61	
	R	36		12	52	
p. Your influence on the arrangement of your work	N	22		31	47	
	R	29		22	49	
q. The extent of work tasks	N	25	⇑	32	43	***
	R	23		15	62	
r. The pace of work	N	23		26	51	
	R	24		16	60	
s. Clarity of your tasks at work	N	23		14	63	
	R	26		11	63	
t. Your possibilities for personal development	N	40		14	46	
	R	37		14	49	

TABLE 9 *Work satisfaction.*

For the sub-questions where significant differences were identified, the employees in Norway were less satisfied with their working conditions than the group of other companies, but this seems in many instances to be related to the fact that more responses from Norway were in the reply category 'indifferent'. However, another way of looking at the results is to identify the distribution of answers from Norway alone for each dimension. In 10 out of the 20 sub-questions, a majority of the employees in Norway reported being satisfied to some degree. In 3 out of the 10 dimensions with less than the majority of responses on a satisfied category, more answers were given to the dissatisfied categories than the satisfied ones. This encompassed cooperation, management, and advancement possibilities. For 3 of the questions (g, l, and t) the distributions were nearly identical for dissatisfied and satisfied, though with a tendency towards the satisfied categories. The 4 remaining questions with less than 50% 'satisfied' responses were concerned with one's immediate supervisor, working time, influence on work arrangements, and extent of work tasks. These results suggest that the participating employees in Norway in general express dissatisfaction with aspects of their working lives that concern management, influence, work organization, and to some extent personnel policies.

CONCLUDING REMARKS

This supplementary report on the Norsk Hydro site in Norway has presented an overview of the research carried out. The nature of the shift systems, the background for the design, the employees' involvement and influence, and also the issues of system and work satisfaction were considered.

Once again it should be emphasized that the results from Norway must be interpreted with particular care due to a response rate of 25% coinciding with a very skewed distribution in terms of there being a disproportionately higher number of shift workers participating in the questionnaire research than day workers (97% of the participants were shift workers with night work, compared to 54% in the other companies). Furthermore, the participants in Norway were younger, even while having levels of seniority in the company similar to the employees from the group of other companies.

With the above reservations in mind, the employees in Norway demonstrated that more respondents reported all the listed reasons for working on the current work schedule – with the exception of 'family life' – to be important or very important rather than not important or of little importance. To the sub-questions concerning possibilities for having work and working at that particular company, pay, and personal freedom, responses showed these to be of greater importance to the employees in Norway than to the respondents from the other companies. These responses can be assumed to influence the answers to other questions in the questionnaire and could be reflected in the attitudes of the shift workers to day work. Thus, a significantly smaller number of the shift workers in Norway than in the other companies reported that they would change to daytime work if they had the opportunity. At the same time, however, more employees in Norway were in doubt about changing even if it would not have consequences for pay or other work conditions. Here a higher number would change under these circumstances, much like at the other companies, but nevertheless a lower proportion in Norway than in the other-companies group. Again, more employees in Norway were doubtful about changing to day work under these conditions than in the rest of the companies.

Fewer employees in Norway reported that, as individuals, they had influence on their current working-hour arrangement. The same tendency, but in a more scattered way, can be found for the employees as a group. However, here fewer in Norway reported having 'no influence' and 'a good deal of influence'. Interestingly, the change in the proportion of employees that stated some degree of influence from the individual to the group level was more dramatic in Norway. No differences could be identified between the groups regarding who should have most influence on the design of shift systems to ensure health and safety. A slight majority in both groups reported a preference for the employees as a group or collective. The next-largest preferences were for employee representatives as works councils and Health and Safety Committees, despite different traditions in the participating countries for employee influence, cooperation and regulations. Moreover, it was noticeable that only about 10% of the employees preferred Health and Safety Committees as the forum for ensuring employee health and safety on shift work.

Finally, less than half of the employees in Norway reported some degree of satisfaction in response to half of the dimensions, and for some satisfaction dimensions a higher number of employees reported dissatisfaction. In particular, the low satisfaction concerned work aspects related to cooperation, management, possibilities for advancement, personal development opportunities, and work conditions such as working time and pay. These findings offer opportunities for initiating discussions at the workplace with regard to practicable new activities and strategies to address the issues raised.

Supplementary report – E Germany
Norsk Hydro

Introduction and background

The research group's reporting on the HAPCA project consists of a main report and a set of appendices that includes company-specific supplements for the companies that participated in the questionnaire research. The study was supported by Norsk Hydro's Research Foundation and NHO's Work Environment Research Foundation, Norway.

In the main, or joint, report we first describe the overarching framework of the project in terms of its purpose and background, design, and methods of data collection, as well as the strategies used in preparing and organizing the project. We then give an account of the investigations, data collection, analyses, and description, followed by our interpretation of the results within the areas investigated.

Originally, the participating companies in the study were Norsk Hydro's factories in Italy, France, the United Kingdom, the Netherlands, former East Germany, former West Germany, Sweden, and Norway. All of these sites were Hydro Agri Europe companies. In addition, we chose to include a site in Denmark, which was from Hydro Aluminium. Before data collection began, the factory in the UK was shut down and was therefore eliminated from the study.

The planned collection of data from different sources was carried out in a variety of ways. This process is described more fully in the main report. In these individual company reports we account for what happened within the individual areas. The interviews were all carried out as originally planned, with at least five interviewees from each company (representatives from management and employees, plus one person from the HR department). The collected data were analysed,

and the results were communicated to outline the tasks and functions of the health and safety committee, the company's handling of work-environment issues when organizing shift work, the related opportunities and limitations, and employees involvement in the process. Furthermore, our analyses determine the nature of the company's existing shift system, and we look at the themes of shift-system responsibility, design background, employee involvement (and its significance), and issues of health and safety. Our intention with the interviews was that the data obtained would enable us to perform general analyses and cross-company comparisons of shift-work issues, and also enable us to analyse at company level to identify features of specific and shared importance. Note that our analyses of interview data is not reported on an individual company level, but only in the main report. This ensures the interviewees' anonymity, as it prevents identification of any single person's utterances and views.

The questionnaire survey was originally initiated on behalf of the employee representatives in the European Works Council, who wanted to give the employees an opportunity to express their views and assessments. The research team and the central project group supported this. Such a questionnaire investigation was then discussed and planned in collaboration with the participating companies. It later turned out that only the companies and employees in E Germany, Denmark, Italy, Norway, the Netherlands, and Sweden wished to participate. The questionnaires were translated from a common version into the different languages of the participating companies and then back-translated, but minor linguistically-based differences between the country-specific versions cannot be ruled out. Questionnaires were handed out by the company and collected by the union representative (steward) in sealed envelopes. The reply rate relative to the questionnaires handed out varied considerably: from 25% to 64%. The rather low response rates diminish the strength of the interpretations and conclusions, and the potential for generalizing our findings. This consideration is especially pertinent here because we have no knowledge about potential respondents' reasons for not participating. These aspects are discussed more fully later, in the section on analyses and descriptions of the questionnaire data, but it is important to view our interpretations and discussions in this light.

In the individual companies, the number of participants is generally too small to further divide the participants in the analyses, for instance

into day and shift workers. Comparative analyses of different groups in accordance with their working hours and other conditions have thus been carried out across all participants. Analyses of these aspects at company level will be prone to statistical uncertainty because of the scattered data. Because this has affected the possibilities for analysis, and the certainty of conclusions on possible differences, these comparative group analyses are only described in the main report.

However, for a number of selected questions, comparative analyses have been made between employees in individual companies versus the rest of the companies. These analyses form the background of the specific supplements for each of the participating companies, since the findings may be used to determine what initiatives the company might take.

Unfortunately, it turned out that the factual data on accidents were too scattered, too sparse, and too variable. The data also reflected insufficient accident reporting in several companies, especially for the collection period in 2000. Consequently, trustworthy analyses could not be undertaken. The quality of these data presumably relates to differences in the evaluation and incidence of events registered as accidents of different severity within different companies. This is reflected in the considerable heterogeneity in the accident data the companies have reported to the project. Thus, accident data were left out, both in the main report and in the supplements.

Similarly, it turned out to be impossible to obtain the necessary data on illness reports, typically because in a number of cases such reports did not exist as digital data or usable files within the project time-frame. Hence, data for illness/absence reports are not a part of this final report or analyses.

We assumed that factual data concerning shift systems (the distribution of staff and the system design) would be known to the participating companies. We therefore considered it unnecessary to report back these data, mentioning them instead in the comparisons and evaluations of the participating companies' organization of shift work, and the design of the applied shift systems.

On this background the supplementary reports have been organized to review the results of the questionnaires with ongoing discussions and a concluding summary. Furthermore, specific appendices with ergonomic rules for designing a good shift system (Appendix 1) and recommendations for implementing or altering shift systems (Appendix 2) have been added, both to the supplements and to the main report.

Hopefully, in line with our intentions, these can be a point of focus for discussions and initiatives about how to organize working hours.

ANALYSES AND DESCRIPTION OF QUESTIONNAIRE DATA

While reviewing the results in the sections below, we sometimes use the expression "significance" or "statistical significance" when referring to differences between groups. "Significant" differences are differences that occur with a certain minimal probability (p). A p-value of, for example, 0.05 indicates that the probability that the differences found are a result of chance is less than 5%. Put simply, the concept of significance helps express one's confidence as to whether there are differences between the analysed groups or not. As noted, a significance level of 0.05 reflects a probability of less than 5% that any differences observed are coincidental. If the significance were 0.01, then the probability of chance would be less than 1%. When referring to the degree of significance in the results sections, a significance of 5% or less is marked by *, 1% or less by **, and 0.1 % or less by ***.

Similar to the presentation of our analyses in the main report and the supplementary reports for the other individual companies, here, in reviewing the results, we focus primarily on the significant findings. Exceptions are made when the results themselves, independently of comparisons with results from other companies, give us important information about issues such as age or attitudes to shift-system alterations. The analyses themselves have been carried out by comparing the employees at Hydro E Germany with the participants from all other companies considered as a total group.

The analyses were carried out at group level, and accordingly the description of results will only be related to group data. The variables examined reflect those questions from the questionnaire that concern characteristics of the participants relating to social conditions such as age, household members, seniority, and working hours. In addition, information about attitudes and wishes for alterations to the current working-time systems in the company are considered. Finally, we present and discuss responses concerning satisfaction and dissatisfaction with different features of the work itself and its organization, and with cooperation and influence.

The response rate is very important in all questionnaire research, since a large drop-out rate means more uncertainty in the interpretations and generalizations of the results – that is, a high response rate means more robust interpretations are possible based on more representative data. This is linked to the lack of knowledge about how people who have not filled out the questionnaires would have responded. This might affect the results, although not necessarily. At the same time, drop-out can be "obliquely" distributed, so that it may be associated with one or more specific groups, such as day workers or shift workers without night shifts. In this case it would be the answers from these groups that primarily confounded the analyses. The degree of uncertainty likewise depends on the whether or not the drop-out is systematic, which could mean that it primarily occurs among people with specific attitudes such as satisfaction with working hours, or dissatisfaction with work conditions. In this way certain attitudes can be over- or underrepresented. We do have some information about the drop-out distribution in groups with different working hours, which we can draw on when interpreting the statistical results of the analyses. Even so, this type of problem, which exists in all investigations, cannot be resolved in this project, because we do not have sufficient information. In addition to this, national differences between labour market, and cultures and traditions, are likely to have influenced some of the responses, which is important to bear in mind when interpreting the differences in the analysis results between the participating companies. At the same time, the strength of these comparative analyses lies in the fact that they have been carried out between companies in the same sector of the chemical industry, which therefore generally have the same kind of production and technology (with the exception of Denmark, as already mentioned). Furthermore, in all the companies most of the employees in production units worked in continuous production, 24 hours a day, which hence applied to the participants in this investigation. In relation to this, the dominating shift systems (again with the exception of Denmark, which operates fixed shifts) are designed as continuous three-shift systems worked by four, five, or six shift teams in the individual companies.

There are differences in the shape of the actual shift systems' design in terms of, for example, their speed of rotation and start and end times, but all share conditions like changing working hours through day, evening and night shifts, and working on weekdays and weekends. (Further accounts of the actual shift systems can be found in the main report.) These shared conditions form the basis for comparing results between and across the companies in order to throw light on the possible influence of national traditions and culture in individual companies, as well as variations in working hours and work-organizational conditions. However, these comparative analyses and interpretations are only partly related to analyses of the questionnaire data and to a large extent rest on our analyses of the interview data.

THE QUESTIONNAIRE PHASE IN E GERMANY

In the following account the results are divided into a number of sections that cover characteristics of the participants or "respondents", factors related to working hours, and work satisfaction. In the analyses, E Germany was compared with the group of other companies as a whole.

The questionnaire process

The questionnaires were distributed and collected in the period from May to June 2000. At the company in former E Germany, 178 questionnaires were handed out and 88 returned, which corresponds to a response rate of 49%. This means that the results have to be interpreted with particular caution. The works council was responsible for taking care of the returned questionnaires and passing them on to the research group. The analyses presented below are thus based on 623 respondents (535 from the other companies and 88 from E Germany). These numbers vary in relation to the analyses, because not everyone responded to all the questions.

Respondents

The majority of the questionnaires were returned by shift workers with night work, with the rest returned by two smaller groups of employees working on call duties and day work. In relation to response rate, no essential differences were found between these working-time groups.

The combined gender distribution for the companies involved was 96% men and 4% women. At Hydro E Germany the same gender distribution applied, with very few women working in the fertilizer production areas. This is certainly related to the nature of production, but cultural traditions may also be of importance. Only Norsk Hydro Denmark involved in aluminium production has a different distribution, with as many women as men, but again, social conditions may be of importance here.

The age distribution in E Germany was different from the group of other companies, where around ⅓ were 40-49 years old. In E Germany nearly half of the employees (48%) belonged to this age group. Both in E Germany and the other companies, approximately ⅓ were 30-39, but in E Germany only 1%, compared to 10% at the other companies, were below 30 years and only 11%, compared to 20% elsewhere, were over 49. There was no difference in marital status between E Germany and the other companies, as around 80-85% were married or cohabiting in both groups, and no reliable differences were identified between the groups concerning the number of children living at home.

Substantial differences (***) in the distribution of seniority were found between E Germany and the other companies, whereby 81% in E Germany had 11-25 years of seniority, compared to 46% at the other companies. This also meant fewer employees in E Germany with both high and low seniority. Regarding involvement in managerial tasks, more respondents (*) in E Germany (43%) than in the other companies (31%), stated that they had such tasks. This number is so large that the responses from E Germany may also include minor tasks with specific responsibility, but not necessarily authority over other employees. No differences were found for attending to representative tasks, as 21% and 22% in the respective groups stated this. Regarding the distribution of roles at work, 32% reported being operators 'both in and outside control room', 24% indicated maintenance jobs, 15% reported more than one role, 14% 'other' roles, and for the rest of the roles 5% or less stated that they belonged to these groups. For most of the roles, a fairly equal distribution with respect to E Germany and the others applies. Variances can be identified, however, regarding maintenance (24% in E Germany and 12% for the rest of the companies) and 'more than one' role, where only 4% reported this in the amalgamated group of companies compared to 15% in E Germany.

Working time
The distribution of the employees in E Germany according to their working-time system is shown in the table below, which shows three main types. The majorities, both at the other companies and in E Germany, have shift work with night shifts, but in E Germany there appeared to be only two other groups of importance, namely day workers and day workers with on-call work. The percentage of day workers with on-call work in E Germany was noticeably higher than for the group of other companies.

Employees' current working hours (in %)	Other companies	E Germany
Day work only	19	11
Shift work without night shifts	9	1
Shift work with night shifts	58	67
Evening work only	1	-
Night work only	6	-
Day work with on-call work	6	20
Weekend work only	2	-
Other	-	-

TABLE 1 *Current working hours.*

Changes in the scheduled working time: The employees in E Germany reported significantly (***) fewer extra hours beyond the normal employment time within the last four weeks. Thus, 74% in E Germany noted no extra hours, compared to 47% elsewhere, and only 9% in E Germany had more than 10 extra hours, against 24% in the other companies. Regarding changes of more than one hour in the working-time schedule itself within the last four weeks, no valid differences were identified, but 29% informed that they had changes at least once, against 39% at the rest of the companies. These two questions can be said to reflect flexibility for the companies as far as organizing and changing the working-time schedules is concerned.

Individual and group influence on the organization of working time: The table below illustrates the distribution in percentages of the replies to the question "To what degree do you experience that you have influence on your current working-hour arrangements?"

Influence for oneself on working-hour arrangements (distribution in %)	None	Not much	Some	A good deal	Complete
The other companies	35	29	20	14	3
E Germany	61	30	8	-	1

TABLE 2 *Personal influence on working hours.*

The table shows that the employees in E Germany reported that, as individuals, they had influence on their working-hour arrangements to a significantly lesser degree (***). Around 90% reported experiencing little or no influence, compared with 64% at the other companies. The following table illustrates the distribution of the replies to the question "To what degree do you experience that the employees as a group have influence on their current working-hour arrangements?"

Influence for the employees as a group on working-hour arrangements (distribution in %)	None	Not much	Some	A good deal	Complete
The other companies	19	33	30	16	2
E Germany	66	22	13	–	–

TABLE 3 *Group influence on working hours.*

Table 3 shows significant (***) differences between E Germany and the others, with considerably less influence being reported in E Germany. Thus, it was not only as individuals but also as a collective that the employees in E Germany stated a significant absence of influence. It is also notable that there was similarity in the number of employees that reported no influence, both as individuals and as a group, in E Germany. At the other companies, the employees as a group reported that the employees as a collective had more influence than the employees as individuals, but still most answers were found in the categories 'none' and 'not much' compared to a 'good deal' and 'completely'. Beyond influence from the actual conditions concerning the organization of working time, it cannot be ruled out that the results may also have been affected by the fact that the main shift systems had been in operation since 1985 with only minor changes.

Attitude to who should have most influence on shift work to ensure health and safety	Other companies	E Germany
You yourself	8	8
The employees as a group	55	39
Representatives / unions	8	8
Health and Safety Committees	12	2
Works councils	15	39
Management / supervisors	3	3

TABLE 4 *Preference as to who should have influence on working hours.*

PARTICIPATION AND PREVENTION

Table 4 illustrates the distribution of replies between E Germany and the others for the question "Who do you think should have the most influence on the design of shift work in order to ensure that the employees' health and safety is taken care of?" (Only one answer could be given.)

The total distribution of the results between E Germany and the other companies was significantly (***) distinct. The differences were expressed particularly in relation to the employees as a group and works councils. These categories accounted for 70% and nearly 80% (E Germany) of the replies, respectively. Except for the Health and Safety Committees, with a very low score for E Germany, no divergences could be identified for the other small categories. The differences may be related to differences between the countries concerning formal structures and provisions for influence. The *Betriebsrat* (the local works council) is given some explicit influence in matters concerning the organization and design of shift work, and all employees elect representatives and can be elected themselves to the works council.

The senior shop steward is also often the chairman in E Germany. This might be reflected in the way that the Betriebsrat represents the formal structure of influence for employees at all organizational levels, whereas the category "employees as a group" may represent one's shift-working colleagues. In this way it could be argued that both categories could be considered to represent the employees, and if so, the participants in E Germany also appeared to want employees to have the most influence.

Conditions of importance (reasons) for working on the actual working time-system: significant differences were found for three reported reasons. In E Germany 42%, against 18% at the other companies (***), stated that the reason "the only possibility if I wanted a job" was very important. 61% in E Germany, against 28% elsewhere (***). reported that the reason "the only possibility of obtaining work at this workplace" had been very important, and the reason "the only possibility to continue at this workplace" was expressed by 68% in E Germany, compared to 27% (***) in the other companies. No differences were found for the other reasons, where 20% in E Germany said that "fits better with my family life", 38% that "pays better", and 16% that "gives greater personal freedom" had been very important. Reasons for having the actual working hours among the employees in E Germany appeared to be most related to the possibilities of having a job, and holding a job at the actual company.

The questionnaire also had a measure that evaluated the current shift system with several sub-questions. The table below shows the distribution of answers in percentages for all the different sub-questions. Examination of these responses at the E German company could give cause to consider potential changes. Comparisons with the other companies are not illustrated, as this would not be so informative because the other companies operated different work schedules.

However, it is worth pointing out that the distribution of answers is very similar, with most responses in the 'not relevant' or 'appropriate' categories. The only deviations were the number of consecutive night shifts and day shifts, where 39% and 37% reported there being 'too many'. Too few (24%) weekends off was reported, and 20% found that the clock-on or start time on day shift was too early.

	Far too few		Appropri- ate number		Far too many	Not relevant
a) Number of day shifts per month	–	3	75	3	3	15
b) Number of evening shifts per month	–	3	80	–	2	15
c) Number of night-shifts per month	–	–	72	2	12	15
d) Number of day shifts in a row	2	2	57	10	27	3
e) Number of evening shifts in a row	2	3	80	3	8	3
f) Number of night shifts in a row	–	–	58	10	29	3
g) Number of week- ends off	12	12	68	–	1	7
h) Number of hours on day shift	–	–	87	3	2	8
i) Number of hours on evening shift	–	2	87	–	3	8
j) Number of hours on night shift	–	2	87	–	3	8
k) Number of hours on weekend shift	–	3	78	3	7	8
	Too early		Appropriate		Too late	Not relevant

Cont. next page

j) Start time for day shifts	12	8	73	2	–	5
k) Start time for evening shifts	3	3	82	3	2	7
l) Start time for night shifts	3	5	78	3	3	7

TABLE 5 *Perceptions of shift-system features.*

Considering the question "Satisfaction with your working hours", the distribution of responses, in percentages, is illustrated in Table 6 below for E Germany compared with the other companies. The differences (*) between the two groups found here were primarily in relation to satisfaction, where a smaller number in E Germany was 'very satisfied', but more were 'generally satisfied'. As a single satisfaction score, no difference of importance emerged. Only 10% indicated that they were dissatisfied.

Distribution in % of answers to "satisfied with working hours"	Very satisfied	Generally satisfied	Neither satisfied nor dissatisfied	Generally dissatisfied	Very dissatisfied
The other companies	16	32	38	10	4
E Germany	6	50	35	5	5

TABLE 6 *Satisfaction with working hours.*

Other research in the area has indicated that this might, at least partly, be a consequence of no vision or knowledge of proper alternatives, because of difficulties experienced in changing applied shift systems. Therefore the answers do not necessarily imply that no alterations would be appropriate (i.e. that the majority are satisfied with their working time), but may also reflect a lack of knowledge about combining health and social considerations.

In order to obtain additional information on the levels of satisfaction with the actual working-time systems in operation, the participants were asked if they would change to daytime if they had the opportunity. A second question asked if they would change to daytime without it affecting pay or other working-time conditions. The distribution of responses to these questions is shown below, and only shift workers participated.

If given opportunity to change to daytime work only (in %)	Yes	No	Don't know
Other companies	36	39	26
E Germany	37	43	20

TABLE 7 *Responses about changing to day work.*

If given opportunity to change to work in daytime without affecting pay or work conditions (in %)	Yes	No	Don't know
Other companies	63	22	15
E Germany	72	21	7

TABLE 8 *Responses about changing to day work with pay and conditions unchanged.*

No differences were found in the answers between E Germany and the rest of the companies for these two questions. However, the results show that, all things being equal, nearly three quarters of the employees in E Germany would like to have only daytime work. Even where no compensations are included, a little more than one third of the employees in E Germany would like to shift to day work – which is in line with the other companies. This may indicate that the question on satisfaction has several dimensions.

Work satisfaction
The question about the degree of employees' satisfaction with their present work situation consisted of a number of sub-questions that covered most aspects of a job situation. We present the distribution of answers for all the sub-questions (see Table 9 below) in the belief that it could facilitate the discussions at the company about introducing change initiatives if certain issues appeared to be problematic.

A seven-point (Likert-type) response scale, ranging from 'very dissatisfied' to 'very satisfied', was applied to each sub-question. In Table 9 the three response categories concerning 'dissatisfied' have been combined into one category and the same applies to 'satisfied', while the neutral category for 'neither satisfied nor dissatisfied' has been maintained. In the analyses the responses from the employees in E Germany (denoted by EG) are compared with the employees at the rest of the companies (denoted by R), and significant differences are indicated with a number of stars ($* \leq 0.05$, $** \leq 0.01$ and $*** \leq 0.001$) depending on the degree

PARTICIPATION AND PREVENTION

of confidence with which the results indicate differences between E Germany and the other companies. Arrows have also been inserted for the sub-questions where reliable differences were found. The direction of the arrows shows the direction of the differences in satisfaction levels. If the direction of the arrow points towards the company in question, which here is E Germany (EG), the level of employee satisfaction concerning that dimension is higher in E Germany than in the rest of the companies, and vice versa if the arrow points towards R.

When interpreting the results it is important to look not only at the differences between the companies, but also at how the responses are dispersed on the different categories for the single sub-question at the given company. In this way, we sometimes found that even a considerable difference in the distribution of responses between satisfied and dissatisfied had no apparent significance, because the same differences occurred in the other companies. Additionally it should be emphasized that, beyond existing differences in conditions for the individual dimensions, variations in culture and traditions are likely to have influenced responses to the questions.

Table 9 presents the results quite clearly. Consequently, only limited additional comments are made here. In all cases where significant differences were found, dissatisfaction was higher in E Germany than the rest (with the exception of sub-question 't', the levels of dissatisfaction were higher than 50%). For all other questions – indeed, the majority of questions except 'k' – the satisfaction categories had the highest proportion of responses. A closer look at the items with a high dissatisfaction score reveals that they are primarily related to the area of personnel or employee policy, and to management issues and relations.

E Germany (EG) compared with the rest of the companies (R) on the dimensions of satisfaction		Very dissatis-fied Dissatisfied Slightly dissatisfied		Indif-ferent	Slightly satis-fied Satisfied Very satisfied	
a. Your phys-ical working conditions	EG	30		14	56	
	R	32		10	58	
b. Freedom to carry out your work	EG	26		10	63	
	R	17		11	72	
					Cont. next page	

c. Your colleagues at work	EG	12		7	81	
	R	14		7	79	
d. The recognition you get for your work	EG	50	⇑	14	36	*
	R	37		12	52	
e. Your immediate supervisor	EG	39		14	47	
	R	29		15	56	
f. The amount of responsibility you get	EG	30		13	57	
	R	21		11	68	
g. Your pay conditions	EG	69	⇑	4	28	***
	R	37		12	52	
h. Opportunities to use your abilities	EG	39	⇑	15	46	
	R	30		12	58	
i. Cooperation between management and employees	EG	62	⇑	8	30	*
	R	46		10	44	
j. Your opportunities for promotion	EG	62	⇑	23	15	***
	R	38		24	38	
k. The manner in which the workplace is run	EG	48		20	33	
	R	48		14	38	
l. The attention your suggestions receive	EG	38		17	44	
	R	37		21	43	
m. Your working time	EG	29		8	63	
	R	34		11	55	
n. Variety in your work	EG	30		13	57	
	R	26		12	62	
o. Security in your employment	EG	62	⇑	13	25	***
	R	31		11	58	
p. Your influence on the arrangement of your work	EG	29	⇑	32	39	*
	R	28		21	50	
q. The extent of work tasks	EG	30		17	52	
	R	22		17	61	
r. The pace of work	EG	18		23	59	
	R	25		16	59	

Cont. next page

s. Clarity of your tasks at work	EG	28			13	60	
	R	25			11	63	
t. Your possibilities for personal development	EG	46		⇑	15	39	
	R	36			12	50	

TABLE 9 *Work satisfaction.*

CONCLUDING REMARKS

This supplementary report on the Norsk Hydro site in former E Germany has presented an overview of the research carried out. The nature of the shift systems, the background for the design, the employees' involvement and influence, and also the issues of system and work satisfaction were considered.

The employees in E Germany experienced considerably less influence than the employees in the rest of the companies. This applied to the influence of both individual employees and employees as a group. The responses regarding employee influence in E Germany must be understood in light of the knowledge that the last change in the shift system took place in 1985.

In E Germany, perceptions about who should have the most influence on the design of shift work to ensure that employees' health and safety is taken care of differed from the other companies. At the E German site, similar numbers of responses were found for employees as a group and for the Betriebsrat, respectively, whereas the employees as a group received by far the most responses in the other companies. The disparities in preferred influence on shift work between E Germany and the others may be related to national differences in formal structures and provisions for influence. The Betriebsrat is given some explicit influence in matters concerning the organization and design of shift work. Thus, the Betriebsrat is a negotiation partner with management in the area of working time. This might be interpreted in such a way that the Betriebsrat represents the formal structure of influence for employees at all organizational levels, whereas the category "employees as a group" may represent perceptions of one's shift-working colleagues. If both categories are assumed to represent the employees, then more than three quarters of the employees in E Germany would appear to prefer the employees to have the most influence. At the same time it could also be argued that the category "employees as a group" reflects a more direct form of participation and influence. On this basis one could suggest that more employees in E Germany than in the other companies preferred the representative system, or that fewer employees have confidence in, or consider direct participation as a solution to shift-work alterations.

Despite the reported lower influence on the design of shift work, more than half of the employees stated that they were generally satisfied, or very satisfied with their working hours. At the same time, around one third of the shift workers would want to change to day work if the opportunity arose. Nearly three quarters of the employees would like to change if it would not affect wages and other working conditions. These findings indicate that there might be good reason to consider possibilities for initiating participatory processes aimed at integrating ergonomic recommendations in the design, which make allowance for both health and social perspectives. The different attitudes to changes in the existing system also point to the potential advantages that could be achieved if systems with increased flexibility and autonomy at group level could be designed and promoted.

Furthermore, the distribution of the replies to the general satisfaction questionnaire with its sub-questions suggests that there may be areas concerning cooperation, management, and personnel policies that hold challenges for both the company and the employees, to initiate discussions about practicable new activities and strategies to address the issues raised.

Supplementary report – The Netherlands
Norsk Hydro

Introduction and background

The research group's reporting on the HAPCA project consists of a main report and a set of appendices that includes company-specific supplements for the companies that participated in the questionnaire research. The study was supported by Norsk Hydro's Research Foundation and NHO's Work Environment Research Foundation, Norway.

In the main, or joint, report we first describe the overarching framework of the project in terms of its purpose and background, design, and methods of data collection, as well as the strategies used in preparing and organizing the project. We then give an account of the investigations, data collection, analyses, and description, followed by our interpretation of the results within the areas investigated.

Originally, the participating companies in the study were Norsk Hydro's factories in Italy, France, the United Kingdom, the Netherlands, former East Germany, former West Germany, Sweden, and Norway. All of these sites were Hydro Agri Europe companies. In addition, we chose to include a site in Denmark, which was from Hydro Aluminium. Before data collection began, the factory in the UK was shut down and was therefore eliminated from the study.

The planned collection of data from different sources was carried out in a variety of ways. This process is described more fully in the main report. In these individual company reports we account for what happened within the individual areas. The interviews were all carried out as originally planned, with at least five interviewees from each company (representatives from management and employees, plus one person from the HR department). The collected data were analysed, and the results were communicated to outline the tasks and functions of the health and safety committee, the company's handling of work-environment issues when organizing shift work, the related opportunities and limitations, and employees involvement in the process. Furthermore, our analyses determine the nature of the company's existing shift system, and we look at the themes of shift-system responsibility, design background, employee involvement (and its significance), and issues of health and safety. Our intention with the interviews was that the data obtained would enable us to perform general analyses and cross-company comparisons of shift-work issues, and also enable us to analyse at company level to identify features of specific and shared importance. Note that our analyses of interview data is not reported on an individual company level, but only in the main report. This ensures the interviewees' anonymity, as it prevents identification of any single person's utterances and views.

The questionnaire survey was originally initiated on behalf of the employee representatives in the European Works Council, who wanted to give the employees an opportunity to express their views and assessments. The research team and the central project group supported this. Such a questionnaire investigation was then discussed and planned in collaboration with the participating companies. It later turned out that only the companies and employees in E Germany, Denmark, Italy, Norway, the Netherlands, and Sweden wished to participate. The questionnaires were translated from a common version into the different languages of the participating companies and then back-translated, but minor linguistically-based differences between the country-specific versions cannot be ruled out. Questionnaires were handed out by the company and collected by the union representative (steward) in sealed envelopes. The reply rate relative to the questionnaires handed out varied considerably: from 25% to 64%. The rather low response rates diminish the strength of the interpretations and conclusions, and the potential for generalizing our findings. This consideration is especially pertinent here because we have no knowledge about potential respondents' reasons for not participating. These aspects are discussed more fully later, in the section on analyses and descriptions of the questionnaire data, but it is important to view our interpretations and discussions in this light.

In the individual companies, the number of participants is generally too small to further divide the participants in the analyses, for instance into day and shift workers. Comparative analyses of different groups in accordance with their working hours and other conditions have thus been carried out across all participants. Analyses of these aspects at company level will be prone to statistical uncertainty because of the scattered data. Because this has affected the possibilities for analysis, and the certainty of conclusions on possible differences, these comparative group analyses are only described in the main report.

However, for a number of selected questions, comparative analyses have been made between employees in individual companies versus the rest of the companies. These analyses form the background of the specific supplements for each of the participating companies, since the findings may be used to determine what initiatives the company might take.

Unfortunately, it turned out that the factual data on accidents were too scattered, too sparse, and too variable. The data also reflected insufficient accident reporting in several companies, especially for the collection period in 2000. Consequently, trustworthy analyses could not be undertaken. The quality of these data presumably relates to differences in the evaluation and incidence of events registered as accidents of different severity within different companies. This is reflected in the considerable heterogeneity in the accident data the companies have reported to the project. Thus, accident data were left out, both in the main report and in the supplements.

Similarly, it turned out to be impossible to obtain the necessary data on illness reports, typically because in a number of cases such reports did not exist as digital data or usable files within the project time-frame. Hence, data for illness/absence reports are not a part of this final report or analyses.

We assumed that factual data concerning shift systems (the distribution of staff and the system design) would be known to the participating companies. We therefore considered it unnecessary to report back these data, mentioning them instead in the comparisons and evaluations of the participating companies' organization of shift work, and the design of the applied shift systems.

On this background the supplementary reports have been organized to review the results of the questionnaires with ongoing discussions and a concluding summary. Furthermore, specific appendices with ergonomic rules for designing a good shift system (Appendix 1) and recommendations for implementing or altering shift systems (Appendix 2) have been added, both to the supplements and to the main report. Hopefully, in line with our intentions, these can be a point of focus for discussions and initiatives about how to organize working hours.

While reviewing the results in the sections below, we sometimes use the expression "significance" or "statistical significance" when referring to differences between groups. "Significant" differences are differences that occur with a certain minimal probability (p). A p-value of, for example, 0.05 indicates that the probability that the differences found are a result of chance is less than 5%. Put simply, the concept of significance helps express one's confidence as to whether there are differences between the analysed groups or not. As noted, a significance level of 0.05 reflects a probability of less than 5% that any differences observed are coincidental. If the significance were 0.01, then the probability of chance would be less than 1%. When referring to the degree of significance in the results sections, a significance of 5% or less is marked by *, 1% or less by **, and 0.1 % or less by ***.

Similar to the presentation of our analyses in the main report and the supplementary reports for the other individual companies, here, in reviewing the results, we focus primarily on the significant findings. Exceptions are made when the results themselves, independently of comparisons with results from other companies, give us important information about issues such as age or attitudes to shift-system alterations. The analyses themselves have been carried out by comparing the employees at Hydro Netherlands with the participants from all other companies considered as a total group.

The analyses were carried out at group level, and accordingly the description of results will only be related to group data. The variables examined reflect those questions from the questionnaire that concern characteristics of the participants relating to social conditions such as age, household members, seniority, and working hours. In addition, information about attitudes and wishes for alterations to the current working-time systems in the company are considered. Finally, we present and discuss responses concerning satisfaction and dissatisfaction with different features of the work itself and its organization, and with cooperation and influence.

The response rate is very important in all questionnaire research, since a large drop-out rate means more uncertainty in the interpretations and generalizations of the results – that is, a high response rate means more robust interpretations are possible based on more representative data. This is linked to the lack of knowledge about how people who have not filled out the questionnaires would have responded. This might affect the results, although not necessarily. At the same time, drop-out can be "obliquely" distributed, so that it may be associated with one or more specific groups, such as day workers or shift workers without night shifts. In this case it would be the answers from these groups that primarily confounded the analyses. The degree of uncertainty likewise depends on the whether or not the drop-out is systematic, which could mean that it primarily occurs among people with specific attitudes such as satisfaction with working hours, or dissatisfaction with work conditions. In this way certain attitudes can be over- or underrepresented. We do have some information about the drop-out distribution in groups with different working hours, which we can draw on when interpreting the statistical results of the analyses. Even so, this type of problem, which exists in all investigations, cannot be resolved in this project, because we do not have sufficient information. In addition to this, national differences between labour market, and cultures and traditions, are likely to have influenced some of the responses, which is important to bear in mind when interpreting the differences in the analysis results between the participating companies. At the same time, the strength of these comparative analyses lies in the fact that they have been carried out between companies in the same sector of the chemical industry, which therefore generally have the same kind of production and technology (with the exception of Denmark, as already mentioned). Furthermore, in all the companies most of the employees in production units worked in continuous production, 24 hours a day, which hence applied to the participants in this investigation. In relation to this, the dominating shift systems (again with the exception of Denmark, which operates fixed shifts) are designed as continuous three-shift systems worked by four, five, or six shift teams in the individual companies.

There are differences in the shape of the actual shift systems' design in terms of, for example, their speed of rotation and start and end times, but all share conditions like changing working hours through day, evening and night shifts, and working on weekdays and weekends. (Further accounts of the actual shift systems can be found in the main report.) These shared conditions form the basis for comparing results between and across the companies in order to throw light on the possible influence of national traditions and culture in individual companies, as well as variations in working hours and work-organizational conditions. However, these comparative analyses and interpretations are only partly related to analyses of the questionnaire data and to a large extent rest on our analyses of the interview data.

THE QUESTIONNAIRE PHASE IN THE NETHERLANDS

In the following the results are divided into a number of sections that cover characteristics of the participants or "respondents", factors related to working hours, and work satisfaction. In the analyses, the Netherlands was compared with the group of other companies as a whole.

The questionnaire process

The questionnaires were distributed and collected in the period from January to February 2001. At the company in the Netherlands, 564 questionnaires were handed out and 203 returned, which corresponds to a response rate of 36%. The shop stewards were responsible for taking care of the returned questionnaires and passing them on to the research group with assistance from the HR department. The analyses presented below were based on 624 respondents (421 from the other companies and 203 from the Netherlands). These numbers vary in relation to the analyses, because not everyone responded to all the questions. On account of the low response rate, and due to a skewed distribution across working schedules, the results must be interpreted with caution.

Respondents

The questionnaires were distributed to 340 shift workers with night work, 287 of whom had continuous shift work, and 53 of whom had discontinuous shift work (without weekend work). In this group at least 159 of the 340 shift workers returned the questionnaire, corresponding to a sub-response rate of 44%. The questionnaire was moreover distributed to 224 day workers, of whom only 42 replied, corresponding to a response rate of 19% for day workers. Two invalid replies concerning the working-time question reduced the numbers slightly.

At Norsk Hydro in the Netherlands, a similar gender distribution applied as in the other companies producing fertilizers (96% male vs 4% female), with very few women working in the production areas, and hence also few women being potential employee participants in the project. In the Netherlands, 99% of the participants were men. Only Norsk Hydro Denmark, involved in aluminium production, has a different distribution, with as many women as men, but again, social conditions may be of importance here.

The age distribution in the Netherlands was different from the rest (***), with a larger proportion of older employees. The Netherlands had 68% in the age groups from 40 to 59 years while the rest had only 48%, and vice versa for the younger age groups. As for marital status, the Netherlands had more (90%) married or cohabiting employees than the other companies (76%) – so the difference was significant (***). No differences were observed with regard to the number of children living at home, which may be related to the above-mentioned differences in age distribution.

Differences similar to those in age distribution were found for seniority in the company (***), with 71% of the employees in the Netherlands having more than 10 years of seniority, compared to 55% in the other companies. More employees in the Netherlands (***) were involved in management tasks than in the other companies. With 44% in the Netherlands and 27% elsewhere, this suggests that minor job tasks with special managerial opportunities may be included here, but the skewed distribution of participants concerning working-time schedules and work roles (see later) may also have had some influence. No differences were found regarding involvement in representative tasks: 23% in the Netherlands and 21% in the other companies reported having such tasks. However, there were also differences (***) regarding the distribution of roles. In the Netherlands, 51% reported being operators both in and outside control rooms, compared to 26% in the other companies. 18% in the Netherlands, compared to 11% elsewhere, were involved in maintenance, and 17% compared to 10% elsewhere reported other work roles. No one working in laboratory or shipments participated in the project in the Netherlands.

Working time

The distribution of the employees in the Netherlands and the other companies according to their working-time system is shown in Table 1. Significant differences (***) were found here. In the Netherlands 79% worked shift work with night shifts, compared to 50% in the other-companies group, and 20% worked day work only or day work with on-call work in the Netherlands, compared to 28% in the rest of the companies. None of the respondents in the Netherlands reported other forms of working-time schedules, and only 1% claimed having another work schedule. These differences may contribute to explaining some of the differences between the Netherlands and the rest of the companies for some of the effect variables connected to working time.

Changes in the scheduled working time: The employees in the Netherlands reported working fewer (*) extra hours in the last four weeks than the employees in the other companies. 60% of employees in the Netherlands and 47% of the employees in the other companies had had no extra hours during the last four weeks. No significant differences were found between the groups regarding changes beyond one hour in the working-time schedule within the last four weeks, but around one third, both in the Netherlands and elsewhere, reported that they had experienced changes in that period. These two questions can be said to reflect flexibility for the companies with regard to organizing and changing the working-time schedules.

Employees' current working hours (in %)	Other companies	The Netherlands
Day work only	20	14
Shift work without night shifts	12	–
Shift work with night shifts	50	79
Evening work only	1	-
Night work only	7	-
Day work with on-call work	9	6
Weekend work only	2	-
Other	-	1

TABLE 1 *Current working hours.*

Individual and group influence on the organization of working time: Table 2 illustrates the distribution, in percentages, of the replies to the question "To what degree do you experience that you have influence on your current working-hour arrangements?"

Influence for oneself on working-hour arrangements (distribution in %)	None	Not much	Some	A good deal	Complete
The other companies	40	27	18	11	3
The Netherlands	34	36	19	11	–

TABLE 2 *Personal influence on working hours.*

PARTICIPATION AND PREVENTION

This table reflects no differences between the employees in the Netherlands and the rest of the companies with regard to individual influence on own working-time arrangements. At the same time it is noteworthy that about 70%, both in the Netherlands and the other-companies group, experienced none or not much influence. The next table illustrates the distribution of reported influence on working-time arrangements for the employees as a group.

Influence for the employees as a group on working-hour arrangements (distribution in %)	None	Not much	Some	A good deal	Complete
The other companies	30	30	26	13	2
The Netherlands	17	35	29	16	2

TABLE 3 *Group influence on working hours.*

There was a significant (*) difference between the Netherlands and the others, where the employees in the Netherlands reported more influence than in the other companies, largely because of the slightly lower proportion in the Netherlands experiencing no influence. This means that a larger proportion of employees in the Netherlands reported influence for the employees as a group compared to their perception of influence as individuals. However, 52% of the employees in the Netherlands and 60% in the other companies reported that they experienced none or not much influence as a group.

The next table illustrates the distribution of responses between the Netherlands and the other companies to the question "Who do you think should have the most influence on the design of shift work in order to ensure that the employees' health and safety is taken care of?" (Only one answer could be given.) A significant difference (*) was found in the distribution of results between the Netherlands and the other companies that appears to reflect the responses for the categories 'employees as a group' and 'works councils'. More employees in the Netherlands (59%), against 49% in the other companies, would prefer the employees as a group to have most influence, and fewer, 12%, compared to 21% elsewhere, want the works council to have most influence. This may reflect different tasks, applications, or authority levels for the works council in the Netherlands concerning working-time issues, or in general. The distribution of responses is even more noteworthy in light of the relatively high proportion of employees in the Netherlands who reported involvement in management tasks. The results suggest that the employees would like to have influence on the design of working-time schedules. The low preference for Health and Safety Committees in relation to taking care of health and safety in shift work is surprising, but similar to the findings for other individual companies.

Attitude to who should have most influence on shift work to ensure health and safety	Other companies	The Netherlands
You yourself	9	6
The employee as a group	49	59
Representatives / unions	7	9
Health and Safety Committees	10	10
Works councils	21	12
Management / supervisors	3	4

TABLE 4 *Preference as to who should have influence on working hours.*

Conditions of importance (reasons) for working the actual working-time system: Significant differences at various levels were found for nearly all the reasons listed, but most of the categories are of less importance for the employees in the Netherlands compared to the rest. In the Netherlands fewer employees than at the rest of the companies (*) reported "the only possibility if I wanted a job" to be an important reason, but for both groups the responses were spread across the reply categories. The same pattern (**) was seen for the reason "the only possibility to continue at this workplace". For the reason "obtaining work at this workplace", no differences were found.

The reason "fits better with my family life" was considerably less important to the employees in the Netherlands than in the other companies (***): 61% in the Netherlands, compared to 37% at the other companies, reported it to be of no importance. The same differences (***) were observed for the reason "gives greater personal freedom". The employees in the Netherlands reported the reason "pays better" to be more important (**) than the employees elsewhere.

The questionnaire also had a measure that evaluated the current shift system with several sub-questions. The table below shows the distribution of answers in percentages for all the different sub-questions.

PARTICIPATION AND PREVENTION

Examination of these responses at the Netherlands site could give cause to consider potential changes. Comparisons with the other companies are not illustrated, as this would not be so informative because the other companies operated different work schedules. Only shift workers were asked to answer these questions.

However, it is worth pointing out that the distribution of answers is very similar, with most responses in the 'appropriate' category. Deviations from this were linked to the number of weekends off, which are assessed as being too few, and to start time for the day shift, where a majority of the employee respondents (56%) reported it to be too early and only 43% noted it to be appropriate.

	Far too few		Appropriate number		Far too many	Not relevant
a) Number of day shifts per month	3	1	73	8	13	3
b) Number of evening shifts per month	6	3	79	3	8	3
c) Number of night shifts per month	1	3	68	6	20	3
d) Number of day shifts in a row	1	1	69	12	16	1
e) Number of evening shifts in a row	4	3	81	4	7	1
f) Number of night shifts in a row	10	3	63	8	15	1
g) Number of weekends off	43	27	28	1	1	1
h) Number of hours on day shift	–	–	75	9	15	1
i) Number of hours on evening shift	3	3	83	4	6	1
j) Number of hours on night shift	8	4	71	3	13	1
k) Number of hours on weekend shift	–	–	67	10	19	4

Cont. next page

	Too early		Appropriate		Too late	Not relevant
j) Start time for day shifts	45	11	43	–	–	1
k) Start time for evening shifts	9	3	77	4	6	1
l) Start time for night shifts	13	4	70	4	8	1

TABLE 5 *Perceptions of shift system features.*

Considering the question "Satisfaction with your working hours", the distribution, in percentages, is illustrated in the table below for the Netherlands compared with the other companies:

Distribution in % of answers to "satisfied with working hours"	Very satisfied	Generally satisfied	Neither satisfied nor dissatisfied	Generally dissatisfied	Very dissatisfied
The other companies	16	35	38	8	3
The Netherlands	11	34	36	13	5

TABLE 6 *Satisfaction with working hours.*

A significant difference (*) was found between the two groups, where a slightly higher proportion of the employees in the Netherlands reported being dissatisfied. It is worth noting here that of all the companies involved in the research, the Netherlands had the largest proportion of participating continuous shift workers with night and weekend work. Around 80% of the employees, the majority in both groups, reported a neutral position (neither satisfied nor dissatisfied), or being generally or very satisfied.

In order to obtain additional information on the levels of satisfaction with the actual working-time systems in operation, the participants were asked if they would change to daytime work if they had the opportunity. A second question asked if they would change to daytime work without it affecting pay or other working-time conditions. These two questions were only for shift workers. The distribution of the answers to these questions is shown below.

PARTICIPATION AND PREVENTION

If given opportunity to change to daytime work only (answers in %)	Yes	No	Don't know
Other companies	35	38	27
The Netherlands	38	41	21

TABLE 7 *Responses about changing to day work.*

If given opportunity to change to daytime work without affecting pay or work conditions (in %)	Yes	No	Don't know
Other companies	60	23	17
The Netherlands	71	19	10

TABLE 8 *Responses about changing to day work with pay and conditions unchanged.*

No significant difference between the groups was observed in terms of the proportions of shift workers who would change to day work if the opportunity should arise. Slightly more than one third would change. Approximately one fifth of the respondents in the Netherlands were in doubt about whether they would change or not. If a change would not affect pay or work conditions, a difference (*) does emerge, with a higher proportion in the Netherlands reporting that they would change to day work. These findings parallel the results that showed the importance of pay as a reason for working shift work, but this may also be a natural reflection of slightly lower satisfaction with the working hours in the Netherlands. In addition, this appears to reflect the findings that for a small group of employees (19%) in the Netherlands, reasons such as compatibility of work with family life and personal freedom were important for working the current shift-work system.

Work satisfaction

The question about the degree of employees' satisfaction with their present work situation consists of a number of sub-questions that covered most aspects of a job situation. We present the distribution of answers on all the sub-questions (see Table 9 below) in the belief that it could facilitate the discussions at the company about introducing change initiatives if certain issues appeared to be problematic.

A seven-point (Likert-type) response scale, ranging from 'very dissatisfied' to 'very satisfied', was applied to each sub-question. In Table

9 the three response categories concerning 'dissatisfied' have been combined into one category and the same applies to 'satisfied', while the neutral category for 'neither satisfied nor dissatisfied' has been maintained. In the analyses the responses from the employees in the Netherlands (denoted by tN) are compared with the employees at the rest of the companies (denoted by R), and significant differences are indicated with a number of stars (* ≤ 0.05, ** ≤ 0.01 and *** ≤ 0.001) depending on the degree of confidence with which the results indicate differences between the Netherlands and the other companies. Arrows have also been inserted for the sub-questions where reliable differences were found. The direction of the arrows shows the direction of the differences in satisfaction levels. If the direction of the arrow points towards the company in question, which here is the Netherlands (tN), the level of employee satisfaction concerning that dimension is higher in the Netherlands than in the rest of the companies, and vice versa if the arrow points towards R.

When interpreting the results it is important to look not only at the differences between the companies, but also at how the responses are dispersed on the different categories for the single sub-question at the given company. In this way, we sometimes found that even a considerable difference in the distribution of responses between satisfied and dissatisfied had no apparent significance, because the same differences occurred in the other companies. Additionally it should be emphasized that, beyond existing differences in conditions for the individual dimensions, variations in culture and traditions are likely to have influenced responses to the questions.

Table 9 presents the results quite clearly. Consequently, only limited additional comments are made here. The factors with significant differences point in both directions. The work aspects with significant differences in terms of the proportion of respondents suggest higher levels of satisfaction in the Netherlands. In 17 out of the 20 sub-questions, a majority of the employees in the Netherlands responded in one of the 'satisfied' categories. For 9 of the sub-questions covering different aspects of working life, significant differences can be identified, with higher proportions of employees in the Netherlands reporting satisfaction compared to the employees in the other companies.

The Netherlands (tN) compared with the rest of the companies (R) on the dimensions of satisfaction		Very dissatisfied Dissatisfied Slightly dissatisfied		Indifferent	Slightly satisfied Satisfied Very satisfied	
a. Your physical working conditions	tN	35		7	58	
	R	30		13	58	
b. Freedom to carry out your work	tN	24	⇑	7	69	**
	R	16		13	71	
c. Your colleagues at work	tN	23	⇑	3	74	***
	R	9		9	82	
d. The recognition you get for your work	tN	42	⇑	6	53	**
	R	37		15	48	
e. Your immediate supervisor	tN	34		10	56	
	R	29		17	54	
f. The amount of responsibility you get	tN	22	⇑	7	72	*
	R	23		13	64	
g. Your pay conditions	tN	28	⇑	5	68	***
	R	47		14	39	
h. Opportunities to use your abilities	tN	30	⇑	8	62	*
	R	31		15	53	
i. Cooperation between management and employees	tN	46	⇑	7	48	*
	R	50		12	39	
j. Your opportunities for promotion.	tN	37	⇑	12	51	***
	R	43		30	27	
k. The manner in which the workplace is run	tN	47	⇑	11	43	*
	R	48		17	35	
l. The attention your suggestions receive	tN	39	⇑	14	47	*
	R	36		23	41	
m. Your working time	tN	33		11	57	
	R	33		11	56	
n. Variety in your work	tN	29		11	61	
	R	27		13	61	
o. Security in your employment	tN	20	⇑	11	70	***
	R	42		12	46	

p. Your influence on the arrangement of your work	tN	32	⇑	15	53	**
	R	27		26	47	
q. The extent of work tasks	tN	21		13	66	
	R	24		19	56	
r. The pace of work	tN	22		14	65	
	R	25		19	56	
s. Clarity of your tasks at work	tN	24		12	64	
	R	26		11	62	
t. Your possibilities for personal development	tN	28	⇑	11	62	***
	R	42		16	42	

TABLE 9 *Work satisfaction.*

However, it is worth noting that for two of these sub-questions, relating to co-operation and management of the workplace, less than half of the employees reported satisfaction and the proportion expressing dissatisfaction was about the same size as the satisfied group. For 3 of the sub-questions (those concerning freedom to carry out the work, colleagues, and recognition for one's work), the employees in the Netherlands reported less satisfaction than in the other companies, but a large majority reported being satisfied, especially with freedom to carry out work and work colleagues. These results suggest that, in general, the employees in the Netherlands were satisfied with their working conditions, although for some dimensions related to cooperation, management of the workplace, influence and recognition, a fairly high proportion reported varying degrees of dissatisfaction.

CONCLUDING REMARKS

This supplementary report on the Norsk Hydro site in the Netherlands has presented an overview of research carried out. The nature of the shift systems, the background for the design, the employees' involvement and influence, and also the issues of system and work satisfaction were considered.

Bear in mind that the results from the Netherlands must be interpreted with caution because of the 36% response rate. At the same time, and undoubtedly related to this, there was a skewed distribution in terms of the proportion of respondents with a higher involvement in management tasks and, probably, also representative shop steward tasks, but the latter is no different from the other companies. Furthermore, the participants in the Netherlands were older and had higher seniority in the company. The question of whether or not this is connected to the response rate could not be evaluated in any more detail. It must also be noted that employees in the Netherlands made up the largest group of respondents with continuous shift work in the project, and also the largest group of shift workers with night shifts among the participating companies.

With these reservations in mind, it is fair to state that the answers from the shift workers in the Netherlands suggested that the reasons for working shift work for most people were not linked primarily to work, social or personal reasons, but to reasons related to salary. This was further supported by the fact that a large proportion (71%), which is larger than at the other companies, would choose to change to day work if this did not affect pay or other work conditions, and if the opportunity was available. Even though the employees in the Netherlands reported that they had somewhat more influence on working-time arrangements as a group than as individuals, it was observed that 70% reported that they experienced 'none' or 'not much' individual influence, and regarding influence of employees as a group, the number was 52%. It was notable that the majority of employees in the Netherlands, regardless the higher number of participants with management tasks, would like the employees as a group to have the most influence on the arrangement of working-time systems in order to guarantee the handling of health and safety issues. Moreover, only a small proportion of the employees indicated Health and Safety Committees as the representatives responsible for shift work health and safety. Furthermore, a smaller group in the Netherlands than at the other companies reported works councils as the forum that should have the most influence. This could be connected to the practice of works councils in the Netherlands, and/or to the basis of their influence and function.

Nearly half of the participating shift workers in the Netherlands, compared to the other participating companies, reported that the time of starting work on the day shift is too early in the shift systems in operation. Almost the same number reported that this time was appropriate, which might indicate a need for considering the possibilities for more flexibility in the design of the shift systems based on the employees' wishes, together with the companies' need for flexibility.

This appears to be supported by reports of the number of extra hours and changes in the employees' shift plans, regardless of the fact that the former are slightly smaller in the Netherlands than in the other companies. At the same time, the fixed times for reporting to work on the day shift in the existing shift systems might be based on wishes or needs that arose earlier in the implementation of the work rota, and which were now carried on as a tradition at the participating companies regardless of changes in attitudes to the working hours, which were possibly connected to societal changes in social functions and cultural conditions.

Finally, the employees in the Netherlands expressed satisfaction with their working conditions in general, but for some dimensions related to cooperation, management of the workplace, influence, and recognition, a fairly high proportion reported varying degrees of dissatisfaction. These findings offer opportunities for starting discussions within the workplace with regard to practicable new initiatives and strategies to address the issues raised.

Supplementary report – Denmark

Norsk Hydro

Introduction and background

The research group's reporting on the HAPCA project consists of a main report and a set of appendices that includes company-specific supplements for the companies that participated in the questionnaire research. The study was supported by Norsk Hydro's Research Foundation and NHO's Work Environment Research Foundation, Norway.

In the main, or joint, report we first describe the overarching framework of the project in terms of its purpose and background, design, and methods of data collection, as well as the strategies used in preparing and organizing the project. We then give an account of the investigations, data collection, analyses, and description, followed by our interpretation of the results within the areas investigated.

Originally, the participating companies in the study were Norsk Hydro's factories in Italy, France, the United Kingdom, the Netherlands, former East Germany, former West Germany, Sweden, and Norway. All of these sites were Hydro Agri Europe companies. In addition, we chose to include a site in Denmark, which was from Hydro Aluminium. Before data collection began, the factory in the UK was shut down and was therefore eliminated from the study.

The planned collection of data from different sources was carried out in a variety of ways. This process is described more fully in the main report. In these individual company reports we account for what happened within the individual areas. The interviews were all carried out as originally planned, with at least five interviewees from each company (representatives from management and employees, plus one person from the HR department). The collected data were analysed, and the results were communicated to outline the tasks and functions of the health and safety committee, the company's handling of work-environment issues when organizing shift work, the related opportunities and limitations, and employees involvement in the process. Furthermore, our analyses determine the nature of the company's existing shift system, and we look at the themes of shift-system responsibility, design background, employee involvement (and its significance), and issues of health and safety. Our intention with the interviews was that the data obtained would enable us to perform general analyses and cross-company comparisons of shift-work issues, and also enable us to analyse at company level to identify features of specific and shared importance. Note that our analyses of interview data is not reported on an individual company level, but only in the main report. This ensures the interviewees' anonymity, as it prevents identification of any single person's utterances and views.

The questionnaire survey was originally initiated on behalf of the employee representatives in the European Works Council, who wanted to give the employees an opportunity to express their views and assessments. The research team and the central project group supported this. Such a questionnaire investigation was then discussed and planned in collaboration with the participating companies. It later turned out that only the companies and employees in E Germany, Denmark, Italy, Norway, the Netherlands, and Sweden wished to participate. The questionnaires were translated from a common version into the different languages of the participating companies and then back-translated, but minor linguistically-based differences between the country-specific versions cannot be ruled out. Questionnaires were handed out by the company and collected by the union representative (steward) in sealed envelopes. The reply rate relative to the questionnaires handed out varied considerably: from 25% to 64%. The rather low response rates diminish the strength of the interpretations and conclusions, and the potential for generalizing our findings. This consideration is especially pertinent here because we have no knowledge about potential respondents' reasons for not participating. These aspects are discussed more fully later, in the section on analyses and descriptions of the questionnaire data, but it is important to view our interpretations and discussions in this light.

In the individual companies, the number of participants is generally too small to further divide the participants in the analyses, for instance into day and shift workers. Comparative analyses of different groups in accordance with their working hours and other conditions have thus been carried out across all participants. Analyses of these aspects at company level will be prone to statistical uncertainty because of the scattered data. Because this has affected the possibilities for analysis, and the certainty of conclusions on possible differences, these comparative group analyses are only described in the main report.

However, for a number of selected questions, comparative analyses have been made between employees in individual companies versus the rest of the companies. These analyses form the background of the specific supplements for each of the participating companies, since the findings may be used to determine what initiatives the company might take.

Unfortunately, it turned out that the factual data on accidents were too scattered, too sparse, and too variable. The data also reflected insufficient accident reporting in several companies, especially for the collection period in 2000. Consequently, trustworthy analyses could not be undertaken. The quality of these data presumably relates to differences in the evaluation and incidence of events registered as accidents of different severity within different companies. This is reflected in the considerable heterogeneity in the accident data the companies have reported to the project. Thus, accident data were left out, both in the main report and in the supplements.

Similarly, it turned out to be impossible to obtain the necessary data on illness reports, typically because in a number of cases such reports did not exist as digital data or usable files within the project time-frame. Hence, data for illness/absence reports are not a part of this final report or analyses.

We assumed that factual data concerning shift systems (the distribution of staff and the system design) would be known to the participating companies. We therefore considered it unnecessary to report back these data, mentioning them instead in the comparisons and evaluations of the participating companies' organization of shift work, and the design of the applied shift systems.

On this background the supplementary reports have been organized to review the results of the questionnaires with ongoing discussions and a concluding summary. Furthermore, specific appendices with ergonomic rules for designing a good shift system (Appendix 1) and recommendations for implementing or altering shift systems (Appendix 2) have been added, both to the supplements and to the main report.

Hopefully, in line with our intentions, these can be a point of focus for discussions and initiatives about how to organize working hours.

ANALYSES AND DESCRIPTION OF QUESTIONNAIRE DATA

While reviewing the results in the sections below, we sometimes use the expression "significance" or "statistical significance" when referring to differences between groups. "Significant" differences are differences that occur with a certain minimal probability (p). A p-value of, for example, 0.05 indicates that the probability that the differences found are a result of chance is less than 5%. Put simply, the concept of significance helps express one's confidence as to whether there are differences between the analysed groups or not. As noted, a significance level of 0.05 reflects a probability of less than 5% that any differences observed are coincidental. If the significance were 0.01, then the probability of chance would be less than 1%. When referring to the degree of significance in the results sections, a significance of 5% or less is marked by *, 1% or less by **, and 0.1 % or less by ***.

Similar to the presentation of our analyses in the main report and the supplementary reports for the other individual companies, here, in reviewing the results, we focus primarily on the significant findings. Exceptions are made when the results themselves, independently of comparisons with results from other companies, give us important information about issues such as age or attitudes to shift-system alterations. The analyses themselves have been carried out by comparing the employees at Hydro Denmark with the participants from all other companies considered as a total group.

The analyses were carried out at group level, and accordingly the description of results will only be related to group data. The variables examined reflect those questions from the questionnaire that concern characteristics of the participants relating to social conditions such as age, household members, seniority, and working hours. In addition, information about attitudes and wishes for alterations to the current working-time systems in the company are considered. Finally, we present and discuss responses concerning satisfaction and dissatisfaction with different features of the work itself and its organization, and with cooperation and influence.

The response rate is very important in all questionnaire research, since a large drop-out rate means more uncertainty in the interpretations and generalizations of the results – that is, a high response rate means more robust interpretations are possible based on more representative data. This is linked to the lack of knowledge about how people who have not filled out the questionnaires would have responded. This might affect the results, although not necessarily. At the same time, drop-out can be "obliquely" distributed, so that it may be associated with one or more specific groups, such as day workers or shift workers without night shifts. In this case it would be the answers from these groups that primarily confounded the analyses. The degree of uncertainty likewise depends on the whether or not the drop-out is systematic, which could mean that it primarily occurs among people with specific attitudes such as satisfaction with working hours, or dissatisfaction with work conditions. In this way certain attitudes can be over- or underrepresented. We do have some information about the drop-out distribution in groups with different working hours, which we can draw on when interpreting the statistical results of the analyses. Even so, this type of problem, which exists in all investigations, cannot be resolved in this project, because we do not have sufficient information. In addition to this, national differences between labour market, and cultures and traditions, are likely to have influenced some of the responses, which is important to bear in mind when interpreting the differences in the analysis results between the participating companies. At the same time, the strength of these comparative analyses lies in the fact that they have been carried out between companies in the same sector of the chemical industry, which therefore generally have the same kind of production and technology (with the exception of Denmark, as already mentioned). Furthermore, in all the companies most of the employees in production units worked in continuous production, 24 hours a day, which hence applied to the participants in this investigation. In relation to this, the dominating shift systems (again with the exception of Denmark, which operates fixed shifts) are designed as continuous three-shift systems worked by four, five, or six shift teams in the individual companies.

There are differences in the shape of the actual shift systems' design in terms of, for example, their speed of rotation and start and end times, but all share conditions like changing working hours through day, evening and night shifts, and working on weekdays and weekends. (Further accounts of the actual shift systems can be found in the main report.) These shared conditions form the basis for comparing results between and across the companies in order to throw light on the possible influence of national traditions and culture in individual companies, as well as variations in working hours and work-organizational conditions. However, these comparative analyses and interpretations are only partly related to analyses of the questionnaire data and to a large extent rest on our analyses of the interview data.

THE QUESTIONNAIRE PHASE IN DENMARK

The questionnaires were handed out and collected in the period from May to September 2000. A special condition applied at the company in Denmark, because this company had previously been a participant in a pilot phase with a view to designing the questionnaire. At that time, 116 questionnaires were handed out and 46 returned (a 41% response rate). On the basis of reports from employees and discussions with the project group, the research team decided to shorten the original questionnaire, even while making a few additions, which ultimately led to the design of the final questionnaire as employed in this project.

Results

In the following, the results are divided into a number of sections that cover characteristics of the participants or "respondents", factors relating to working hours, and work satisfaction. In the analyses, Denmark was compared with the group of other companies as a whole.

The questionnaire process

At the company in Denmark, 160 questionnaires were handed out. 102 were returned and 100 satisfactorily filled out with information about working-time systems, which gave a response rate of 63%. The highest response rate was found among day workers and permanent night workers, and correspondingly, a lower response rate was found among employees with day and evening shifts, and among those with permanent weekend work. The analyses presented below are based on 623 respondents (523 from the other companies and 100 from Denmark). These numbers vary in relation to the analyses, because not everyone responded to all the questions.

Respondents

In Denmark, there was a different gender distribution than in the rest of the companies, with an almost equal proportion of men and women.

At the other companies in total, the distribution was 96% men and 4% women. This reflected the differences in trade and production conditions between Denmark as an aluminium producer, and the others as chemical factories, but differences in social and cultural conditions may also be of importance. The age average was lower in Denmark than in the group of other companies. In Denmark and the other companies, around one third were 40-49, but in Denmark 59% were younger and just 8% older than this age band, while in the other companies 40% were younger and 23% were older than the 40-49 age group. There was no difference regarding marital status between Denmark and the other countries, where around 80% in both groups were married or living with someone and, conversely, 20% reported being single.

Seniority was also lower among employees in Denmark than in the other-companies group. There was a considerable difference between Denmark and the others in relation to the handling of management tasks. Only 4% in Denmark stated that they had management tasks, whereas this applied to 39% in the group of other companies. The differences here were so marked that it is reasonable to suppose that production conditions, and also differences in the organization of work, exert an influence. In addition to this, we cannot ignore the possibility that differences in culture in the companies in relation to management tasks could have some influence. On the other hand, there were no differences between the other companies and Denmark regarding involvement in union representative tasks (reported by 22% of respondents both in Denmark and elsewhere).

Regarding work tasks, the participants in Denmark split into three primary work functions consisting of packaging operators (27%), press/tool operators (34%), and 'working up' (24%). Of the rest, most (7%) reported having other tasks.

Working hours
The distribution of employees in Denmark according to their working-hour system is illustrated in the table below. Participants in Denmark fall in three main groups consisting of: day work only, shift work without night shifts, and night work only, plus a smaller group with weekend work only. The table clearly shows the differences between work schedules in Denmark and the other companies, where the large majority have continuous shift work with night shifts (71%), and a smaller group with day work only (18%), which was similar to Denmark.

Employees' current working hours (in %)	Other companies	Denmark
Day work only	18	20
Shift work without night shifts	2	36
Shift work with night shifts	71	–
Evening work only	–	3
Night work only	–	30
Day work with on-call work	9	2
Weekend work only	–	9
Other	–	–

TABLE 1 *Current working hours.*

Changes in the scheduled working time: The employees in Denmark had worked a significantly (***) larger number of extra hours, in addition to the normal hours of employment, during the four preceding weeks: 28% in Denmark reported 'none', whereas 56% reported 'none' in the other companies. Moreover, 27% had 6-10 hours and 23% had 11-20 extra hours in Denmark, while elsewhere, the corresponding proportions were 12% and 14%, respectively. Regarding changes of more than 1 hour in the working-hour plans during the last four weeks, no differences were observed, and 63% in both areas stated 'none', followed by a gradually declining distribution from 1 to 4 times. This indicated that 37% had experienced changes at least once. These two questions can be said to reflect flexibility for the companies with regard to organizing and changing the working-time schedules.

Individual and group influence on the arrangement of working hours: The table below illustrates the distribution of answers to the question "To what degree do you experience that you, yourself, influence the arrangement of the working hours?"

Influence for oneself on working-hour arrangements (distribution in %)	None	Not much	Some	A good deal	Com-plete
The other companies	42	31	17	9	2
Denmark	27	19	25	24	5

TABLE 2 *Personal influence on working hours.*

Table 2 shows that a slightly larger proportion of employees in Denmark reported that they, as individuals, had 'some' to 'complete' influence on the arrangement of their working hours (the difference was significant at the *** level). However, in Denmark almost half (46%) reported little or no influence, but this was compared to 73% elsewhere. The following table shows the distribution of answers in percentages to the question "To what extent do you experience that the employees as a group influence how the current working hours are arranged?"

Influence for the employ-ees as a group on work-ing-hour arrangements (distribution in %)	None	Not much	Some	A good deal	Com-plete
The other companies	26	32	27	13	2
Denmark	21	29	29	18	3

TABLE 3 *Group influence on working hours.*

In Table 3 no major differences in the proportions of responses between Denmark and the group of others were observed regarding the influence of employees as a group. Here 58% in the other companies, and 50% in Denmark, reported the employees as a group as having little or no influence on the arrangement of working hours. The changes that can be seen in comparison with experience of individual influence was notable, since an increase in the influence from oneself to the group of 28%–42% in the proportion of responses was observed for the other companies, (the answers encompassing 'some', 'a good deal', and 'complete'). In comparison, for Denmark a small decrease in the proportion of responses for individual to group influence from 54% to 50% was found. A possible explanation for the larger degree of influence experienced by individual employees in Denmark could be connected to their experience of being able to choose between different working-hour systems. In Denmark this encompasses, for example, people with night work only and weekend work only who had the same work tasks as those on other shifts. This was not the case in the other companies for employees with the same work function, since they entered into the same system of continuous shift work. Furthermore, it is reasonable to assume that the perception of group influence may be connected to the experience of the influence on the design or shape of the specific systems, since there are typically issues connected to this that are discussed and negotiated. This interpretation is supported by the fact that there are no differences between the participating companies, which seemed to support the idea that employees in general wish to have more influence on the design of individual systems.

The next table illustrates the distribution of replies between Denmark and the others for the question "Who do you think should have the most influence on the design of shift work in order to ensure that the employees' health and safety is taken care of?" (Only one answer could be given.)

Attitude to who should have most influence on shift work to ensure health and safety	Other companies	Denmark
You yourself	7	16
The employees as a group	52	56
Representatives / unions	8	6
Health and Safety Committees	10	9
Works councils	20	9
Management / supervisors	3	3

TABLE 4 *Preference as to who should have influence on working hours.*

The overall difference between Denmark and the group of other companies was significant (*). Differences were particularly noticeable in the preferences for personal influence and for works councils to have influence. No major differences were found for the other options. Among employees in Denmark, compared with the other companies, a larger proportion expressed a preference for personal influence. Almost twice the proportion of employees in the other companies would prefer to give the most influence to works councils. Explanations of this may be related to the differences found in the responses to the question about experiencing individual influence. As the works-council preference, the responses might express the difference between functions and members of "works councils" for the other companies' and the work councils' activities in the field of working hours in Denmark. In the interviews we found that there was a tradition that specific themes related to working hours were directly negotiated between management and union representatives, while other discussions on, say, design and employment, took place in certain ad hoc committees. This might be connected to perceptions of who one feels is the best qualified to handle these questions, but both in Denmark and in the other companies, the majority (just over half) would prefer the influence on shift work, health, and safety to lie with the group of employees.

Conditions of importance (reasons) for working on the actual working-time system: We found the largest significant differences between Denmark and the group of other companies for the reasons "fits better with my family life" and "gives greater personal freedom". These were the reasons indicated by the largest proportion of employees in Denmark as having great or very great importance. For the reason relating to family life, the proportion was 55% in Denmark versus 31% elsewhere. These responses are likely to reflect the possibility of choosing a specific system with more fixed arrangement of working hours, or becoming employed in the given system. That is, in Denmark, a selection has occurred between people who, for example, want to have fixed night work and others who do not, and therefore the given group of people might be more suited to the conditions. At the same time it must be recognized that there is no universal free choice here, but that the given working hours were connected to the possibility of having a job, or of working in the company. Regarding pay, 47% in the other companies versus 28% in Denmark reported that this reason was of great or very great importance. Compared to Denmark, a greater proportion of employees from the group of other companies reported that "the only possibility of working" or "working in other firms or staying there" were important or very important reasons for working the existing shift system.

The questionnaire also had a measure that evaluated the current shift system with several sub-questions. The table below shows the distribution of answers in percentages for all the different sub-questions. Examination of these responses at the Denmark site could give cause to consider potential changes. Comparisons with the other companies are not illustrated, as this would not be so informative because the other companies operated different work schedules. However, it is worth pointing out that the distribution of answers is very much similar to most responses in the 'not relevant' and 'appropriate' category.

	Far too few		Appropri-ate number		Far too many	Not relevant
a) Number of day shifts per month	10	9	30	1	1	48
b) Number of evening shifts per month	2	3	20	8	9	48
c) Number of night shifts per month	2	0	23	4	4	68
d) Number of day shifts in a row	5	5	29	2	3	56
e) Number of evening shifts in a row	2	3	21	3	10	61
f) Number of night shifts in a row	0	0	32	5	3	60
g) Number of week-ends off	5	0	34	2	0	59
h) Number of hours on day shift	3	0	39	8	1	48
i) Number of hours on evening shift	0	3	41	0	6	50
j) Number of hours on night shift	0	0	30	10	3	55
k) Number of hours on weekend shift	2	2	7	7	5	77
	Too early		Appropriate		Too late	Not relevant
j) Start time for day shifts	17	11	35	0	0	38
k) Start time for eve-ning shifts	0	5	42	3	6	44
l) Start time for night shifts	8	3	40	2	2	45

TABLE 5 *Perceptions of shift-system features.*

The schedule of answers is shown in Table 5. The only two sub-questions that diverge from the others in the responses concern the number of hours on weekend shifts, where just slightly more reported there being too many hours (12%, compared to 11% who said the hours were too few or appropriate). Clearly, these are small numbers. In addition, the start time for day shifts was reported to be too early by 27%, while 35% reported it being appropriate, and the largest proportion, 38%, responded that it was not relevant.

Considering the question "Satisfaction with own working hours", the distribution of answers is illustrated in the table below for Denmark and other companies:

Distribution in % of answers to "satisfied with working hours"	Very satisfied	Gener- ally satisfied	Neither satisfied nor dis- satisfied	Gener- ally dis- satisfied	Very dissatis- fied
The other companies	10	39	40	10	4
Denmark	42	22	23	8	4

TABLE 6 *Satisfaction with working hours.*

Only small proportions of the employees in the other companies and Denmark (14% and 12%, respectively) reported dissatisfaction with the working hours. The distribution should be considered in relation to employees' experience of a lack of opportunity for, or limitations in, potential new working-time patterns within the given frameworks in the companies. Therefore, it could be suggested that the responses do not necessarily mean that employees do not wish for changes, or would not want to avoid shift work. A large proportion in Denmark indicated that they were very satisfied with their working hours, which is presumably related to the opportunities for many of them to choose what hours they worked under the conditions imposed by shift work; probably to accommodate social preferences.

In order to obtain additional information on the levels of satisfaction with the existing working-time systems, the participants were asked if they would change to daytime work if they had the opportunity. A second question asked if they would change to daytime work without it affecting pay or other working-time conditions. These two questions were only asked of shift workers.

If given opportunity to change to daytime work only (in %)	Yes	No	Don't know
Other companies	35	39	26
Denmark	39	39	22

TABLE 7 *Responses about changing to day work.*

If given opportunity to change to daytime work without affecting pay or work conditions (in %)	Yes	No	Don't know
Other companies	65	21	14
Denmark	57	28	16

TABLE 8 *Responses about changing to day work with pay and conditions unchanged.*

There were no significant differences between Denmark and the other companies. For the first question, there were two almost equally large groups of a little more than a third who would and would not change if the opportunity arose. However, if a change to day work could happen without alterations in pay or work conditions, a larger proportion indicated that they would change to daytime work. Given this opportunity, the proportion recording 'don't know' became noticeably smaller, but at the same time there was still, in Denmark, a group of 28% that would not want to change. These answers support the themes that were discussed earlier concerning the existence of a small group among employees in Denmark that apparently had the opportunity to choose the system that was optimally suited to their social life. Moreover, they could also be said to support the conjecture that satisfaction with the shift system, as stated, is not related to having shift work instead of day work, for the majority, but that the given system within the existing framework is perceived as satisfactory.

Work satisfaction
The question about the degree of employees' satisfaction with their present work situation consists of a number of sub-questions that covered most aspects of a job situation. We present the distribution of answers on all the sub-questions (see Table 9 below) in the belief that it could facilitate the discussions at the company about introducing change initiatives if certain issues appeared to be problematic.

A seven-point (Likert-type) response scale, ranging from 'very dissatisfied' to 'very satisfied', was applied to each sub-question. In Table 9 the three response categories concerning 'dissatisfied' have been combined into one category and the same applies to 'satisfied', while the neutral category for 'neither satisfied nor dissatisfied' has been maintained. In the analyses the responses from the employees in Denmark (denoted by D) are compared with the employees at the rest of the companies (denoted by R), and significant differences are indicated with a number of stars (* ≤ 0.05, ** ≤ 0.01 and *** ≤ 0.001) depending on the degree of confidence with which the results indicate differences between Denmark and the other companies. Arrows have also been inserted for the sub-questions where reliable differences were found. The direction of the arrows shows the direction of the differences in satisfaction levels. If the direction of the arrow points towards the company in question, which here is Denmark (D), the level of employee satisfaction concerning that dimension is higher in Denmark than in the rest of the companies, and vice versa if the arrow points towards R.

When interpreting the results it is important to look not only at the differences between the companies, but also at how the responses are dispersed on the different categories for the single sub-question at the given company. In this way, we sometimes found that even a considerable difference in the distribution of responses between satisfied and dissatisfied had no apparent significance, because the same differences occurred in the other companies. Additionally it should be emphasized that, beyond existing differences in conditions for the individual dimensions, variations in culture and traditions are likely to have influenced responses to the questions.

Table 9 presents the results quite clearly. Consequently, only limited additional comments are made here. In all the places where significant differences were found, the arrows show that the greater satisfaction was found among employees in Denmark. For most of the questions, 60% or more of the employees reported being satisfied. A varying number in the individual sub-questions were neutral. However, it is noticeable that in relation to question 'i' concerning cooperation between management and employees, and question 'k' concerning the manner in which the company is managed, there were relatively small differences in the proportions of employees who reported being satisfied and dissatisfied. Indeed, this is where the degree of dissatisfaction was greatest. It should be stressed, however, that this applies even more notably to the other companies as a group. Moreover, it should be noted that regarding the item about satisfaction with the possibilities for promotion, the proportion reporting satisfaction was 44%, which was the lowest among all the work-satisfaction items (but note that a larger group here reported that they were indifferent).

Denmark (D) compared with the rest of the companies (R) on the dimensions of satisfaction		Very dissatisfied / Dissatisfied / Slightly dissatisfied		Indifferent	Slightly satisfied / Satisfied / Very satisfied	
a. Your physical working conditions	D	33		9	58	
	R	31		11	58	
b. Freedom to carry out your work	D	16		9	75	
	R	19		11	70	
c. Your colleagues at work	D	5	⇑	6	89	*
	R	16		7	78	
d. The recognition you get for your work	D	27	⇑	8	65	**
	R	41		13	46	
e. Your immediate supervisor	D	29		10	61	
	R	31		16	54	
f. The amount of responsibility you get	D	15		10	75	
	R	24		11	65	
g. Your pay conditions	D	23	⇑	13	64	***
	R	44		10	45	
h. Opportunities to use your abilities	D	22	⇑	9	69	*
	R	33		14	54	
i. Cooperation between management and employees	D	45	⇑	4	51	*
	R	49		11	40	
j. Your opportunities for promotion	D	22	⇑	34	44	***
	R	45		22	33	
k. The manner in which the workplace is run	D	40	⇑	8	52	**
	R	49		16	35	
l. The attention your suggestions receive	D	26	⇑	20	54	*
	R	39		20	41	
m. Your working time	D	24	⇑	8	68	*
	R	35		11	54	
n. Variety in your work	D	11	⇑	12	77	***
	R	30		12	58	

Cont. next page

o. Security in your employment	D	16	⇑	7	77	***
	R	39		12	49	
p. Your influence on the arrangement of your work	D	23	⇑	9	68	***
	R	30		25	45	
q. The extent of work tasks	D	15	⇑	9	76	**
	R	25		19	56	
r. The pace of work	D	19	⇑	10	71	*
	R	25		19	57	
s. Clarity of your tasks at work	D	15	⇑	8	77	**
	R	28		12	60	
t. Your possibilities for personal development	D	28		15	57	
	R	39		14	47	

TABLE 9 *Work satisfaction.*

CONCLUDING REMARKS

This supplementary report on the Norsk Hydro site in Denmark has presented an overview of the research carried out. The nature of the shift systems, the background for the design, the employees' involvement and influence, and also the issues of system and work satisfaction were considered.

The analyses of the questions regarding working hours appear to point to the implementation and importance of flexibility concerning working hours. Flexibility can be designed at different levels, and be guided by the company's and employees' needs, respectively, and also by the influence they might have at different levels. Some questions reflected the importance of flexibility in relation to the company's need for continuous adjustment and change. On the other hand, other responses appeared to support the contention that it is valuable for employees to have flexibility, which was expressed here as opportunity for choosing a specific system when being hired, or perhaps later, in accordance with social and individual preferences. This was certainly related to working fixed nights and weekends. It should also be noted that this could be an option for some, while being unrealistic for others. At the same time it was not a completely free choice for all individuals, as economic and work opportunities would have some influence on choice. Making a choice to accommodate social factors does not necessarily protect against the illness risks of shift work, but by taking account of social factors the risks might be experienced as putting less strain on the individual. Regardless of these problems, the employees' responses could be suggested to point to the value for the employees of having a kind of flexibility that is influenced by the employees themselves. Such flexibility could, in principle, also exist in relation to the time of going to work, preferences for working specific days, and opportunities for taking time off in lieu of unpaid overtime, all of which presumably influence the degree of satisfaction reported. It is worth emphasizing that by far the largest proportion of employees reported satisfaction with working hours.

In Denmark, and in other companies, there was a preference for giving the employees as a group the largest amount of influence on the arrangement of working hours to ensure health and safety. This could give rise to some reflection on the opportunities for working with a different integration of the company's needs, and employees' social preferences and health considerations, by giving the employees more influence on working-hour design within a given framework decided by the companies. This could take place through work groups constituted for that particular purpose, but could perhaps also be instigated through autonomous working-hour groups. In Appendices 1 and 2, we have presented some recommendations on designing shift work, and some information useful to the process of implementing, or altering, shift-schedule designs or working-hour systems.

The questions concerning work satisfaction show that compared with the other companies, a larger proportion of employees at the Denmark site were satisfied with the different work themes. If we focus exclusively on the distribution of employees in Denmark, most of the responses indicated varying degrees of satisfaction. The challenges for the company and employees could be said to relate to the themes of cooperation and running the workplace, where the dissatisfaction appeared to be greater than for the other areas of work satisfaction.

CONTRIBUTORS

HANS JEPPE JEPPESEN
Department of Psychology,
University of Aarhus,
Denmark

MAGNAR KLEIVEN
Vivilja AS,
Stathelle,
Norway

HENRIK BØGGILD
Centre for Working Time Research,
Department of Occupational Medicine,
Aalborg Hospital,
Aarhus University Hospital,
Denmark

COLIN GILL
Manufacturing and Management Division,
University of Cambridge,
United Kingdom